ON BEING A MASTER THERAPIST

ON BEING A MASTER THERAPIST

PRACTICING WHAT YOU PREACH

JEFFREY A. KOTTLER
AND JON CARLSON

WILEY

Library of Congress Cataloging-in-Publication Data:

Kottler, Jeffrey A.
  On being a master therapist : practicing what you preach / Jeffrey A. Kottler and Jon Carlson.
    pages cm
  Includes bibliographical references and index.
  ISBN 978-1-118-22581-3 (pbk.)
  ISBN 978-1-118-28694-4 (ebk.)
  ISBN 978-1-118-28241-0 (ebk.)
  1. Psychotherapists. 2. Psychotherapy—Practice. I. Carlson, Jon. II. Title.
  RC480.5.K6788 2014
  616.89'14—dc23

                                                2013048874

CONTENTS

PREFACE

This is a *very* different book about counseling and psychotherapy, one that we hope is quite unlike others you have encountered before. We can tell you with assurance that among the
dozens of volumes we have written on this subject previously, this
one represents our definitive word on what we think matters most
in creating and sustaining superlative therapeutic practice. It is also
our most personal book.

We are hardly the only ones to tackle the job of distilling more
than 100 years of clinical experience between us (and an equal
number of published books) to make sense of what matters most in
the practice of a profession. We have been investigating nuances of
our field all our lives, each a study of a particular aspect of the work
that interests us most, whether that includes a discussion of ethics,
failures, lies and deception, relationships, loneliness, creativity, social
justice, self-care, reciprocal changes, professional identity, indigenous
healing, self-supervision, group work, conflict resolution, difficult
cases, and so on. Among all our attempts to make sense of what we
do, and how we do it, we have yet to come to terms with what really
leads to mastery in our field. There is much talk about evidence-based
practice, empirically supported treatments, manualized strategies,
and consensual standards, all of which settle for mere *competence*
in particular domains. And yet we have been struggling to go far

beyond minimally acceptable standards to attain a level of mastery in our work with clients. We suppose the same could be said for our writing and teaching as well: If our goal is to truly help people to grow and learn and change, why would we accept only proficiency, if not mediocrity? Just as our clients want so much more from their lives, so, too, do we strive for a degree of excellence.

Although we have consulted hundreds of sources, research studies, and books by esteemed writers and scholars who have investigated facets of mastery in the practice of therapy, we have adopted a more informal, narrative tone in this book, one that allows us to speak informally and frankly about what we think we know and understand, as well as what puzzles and disturbs us the most. Rather than using a conventional citation style, we have instead referred to particular authors and studies by name and then included the sources in our reference list (this allows us to keep the conversation with you more personal). You will also find direct quotations from some of our field's most esteemed theorists and practitioners inserted throughout the book, most of them based on direct communications with them. We have reached deep to talk about some of the taboos, secrets, and forbidden aspects of the profession, or at least those that have been rarely discussed in a public forum rather than behind closed doors. As such, we have tried to be honest, transparent, and even vulnerable in what we say and how we say it. In short, this is the book that contains within it all we have ever hoped to say but perhaps never had the courage to speak quite so bluntly about many of the issues.

We acknowledge that the choice of the word *master* to describe extraordinarily accomplished therapists is somewhat problematic. Although it is most often the term applied in this context, it also comes with some colonial baggage in that it's associated with slavery. While it is hardly our intention to conjure such associations, the word is usually the preferred choice to identify an especially skilled technician (master plumber or electrician) or professional. It denotes a practitioner who has moved beyond a journey-(wo)man or even an "expert" status, someone who is, in one sense, part of an elite group that includes an expert's expert. We continue this discussion in the first chapter, defining in a multitude of ways the different conceptions of what it means to be an extraordinary practitioner.

Chapter 2 sets the stage for what follows by reviewing what we mostly know is true about excellence in the practice of therapy, or at least what we *think* we know and understand. In the chapters that are sequenced afterward, we cover some of the important facets of mastery including the practice of deep compassion and caring (Chapter 3); a set of sophisticated interpersonal skills (Chapter 4); remaining fully present in therapeutic encounters (Chapter 5); demonstrating a high level of domain- and subdomain-specific knowledge (Chapter 6); being clear-headed and honest with clients (Chapter 7), as well as with oneself in acknowledging mistakes (Chapter 8); and processing feedback (Chapter 9). As important as knowledge, wisdom, and skills are in helping people, we also insist that who we are as human beings is just as critical, especially with regard to modeling the qualities we would most like our own clients to develop (Chapter 10).

Next, we move on to discussing some of the attributes that truly distinguish excellence in clinical practice. This includes not only the mandated and critical responsiveness to cultural and individual differences of our clients, but also the deep understanding of commonalities that link all human experience (Chapter 11). Chapter 12 delves into one of the most taboo subjects in our field—a four-letter word that is rarely uttered aloud because of its associations and yet, we believe, forms the essence of what we do: the expression of nondemanding, platonic *love*.

Whereas extremely skilled and competent therapists have shown an ability to demonstrate consistent and reliable outcomes in their work, we believe true mastery is evidenced by those who go beyond what is known and show a level of creativity and originality that is truly remarkable (Chapter 13). Master therapists are innovators and deep thinkers, those among us who advance our knowledge through their scrupulous critical reflection and experimentation, always searching for more effective ways to be helpful to their clients. We also hold dear to our hearts the belief that truly great professionals feel a commitment to something far greater than their own clients and become actively involved in advocacy within their own communities or on a global scale (Chapter 14). There is much talk, even scolding, in our field about the obligation to promote social justice even if many of the actions remain short-lived or token efforts. We maintain that masters are those who sustain their advocacy over time, launching projects that make a difference in the lives of those who are most marginalized and who would ordinarily never seek help in our offices.

We close this exploration of mastery in therapy by talking about the ways we always fall short no matter how hard we strive for mastery (Chapter 15) and how we are all "works in progress" doing the best we can.

Acknowledgments

We are most grateful to many of our distinguished colleagues, representing a variety of theoretical orientations, who were willing to talk to us about their beliefs, thoughts, and experiences related to being a master therapist. You will find many of their ideas and wisdom sprinkled throughout the pages of this book. We are especially indebted to: Diana Fosha, Michael Yapko, Nancy McWilliams, Scott Browning, Laura Brown, Michele Weiner-Davis, Michael Hoyt, Scott Miller, Bradford Keeney, Kirk Schneider, Judy Jordan, Les Greenberg, Roger Walsh, Frances Vaughan, Keith Dobson, Pat Love, David Cain, William Doherty, Robert Wubbolding, Melba Vasquez, Bruce Wampold, Albert and Debbie Ellis, and Barry Duncan. In addition to those who specifically offered their input on the subject of mastery in the practice of therapy for this book, we have been privileged to interview some of the most noted figures in the field during the past decade, many of whom have been highly influential helping us to develop our own ideas on this subject. We appreciate the contributions over the years from a number of noted figures who spoke with us about their best and worst work, including: Albert Ellis, Jay Haley, William Glasser, Jim Bugental, Susan Johnson, Insoo Kim Berg, Alan Marlatt, Len Sperry, David Scharff, Patricia Arredondo, Ken Hardy, Violet Oaklander, Harville Hendrix, Arnold Lazarus, Frank Pittman, Nick Cummings, John Norcross, Bill O'Hanlon, Cloe Madanes, Jeff Zeig, Steve Madigan, Robert Neimeyer, Alvin Mahrer, John Krumboltz, and Peggy Papp.

As you will see in the pages that unfold, it has been a long and challenging journey to complete this book, given a number of crises and health issues that cropped up along the way. We appreciate the patience and support of Rachel Livsey, who has been so very understanding during the eventual completion of this project that represents our life's work.

Jeffrey Kottler, Huntington Beach, California

Jon Carlson, Lake Geneva, Wisconsin

Introduction:
Two Variations on a Theme

Jon Carlson

I am dying.

I've been told there's only a 20% chance that I will survive the next year so I will likely not see the publication of this book.

Cancer has penetrated my bones, circulating throughout my blood, infesting my lymph glands, growing tumors along my spine. My vertebrae are being crushed by the tumors, causing unrelenting agony.

Of course, I've always been dying. So have you. It's just likely to happen sooner for me than for you.

Jeffrey Kottler

There's nothing like the casual mention of impending death to scare the heck out of me; it's even worse when it is one of my oldest and dearest friends who seems determined to treat the diagnosis as an inconvenient annoyance, a mere interruption of our latest project to explore what it means to be a master therapist.

It's not like I've pretended I would live forever. I was given a death sentence when I was 25 years old, told I'd be lucky to live another 20 years. Bad genes, the doctor said. My mother had just died of lung cancer. As I sat in the hospital, grieving her loss, my father was critically ill in another hospital. His heart was failing and he needed a transplant, or perhaps a quadruple bypass, during a time when these were pretty radical procedures. Although he survived that immediate crisis, a few years later he had a stroke that left him paralyzed and brain damaged. The doctor said I'd be fortunate if I lived to be 40.

JC Let's talk about pain. I've been a competitive athlete most of my life. I ran track and cross-country in high school, coached at college level, and continued training throughout my adult years running marathons and even winning national awards. Long-distance running is essentially about tolerating pain, and I was pretty good at that. I learned that pain is just an annoyance, something to be tolerated for some ultimate goal or greater good. This realization fit quite well with some of my later thinking as a Buddhist, in which suffering is just accepted as a normal, natural part of life.

It absolutely devastated me to face the limits of my pain tolerance these past months. I have been filled with despair. I have been in and out of a kind of coma, sometimes half-conscious, while they tried to figure out what was wrong with me. Tumors were literally cracking my ribs, consuming the marrow. The pain I felt deep in my bones was so excruciating I couldn't sit, couldn't move, couldn't lie still, without wishing that the end would come sooner rather than later.

As a therapist, I'm no stranger to unremitting agony. During the past 40 years I have sat with thousands of clients, many of whom struggled with grief, losses, disappointments, depression, mental disorders, and a host of other life challenges. Pain is my business, as it is yours.

JK Like most therapists, I'm pretty good at holding other people's pain; it's my own struggles that lead me to question the extent to which I can truly practice what I teach to others.

I became a therapist in the first place because I wanted to be immortal. As a child, I yearned to be special in some way, to have some skill or ability that would stand out. Alas, it was not to be. I would die young—worse yet, my brief life would be filled with mediocrity.

I was an awful student, undistinguished in every way that mattered to me. I couldn't run fast or catch a fly ball. The girls I liked never seemed to like me back the same way. I had terrible vision but didn't know it at the time: The consequence was that I could never see the board at school, meaning that I could never really catch on to math, grammar, or anything else that was written in chalk. By the time I got glasses in high school, it was too late to catch up.

I had been told most of my life that I wouldn't amount to much. My only dream was to do something, or be someone, who was worthwhile, who helped people. If I wasn't going to live very long, I at least wanted to make my mark in the world. I figured that being a therapist would allow me to live beyond my own mortality in that those I helped would remember me. In some small way, my soul would live on. I never aspired to be a master therapist; I'd have settled for being merely competent. Most of all, I wanted to find some way to live with myself and feel useful.

JC One thing I've learned is that pain and suffering are a part of life—no one escapes them—although we try so hard with denial, antidepressants, cosmetic surgery, and hair coloring. Buddhists believe that suffering is just an ordinary part of life; the only cure for the discomfort is acceptance. Things happen in life that we don't like and can't control, but, oh well, that's part of the deal. I suppose one of the things we learn as therapists along the way is to help our clients accept the things they can't do anything about and concentrate instead on what is within their power to change. I've always thought that is what truly distinguishes a master therapist, or a master anything— professionals who can actually apply in their lives what they do for others.

It is interesting to me that others are so troubled by the calm way in which I appear to accept my fate. I accept cancer as part of me since it also has a right to life. I don't much like the agony I suffer physically, or the stricken reactions I see in others in response to my condition, but I understand that my predicament triggers crises of mortality for others, who often pretend that they will live forever. Sometimes I wonder if therapy isn't counterproductive when we encourage people to change anything they don't like instead of increasing tolerance for pain and greater acceptance of things outside of one's control.

JK I didn't delude myself that this dialogue between us would be one in which we thoroughly agree with one another. We have collaborated on many projects over the years precisely because we are so different in the ways we walk through life and how we conceive of and practice therapy. Our theoretical orientations, therapeutic styles, lifestyles, even core values in some areas, are compatible yet very different.

I feel my heart pounding and perspiration percolating just thinking about acceptance of hardly anything. Call it delusion or denial, but I prefer to believe that we do have the capacity to change almost anything. Perhaps willing cancer away is beyond realistic limits, but as Jon suggests, we can choose our attitude.

I know we are throwing around a term, *master therapist*, that we haven't yet defined, but whatever it turns out to be, and however it is conceived, it means that practitioners have found their own voice. They have found a way of working with others that feels fluid and natural, consistent with their unique personalities and styles. They aren't imitating anyone else but rather following the lead of their clients—with sensitivity, caring, and respect.

As different as we might be in the ways we express ourselves and talk about what we do, I think we both share a vision of what it means to help others. We use different language, ground ourselves in different traditions, and speak with singular voices, yet we basically agree on the important stuff: It is indeed senseless to focus on things that are beyond our control.

JC Before we begin to speak in subsequent chapters about what distinguishes extraordinary therapeutic practice, we have to arrive at some consensus about what any good therapy involves. What *is* therapy anyway? Is it just a form of conversation where we convey information and share emotions? Is it a process where the therapist attempts to put new ideas or thoughts into the client's head?

It's clear that therapy involves far more than just an exchange of ideas or imparting of wisdom. It is a process in which perceived facts are changed and transformed, creating new ways of being, new ways of thinking and behaving, even creating neural and life pathways. Sometimes novel solutions are discovered for lifelong problems, possibilities that had never before been considered. That is one reason we are writing this book, not just to shuffle the cards a bit, hoping for some new configurations, but perhaps bringing new cards to the deck, as well eliminating those that have long been overused. Just as our clients subscribe to certain beliefs that limit them and keep them stuck, so, too, do therapists embrace particular attitudes that may compromise greater effectiveness.

JK I used to rarely question some of the most fundamental principles of our profession. I'm talking about basic things like scheduling 50-minute sessions, having conversations about whatever is most disturbing, collaborating on therapeutic tasks that relate directly to the client's stated goals, sitting in chairs—as I said, basic stuff. But then a few years ago, Jon and I had the opportunity to work with shamans in a remote part of the Kalahari Desert in Namibia. This experience changed everything about what I think I know and understand about healing.

Although we've written about the experience previously, it bears a brief mention in this context. I had been interviewing the elder shaman of a Bushman village, talking to him about his sacred healing rituals, when he turned the tables and asked me what I do as a shaman among my own people. I explained how someone comes to see me and then tells me about his or her troubles.

The shaman interrupted me immediately, more than a little confused. He wondered where the rest of the village was during this talk. He asked me about why there was no fire lit during this ritual, why there was no music or drumming or dancing. All I could do was shrug and say that we didn't do things that way among my tribe.

"What about the spirits?" he asked me. "How can they be present if they are not invited?" I explained that I didn't use spirits in my work—nor did I dance or chant with my clients.

Increasingly confused, he finally asked me what I actually do to help people if we don't dance, shake, and sing in the presence of the whole village and their spirits.

"Well," I tried to explain, "we have a conversation. The person tells me what's wrong and then we try to figure out what to do about it."

The shaman looked at me, giggling, then outright laughing. When he finally caught his breath, he asked me a question I'll never forget: *Have you ever helped anyone doing that?*

It sure got me thinking about what we do as therapists, especially compared to what indigenous cultures have been doing as healing rituals for the past 10,000 years. It takes more than mere talk to help clients to not only make important changes in their lives but also to make them last over time. The best among us find ways to "dance" with their clients. The masters in our field have thought long and hard about what matters most—to their clients but also to themselves.

JC I've been thinking long and hard about these issues Jeffrey mentioned and it leads me to wonder why I would want to write another therapy book when I am dying. I've been told I probably only have a few months, maybe a year to live, so why would I want to use that time to reflect on what it means to be a therapist? This is because I'm not *dying from* cancer, but rather *living with* it as my companion.

Psychotherapy is what I know and what I have practiced all of my adult life. This is likely my last book, my last shot at saying what I think is most important about our work. It is my final attempt to speak with the most honesty about what I have witnessed and experienced with my clients. I am working hard at not regurgitating someone else's ideas but rather to share what I have actually seen and felt in working with others. Much of today's therapy world is taking what others say as immutable truth, without critically examining the assumptions for themselves.

I've been seeing an average of 50 clients per week for many decades, logging over 60,000 sessions in that time. That doesn't by any means qualify me as a "master" just because I have a lot of experience. I've known all kinds of people who have practiced their profession all their lives but they're still not very good at what they do. I'd like to think I've continued to improve because I pay such close attention to what my clients want and need. Although I have learned some important things from research studies, conferences, workshops, and even books like this, most of my best supervisors and teachers have been my clients.

It is my wish, maybe one of my last wishes, that I make a clear statement about what I've learned over the years. Like most everything in my life, I am essentially relational: I prefer to work with collaborators. Jeffrey and I have been partners in mischief, having known each other since our days as graduate students in the 1970s. The idea of this book is to make a seminal statement, not as a collection of wisdom but my last word—*our* last word as a team.

I have never been in a place like this, a place where tomorrow might not come. It has affected many areas of my life, especially my worldview and what is important. I seem to be more interested in smaller satisfactions rather than larger accomplishments. I am not sure if anyone other than Jeffrey will read what I'm writing, but it still feels like the right place to put my energies.

JK It's always been a bit of a mystery, Jon, how you manage to do so much, for so long, without burning out. I'm certainly no slouch when it comes to being productive, but I have needed constant variety in my work and my life; I get bored easily. Yet you have stuck with your commitments and your five(!) different jobs as a full-time professor, full-time therapist, film producer, author, elementary school counselor, not to mention your role as a devoted husband, father, and grandfather to your brood.

During my best days I could see 30 to 34 clients each week—when it was my full-time job. Yet you have sometimes seen almost double that number, as a second (or maybe third) job. Even more remarkably, you absolutely love the work. I honestly don't know how you do it, but somehow you have managed to remain energized in your sessions, rarely stale or bored, and always appearing excited about some new development in your craft.

I have teased you over the years because of your devotion to your mentor, Alfred Adler, even though I insist that you have never been an Adlerian except in your own mind. I don't doubt that Adler's theory and ideals have inspired you, but I think you have gone way beyond the orthodoxy to develop your own unique voice. And I think one reason for this evolution is that, like so many others who have attained a degree of excellence in their skills, you work so damn hard at it. You've conducted over 300 interviews on video with the world's greatest living theoreticians and clinicians, including their accompanying live demonstrations. From each of these you have taken something and made it yours. Even more critically, you've been able to challenge their ideas face to face, a fantasy that many of us could only imagine.

Whereas your retrospective looking back on your life's work, staring death in the face, leads you to a certain modest acceptance of the stature you've attained from so much direct experience, by contrast, I'm uncomfortable even using the term master therapist. First of all, I don't know what that means (which is one reason we are doing this book). Second, mastery implies some sort of definitive expertise of a craft, which I suppose I must have as a function of having practiced so long and written so much about what it is that therapists do. But here's the thing: My felt experience of doing therapy is that I don't feel all that masterful some of the time; I feel confused, tentative, and sometimes clueless.

JC We are indeed different in our outlooks, a familiar realization that I so enjoy in our collaborations. Come on, Jeffrey, you've been writing about your insecurities for years; it's time to get over them and accept the realization that most of the time you really do know what you're doing and you're really, really good at what you do.

I never intended to become a master at this work. I just thought this was a cushy job that might be lucrative, or at least a way to earn a living and do some good. I wasn't interested in saving the world, just a little bit of myself. And here I am so many years later, perhaps at the very end of my life, grateful for what my clients, mentors, and friends have taught me.

Now that I have closed my practice, quit my other part-time jobs, and settled into a mode of daily coping that involves constant blood and bone marrow tests, chemotherapy, blood transfusions, stem cell transplants, and all sorts of drugs mainlined into a permanent hole in my arm, I have a new perspective on what matters most. In part I think that . . .

We Interrupt This Introduction With a Special Bulletin

JC I just got some amazing news! Although I have a rare form of cancer that had invaded my blood and bones, my body has responded spectacularly well to the chemotherapy. The tumors have reduced in size and seem to be on the run. Of course, I'm still dying (so are you!) but just not as quickly as I had been told originally when we first started this introduction several months ago.

I had fully accepted my impending death, although I'm not that pleased with the mind-numbing pain that accompanies every breath. Things are still a bit sketchy for the future, whether I will respond to stem cell transplants, whether my body can pull itself together after having lost almost half my body weight, whether the cancer will return in greater force.

I feel more committed than ever to want to complete this project. What follows is our understanding of what it takes to be a master at therapy. The conclusions come from our reading, observations, and experiences. It will be a personal rather than research-laden book that we hope touches you at a deeper level—not just to pass an exam or make conversation with colleagues, but to actually learn how to help others in a much more meaningful and satisfying way.

Chapter 1

What *Is* a Master Therapist Anyway— And How Do You Get to Be One?

Raise your hand if you consider yourself a "master therapist."

If you're feeling uncertain, or perhaps too modest, then consider someone you know—a former teacher, supervisor, mentor, or perhaps a cherished colleague—whom you consider to be of extraordinary skill and expertise.

What qualifies someone to be identified in this lofty category of exemplary professional? Often, such judgments are made based on so-called "reputation" in the community, or the recommendation of colleagues, or perhaps acknowledgment of scholarly achievement, none of which may have a direct connection to clinical excellence. As we begin our journey together to explore what it means to be a therapeutic "master," we must acknowledge at the outset that there is hardly a consensus in our field about what exactly this means. Are master therapists those who have attained eminence as a function of their longevity, position of power and influence, or publication record? Do they represent clinicians with a full caseload and long waiting list? Are they perhaps those whose clients and ex-clients sing their praises with wild passion and enthusiasm?

Even should we agree on what constitutes excellence in therapy, is this assessment based on the mastery of certain clinical skills, particular personal qualities, or professional characteristics? Perhaps it includes those with the deepest possible understanding of a conceptual framework or the most successful positive outcomes in the most efficient period of time?

Whether or not you feel comfortable including yourself among this illustrious group, on what basis would you consider nominating a colleague? Perhaps a therapist talks a good game, appears wise and knowledgeable, even reports dramatic success with intractable cases, but how do you *really* know what goes on beyond closed doors when sessions are in progress? Is a therapist's reputation in the community or among peers actually a reliable measure of mastery? Can we even trust the critical judgment of their clients, who may report tremendous satisfaction with services? Perhaps this assessment is based on factors that have little to do with the therapist's expertise or skill and more to do with other things, such as how much he or she is liked.

Historically in our field, those who have received the most attention, even deification, are largely a group of elderly white male theorists (like the two of us!) whose main attributes may be the ability to sell their particular ideology and portray themselves in writing or public speeches as charismatic and wise. Such abilities are certainly laudable but may not directly translate into mastery as a clinician. The fact that someone developed new ideas, can explain things well, or is a persuasive speaker or gifted writer does not necessarily mean that he or she is all that effective in sessions. In fact, often quite the opposite is true. Whereas there are notable exceptions, we have learned over the years from our own interviews with over 100 of the most famous theoreticians in the field, as well as observing them in sessions, that many of them struggle working with clients just like everyone else. Whether you agree with that assessment or not, our point is that just because someone is well known in the field for the ability to promote a particular theoretical perspective does not necessarily mean that they are master *practitioners* of that framework.

Some of the world's greatest therapists labor in relative obscurity. They don't enjoy the limelight. They may not care to speak or write about their work. They just adore working with their clients, have attained an extraordinary degree of competence, and don't choose to talk much about what they're doing. We hardly know they exist.

What Is a Master Therapist?

As a counterpoint to this project, we have completed a previous investigation of what constitutes "bad therapy" and discovered there was hardly a consensus among our field's leaders. We may have some idea that a certain percentage of clients become worse as a result of treatment (estimated between 10% and 40%, depending on the diagnosis), but there isn't necessarily agreement on what most often leads to negative outcomes. Some theorists we interviewed said with great authority that bad therapy is a negative outcome for the client, which makes perfect sense. But others described it as occurring when: (1) the therapist loses control of him- or herself, (2) invalid assumptions are made, (3) the same mistakes are repeated over and over, (4) obsolete or untested methods are employed, (5) the therapist just goes through the motions, (6) there is an inadequate alliance, (7) the client doesn't feel understood, (8) the therapist is overly arrogant or unjustifiably overconfident, or (9) the therapist isn't satisfied with the result even though the client may be perfectly content. It is therefore not surprising that there would be just as much debate about what qualifies an extraordinary practitioner.

Do we rely on self-identification of the most accomplished among us? According to one study by Jeffrey Sapyta and colleagues, 9 out of 10 clinicians describe themselves as "above average." This is consistent with other studies in which the vast majority of drivers (80%) describe themselves as more skilled than others. Even more interesting (and amusing) are the 90% of graduate business students at Stanford (who we assume would be well prepared to understand statistics) who all described themselves as better qualified and prepared than their peers. This "illusory superiority effect" is consistent among our species across a range of behaviors in which almost all of us consider ourselves to be masters in our chosen fields. After all, who is willing to admit that they are only average, or even less than fully competent?

Assessing one's own level of competence in almost any area is notoriously unreliable, especially in those dimensions that are most integrally tied to our self-esteem, such as our professional practice. There is overwhelming evidence that self-confidence has absolutely no relationship to mastery of a skill or behavior. In his studies of self-deception, for example, evolutionary biologist Robert Trivers observed that there is often an *inverse* correlation between professed knowledge and confidence versus actual performance. In other words, those who most loudly and passionately claim they are extraordinary in their work are often those who are the *least* effective.

If self-selection of excellence is subject to cognitive bias and exaggeration, should we use other criteria such as recognition by colleagues, including the conferring of awards or "fellow" status? While certainly an indication of respect, does such recognition really mean that the professional is truly exemplary as a therapist? Such awards usually represent scholarly, academic, or political accomplishment.

Of course, there have also been numerous attempts to apply more objective, quantitative measures to the assessment of mastery. While empirical studies of treatment outcomes do provide a degree of precision to the discussion, they also tend to focus on rather definable factors in the process that may or may not represent ultimate, meaningful progress. Do we simply ask clients to report on their own satisfaction, a strategy often recommended by a number of researchers in the field? That brings up the interesting question of whether some clients are actually the most reliable judges of their own experience. How often have you seen clients who say they are not happy with therapy, yet appear to be making remarkable progress? Likewise, how often have clients claimed they are totally satisfied with the way things are going, yet there doesn't seem to be any noticeable change in their behavior outside of sessions? Time and time again, some clients say how much they appreciate their treatment, how much they are learning and growing, yet other reports by family members dramatically contradict this report.

There are many other ways that we might identify exemplary clinicians—whether they are in great demand, whether their clients refer others, evaluations by supervisors, stature in the community, respect of colleagues and peers, demonstrations of their work in public forums. Yet each of these methods has limitations, in part, because we can't really agree on a consistent definition of mastery. Another significant reason for the confusion is all the different ways it is possible for therapists to operate at peak performance, depending on their style, personality, theoretical orientation, client population, and clinical context. This is really not that different from the ways that mastery is demonstrated in other fields.

Consider, for example, two baseball pitchers. The first is in his twenties, tall, strong, muscular, intimidating, featuring a blazing 97-mile-an-hour fastball. The second pitcher, in his twilight years, a bit stooped and slow in his movements, commands a variety of "junk" pitches that are off-speed and move all over the plate. Each of them is regarded as superior in their performance, but they have evolved very different ways of achieving their outcomes, relying on particular strengths and resources at their command. This is exactly the case with regard to extraordinary therapists, each of whom has figured out a unique way to persuade and influence their clients.

Different Standards of Mastery

One of the accepted myths in our field is that there are a discrete number of theoretical models, perhaps a half-dozen popular ones, that most therapists employ in their work. Whereas it is not surprising that a number of practitioners identify themselves closely with cognitive behavioral, psychodynamic, existential, narrative, feminist, or other orientations, the reality is that very few of us apply these in pure form. Each of us has evolved our own unique style of practice that resembles nothing else exactly like it. In addition, depending on your chosen approach, each with its own most valued skills and interventions, effectiveness will be assessed differently. An accomplished cognitive-behavioral therapist may work in a business-like fashion and follow a treatment protocol, depending on what the client wants to address. A more psychodynamic therapist might judge mastery based on the quality of interpretations that reveal underlying core issues in need of attention. A humanistic-existential therapist might be less interested in identifying a specific presenting problem and more concerned with creating a deep connection with clients in the context of a warm, caring, and supportive relationship.

Although there are certainly some features that would cross all boundaries, no two master therapists perform therapy in the same way. You've confirmed this over and over again each time you watch an identified master therapist working with a client. It is one of the true mysteries of the therapy universe that historical figures as diverse as Carl Rogers, Albert Ellis, Virginia Satir, Fritz Perls, and Sigmund Freud could have all been effective in their work given their *apparent* extreme differences in values, style, and approach. Of course, one possible explanation is that although their espoused ideas and approaches appeared to be polar opposites, what made them truly great were other, more personal characteristics that empowered their chosen methods.

As we've mentioned, people consistently overestimate their own competence, especially in domains that are integrally tied to their core being. Moreover, what therapists *say* they do in their sessions may bear only a remote resemblance to what actually transpired. You may think that it was a particular confrontation or elegant interpretation that made the most difference to a client, but, more often than not, the client will hone in on something else entirely that you may not even remember.

JC I remember one time when my five children were young and I was working long hours, basically burning the candle at both ends and getting very little sleep. It was during a particularly boring afternoon session with a woman who was complaining about her teenage daughters that I must have dozed off.

"Excuse me?" I heard a voice say, startling me awake. "But were you sleeping just now?"

"Actually, no," I said to her. "I was just closing my eyes for a moment to concentrate more deeply on what you were saying."

The client knew that I was lying to her, but rather than seeming irritated or disappointed, she seemed to just accept this feeble explanation and ignore it. It bothered me that her expectations were so incredibly low that she refused to become angry or dissatisfied with the poor level of care I was providing. In fact, she was wildly enthusiastic about what a great therapist I was and referred many of her friends and family over the years. She described me as a "wizard" and a "miracle worker," even though I was rarely fully present with her and felt ashamed of my lack of attentiveness.

JK Similar to Jon's story, one of the seminal cases of my professional career, one that completely changed the way I think about what is good and bad therapy, occurred with an older woman I'd been seeing for many months with little, if any, noticeable change in her behavior during that time. Even more frustrating is that she talked constantly in a rambling monotone, retelling the same stories over and over again, and never taking a breath to even give me a minute to say something in return. When I would interrupt her to make some comment or offer an interpretation, she would just totally ignore me as if I weren't even in the room. In fact, during most of our sessions together, I rarely stayed in the room at all and instead retreated into fantasy. I stopped listening to her. At one point, I even became punitive and didn't even pretend to listen, yawning in boredom. I felt little compassion and caring for her; instead, I was filled with annoyance and frustration.

I consider this case to exemplify some of the worst therapy I've ever done in my life. In fact, I was so disappointed with my miserable attitude that it led me to stop practicing for a number of years until I recovered my passion and commitment once again. But here's the thing: This woman absolutely loved me! I know this not only because she kept saying so over and over about how delighted she was with our sessions (I kept trying to push her away, but she still kept coming back). Even more confusing is that, like Jon's case, she continued to refer many family members and friends, who sang my praises.

Client and Therapist Perceptions of Outcomes

Both of these examples illustrate the uncertainty, confusion, and complexity involved in deciding what leads to extraordinary professional effectiveness. And if we can't trust our own judgments, we have already made a strong case for why it is equally problematic to rely purely on client statements. After all, clients lie. A lot. They lie about what they did—or didn't do—during the preceding week, whether they completed assignments or not. They lie to themselves about what is really happening in their lives. Most of all, they tend to exaggerate the extent to which others are responsible for their suffering.

Far more perverse and disturbing are those instances when clients present themselves in ways that are deliberate, strategic falsifications in order to manage their image or even play games with their therapists. In one project, we collected dozens of cases in which therapists were duped by their clients in extreme ways by their claiming they were dying of cancer, actively suicidal, or even presenting whole fictitious lives that were simply invented to manipulate, control, or deceive their therapists.

Lest we become too critical of the milder forms of client exaggeration or deceit, they aren't the only ones concerned with image management. We have seen how therapists tend to exaggerate their effectiveness, believing they are working wonders in cases in which their clients may have a different opinion. We can think of a few instances in which clients have complained to us about a previous therapist who was less than appreciated. After signing a release and contacting the former therapist, we hear glowing accounts from that professional about how well they clicked with their client and how well they worked together.

Therapists have all kinds of reasons to account for results that are not what was expected or hoped for. The client wasn't yet ready to change. The client externalized the problems. The client was resistant or obstructive. Rarely will we fully own and accept responsibility ourselves for a less-than-stellar performance because there are too many other factors that could be at work to sabotage progress—limited resources; dysfunctional family; lack of outside support; intractable, chronic problems; poor client motivation; preexisting conditions; and so on.

JC I have been privileged over the past several decades to produce hundreds of therapist demonstration videos with the greatest living practitioners (or at least the most prominent theorists). We have completed a series on major theories, addictions, consultation, couples therapy, and even a set of films in which each therapist worked with a client for six sessions. During each of these productions, I had the opportunity not only to observe each master therapist in action but also to critically reflect on the sessions and challenge the theorist to explain what he or she was doing and why.

As impressed as I have been by watching eminent therapists in their sessions up close and personal, I have also been occasionally surprised by how poorly some of them do when they are working with clients. I remember one well-known master therapist struggling terribly once the cameras were rolling. I had long admired this person for his groundbreaking ideas in the field but was shocked that he didn't seem to know how to conduct a session. This was all the more confusing because I had previously seen tapes of him working and he seemed pretty impressive (which was why I invited him the first place).

I asked the gentleman about the discrepancy, and he explained sheepishly that the previous sessions I had watched had actually been staged, with some of his assistants pretending to be clients, and a teleprompter had been used so he could read from a script! This may be an extreme example, but I mention it in order to suggest that we approach our subject of mastery with a certain humility and open-mindedness.

Definitions of Mastery by Experts on the Subject

We now return to our original question that began this chapter: What exactly is a master therapist and how do we define this term that will be used repeatedly throughout this book?

At its most basic level, a "master" in any profession is someone who is qualified to teach others, especially those who are novices or apprentices. Compared to their peers, masters are able to produce consistently better results in a shorter period of time. They can do this, in part, not only because of their extensive experience, but because they have attained the ability to perceive the underlying structure of situations and the deeper issues that are part of chronic problems. They are largely responsible for setting the standards or ideals of practice, to which others may aspire.

There have been many scholars and researchers in our field who have taken on the challenge of developing some level of precision when talking about exemplary therapeutic practice. David Orlinsky describes them as more inventive in such a way that they model masterful behavior for others. Michelle Chi and Robert Glaser believe extraordinary therapists monitor themselves more carefully, analyzing problems they face with deep reflection. They are also much faster and more efficient in finding and making sense of meaningful patterns. Len Jennings and Thomas Skovholt conclude that the subject is so complex and multifaceted that they provide a long list of definitional features that include personal characteristics such as insatiable curiosity, accumulated wisdom, and a nuanced ethical compass.

Among the dozens of therapists we interviewed for this book, identified as masters because of their stature in the field—at least as it is defined by their positions of influence from their writing and research—we were surprised how reluctant most were to acknowledge this status of excellence. Many specifically mentioned humility as a key characteristic of extraordinary professionals, whether applied to themselves or others who might qualify for exalted status.

Barry Duncan, along with several colleagues, has been one of the groundbreaking researchers in studying mastery in therapy, yet he is uncomfortable with that term. "While your description makes sense," he told us, "the notion itself is troublesome because it seems to connote that an elite group of so-called masters possess something special that others do not have. I don't possess anything that others don't have or can't develop." Duncan, along with Scott Miller, Bruce Wampold, and Mark Hubble, have made this point repeatedly, based on their research findings that what most distinguishes experts aren't necessarily their "gifts" as much as their dedication and commitment to flat out work harder and prepare better than others. What they describe as "supershrinks" just know more, perceive more, and remember more than others.

Sharing this position, Bruce Wampold also adds that the most effective therapists, who may span a range of different approaches and interpersonal styles, nevertheless have "a sophisticated set of interpersonal skills and use them deliberately to help their patients."

These might be framed as the core relational skills that form the heart of building an effective alliance, identified by Carl Rogers, Robert Carkhuff, Charles Truax, and others decades ago.

Psychodynamic theorist Nancy McWilliams is intrigued by all the different ways that masters of our profession can manifest so many varied styles of practice: "I have known many very good therapists, and I am struck by how different they are from one another. Some clinicians I know, who seem to me to have fairly serious psychopathology, are nevertheless remarkably helpful to their clients. Yet I think that one thing that all good therapists share is an authentic wish to understand people. They orient themselves toward what is true and prefer a difficult truth to a comforting illusion. They are emotionally honest with themselves and with their clients. Their courage in facing painful realities, both internally and externally, also gives their patients courage to look at themselves unflinchingly."

According to health psychologist Michael Hoyt, a master, in any context, is someone who repeatedly gets excellent results, across a variety of situations: "A master is someone who takes on difficult and complex challenges instead of just sticking with the easy, routine ones. I sometimes consult with a couple of colleagues when I'm stuck. I'm impressed with how quickly they each seem to have a grasp of the situation and specific ideas on how to proceed—and not the same ideas either." Hoyt's views are consistent with several others who have mentioned before that master therapists not only perceive things that others miss, but they do so very quickly.

Finally, Roger Walsh, a psychiatrist and transpersonal therapist, does not accept the label that he is a master of anything, since even with consistently good outcomes in his work, he has also experienced his fair share of failures. "Therapists are highly biased about their outcomes," he cautions, citing studies that support this, "and can be very poor at accurately assessing them." Yet if he were to agree that he has attained some degree of excellence in his work,

Walsh attributes that primarily to his 30 years of meditative practice that has allowed him to hone his perceptual sensitivity, empathy, and presence with others. This is one consistent theme that seems to run through all the beliefs about mastery that have been expressed. We will be returning to many of these ideas later, as well as providing input from dozens of other contributors.

Each chapter in this book explores a different attribute of a master therapist, regardless of the particular theoretical orientation or therapeutic approach. We will rely on a broad definition of a master therapist as a professional with extraordinary skill and effectiveness who consistently produces successful outcomes in collaboration with his or her clients. In addition, such professionals are characterized by extreme flexibility in their approach, the ability to adapt their style and strategies to fit the unique needs, interests, and requirements of each client and therapeutic context. Finally, true masters of their craft live what they teach to others.

The key features of our working definition are that a master therapist:

- Demonstrates superior clinical skills with regard to creating and maintaining a solid therapeutic relationship and treatment alliance, as well as the core skills of helping.
- Knows things, sees things, perceives, intuits, and feels things that others might miss because of their ability to discover deep, underlying structures and patterns.
- Collaborates with clients to reach their stated goals in an efficient period of time.
- Shows a high degree of flexibility and willingness to alter the nature of treatment and style of practice, depending on what a given client requires at a particular moment in time.
- Practices in his or her own life that which is taught to others. This last point is hardly universal in discussions of therapist excellence and may not even be supported by empirical

research. Nevertheless, we feel very strongly that a true master applies to her own life those cherished ideals, values, and behaviors that she considers so important for her clients to learn.

There are a *lot* of other things we could add to this general definition related to ethical standards, personal characteristics, reliability and responsibility, and perhaps 100 (or 10,000) other factors. We will take up many of these in the chapters that follow, beginning with some things that we already know for sure (or reasonably sure). Keep in mind that one characteristic of masters in most fields is that they have a high tolerance for ambiguity and complexity; rather than reducing phenomena to simplistic formulae, they are able to tolerate and hold a far more sophisticated, intricate model of the world and the ways things operate within it.

It was the great Russian novelist, Ivan Turgenev, who once explained to his friend and fellow writer, Leo Tolstoy, that truth remains out of reach when one is limited to a single framework to find a simple answer to a complex question: "The people who bind themselves to systems are those who are unable to encompass the whole truth and try to catch it by the tail; a system is like the tail of truth, but truth is like a lizard; it leaves its tail in your fingers and runs away knowing full well that it will grow a new one in a twinkling."

The concept of a master therapist is neither easy to define nor easy to grasp, especially considering all the different ways such excellence might be manifested.

CHAPTER 2

WHAT WE (THINK WE)
KNOW SO FAR

This is the place where we are supposed to review the literature and knowledge related to our subject of mastery, especially as gleaned from empirical research and experimental studies. We could easily devote a lifetime to reviewing all the studies that have been completed so far regarding what makes a professional extraordinarily effective and what leads to the best outcomes. We could review meta-analyses, literature reviews, study research published in flagship and obscure journals, even review our own studies, and still not come close to making sense of the often-discrepant results. We've heard throughout our careers that it's all about insight—or action, or thinking, or feeling, or behavior. We've been introduced to theories that have guided us in often opposite directions—to work with individuals, families, groups, or communities; to promote autonomy or cohesion; to work in the past, present, or future; to use intuition or deductive reasoning—we could go on and on, but you get the idea.

Since we have colleagues we've already mentioned (and who will be profiled throughout the book) who are already engaged in the systematic study of masterful therapeutic behavior, we intend to approach the subject in quite a different way by drawing on the experiences of the distinguished theorists we've interviewed during the past decade. We are pretty sure you will be as surprised as we were by what was discovered.

A Movement Toward Consensus

There are some cherished assumptions about our field that seem to have been accepted as gospel without sufficient critical judgment.

This is to be expected in a profession that is still relatively young, and especially one that straddles the boundaries between science, education, religion, philosophy, and art. For many of the earliest years it was simply accepted that psychological problems or mental illness were attributed to any number of causes—an ailing heart, an imbalance of bodily fluids, impure blood, witchcraft, masturbation, and disrespect of the gods, to mention a few. Whereas we now consider such explanations to be comical in their naiveté and misguided beliefs, it's interesting how we simply accept that certain policies currently in popular use are above reproach.

It is assumed, for instance, that master therapists have attained that status as a function of advanced degrees and thousands of hours logged under close supervision and continuing education. Likewise, we have spent the better part of the past century arguing which theoretical approach is superior to the rest, which professional discipline is most advantageous, and which license best qualifies someone to do psychotherapy. But here's the interesting thing: We aren't aware of any definitive studies, replicated consistently and accepted universally, that demonstrate that therapist excellence is determined by any of these variables. There's no evidence, for instance, that social workers, psychologists, family therapists, counselors, or psychiatrists have the best preparation; that one's theoretical orientation best predicts superior clinical functioning across a broad spectrum of problems; or that the number of workshops you've attended, supervision or personal therapy you've received, continuing education units (CEUs) you've accumulated, or even books that you've read like this one determine clinical effectiveness. Even years of experience don't predict excellence.

There have been several researchers and writers over the years who have attempted to synthesize what we think we know about what makes a master therapist. Such a list represents a researcher's "hall of fame" since these seminal studies were instrumental in the movements toward pragmatism, eclecticism, and integration of our field's often contradictory theories into a useful synthesis of guidelines that are currently in practice.

Sitting on panels with many of the field's most visible spokespersons, we have personally witnessed the dramatic transition from single-theory allegiance that was common many years ago to the now far more popular flexibility in which therapists routinely rely on several different frameworks to inform their practice and guide their clinical choices. When a handful of passionate advocates for their respective approaches are forced to sit next to one another and talk about their ideas, a funny thing happens: They listen to one another! Their ideas begin to blend together. The boundaries between their differences collapse. And what we are thankfully left with are previously contradictory positions that are blended during these collaborations.

JK It was while moderating a panel discussion among several theoreticians I greatly admire that I completely changed the way I teach a theories course to graduate students. For most of my career I have followed the curriculum established long ago in which we introduce a different therapeutic approach each week and then require students to select one that seems to best fit their own preferences and style. During the early part of my own development, I had been forced to choose a theory with the idea that it would become the dominant framework from which I would owe allegiance and loyalty.

This particular panel was composed of theoreticians who held diametrically opposite ideas on almost everything. Through their published writings, they disagreed on the nature of the human condition, the mechanisms by which change takes place, the preferred focus of treatment, the ideal modalities and interventions that should be employed, even the primary role of a therapist as a consultant, teacher, parent, doctor, or coach. I volunteered for this particular assignment because I was perversely looking forward to the sparks flying.

My first hint that things would not unfold as expected was when I noticed how friendly and respectful the competitors were with one another while sitting at the table. They bantered and teased one another, traded stories about their families, and planned the areas in which they would focus. Once the debate began, I noticed something even more surprising: Rather than searching for areas to engage in heated combat, they ended up finding quite a number of points of agreement. It turns out that these writers, who make a living advocating positions of theoretical purity, actually borrow one another's ideas! They are all integrative in their work, just like the rest of us.

What Does Make a Difference?

It has been in the past few years that not only have theorists with extremely different positions identified universal points of agreement, but also researchers are rediscovering the so-called common factors discussed by Jerome Frank, Marvin Goldfried, John Norcross, Michael Lambert, David Orlinsky, and others many years ago. It turns out that in spite of passionate claims to the contrary, our specific techniques and strategies that we so adore don't matter as much as we think they do.

Exceptional therapists do happen to have more than a working familiarity with several different therapeutic options at any moment in time, and this flexibility is what helps them to function at such a high level. Let's review a few of the other things that we are reasonably sure lead to successful outcomes.

What Clients Bring to the Table

Although we may often blame the client when things go wrong, there is a certain truth to the matter that unless someone is sufficiently motivated and possesses certain basic resources, it is very difficult to promote lasting change. Even among so-called resistant clients, it is their capacity for resilience and hope that best predicts their prognosis.

A number of studies have found consistently that what best predicts successful outcomes may have a whole lot less to do with what therapists do in sessions than we think. Likewise, it isn't so much what theory the therapist subscribes to as the one preferred by clients that guide their perceptions and interpretations of experience. Depending on the client's personality configuration and preexisting conditions, prognoses can be more or less favorable. Their motivation and level of desperation to change will make a difference. Clients who feel a sense of personal responsibility and internal control will likely do better, as will those with a fair degree of resilience and hardiness. Finally, what clients believe about therapy and possibilities for change will have some influence on how far things will go in sessions.

Personal Attributes of the Therapist

We spend all kinds of effort focusing on improving our basic skills, techniques, and interventions. We attend workshops primarily to learn new methods for increasing efficiency and effectiveness. We read books like this in order to grab a few new ideas that may be useful in sessions. Yet much of our persuasive power emanates not from what we *do* but who we *are*. There might be some disagreement as to exactly *which* qualities are most important, but it's safe to say that in all the many personal features that might be mentioned—charisma, essential kindness, wisdom, interpersonal sensitivity, integrity—it is critical for therapists to be compassionate and caring, not to mention persuasive in their own unique ways.

Great therapists think differently in a multitude of ways. They often recognize and make connections that mere mortals would miss. They are able to apply a variety of complex theoretical constructs and then adapt them to any particular case. It isn't so much what they know, and can do, as the ways they are able to personalize and customize such knowledge with a given client and situation. Over time, they are able to develop, test, and refine their working hypotheses as they become progressively more accurate and useful. All the knowledge and skills in the world are hardly useful if the therapists can't understand what is going on and what it means.

The Importance of Knowing Stuff

Being a good, moral, and kind person is hardly enough; otherwise, we could do away with training altogether and just select people for the profession who have desired qualities. Therapists have to know stuff and be able to do stuff. This "stuff" may vary a bit according to one's approach and style, but there is still a level of expertise, knowledge, and mastery associated with effective change agents. We possess ideas, skills, and expertise that others want from us. We know things that others find interesting and useful. And we can do things that are beyond the capacity of others, meaning that we have learned to be sensitive, attentive, and responsive in ways that are not part of normal conversational discourse.

It isn't surprising that Michael Yapko, master of creative interventions, sees the importance of knowing how to do stuff. "I think it also helps to recognize that the foundation of any therapeutic intervention includes suggestions given within the context of a therapeutic alliance, and that mastery of suggestive language is therefore essential to doing effective therapy."

Multicultural theorist Melba Vasquez acknowledges that although there are many different ways to do therapy, and thus different ways of defining excellence within those models, one thing that all great practitioners have in common is their ability to engender trust in their clients. This does not happen through faith but because they know "the therapist understands their problems and situation, as well as has an idea of how the situation occurred, and a plan to help alleviate the problem." Indeed, great therapists do have a plan, an ever-changing template that is co-created with their clients.

Whereas knowledge may be domain specific, one thing that distinguishes truly distinctive professionals is their greater wisdom. Such individuals study widely, *way* outside the parameters of the social sciences, reading fiction, science, and a dozen other fields that interest them. They find inspiration and truth in great novels just as Freud did during the earliest years of the profession. When Ronald Siegel asked notable therapists what wisdom meant to them, they defined this attribute as a deeply reflective way of being, struggling with addressing life's ultimate questions and challenging so-called conventional thinking in a variety of areas. This actually flies in the face of the current zeitgeist in which we are discouraged from pursuing excellence and instead settling for mere competence to conform to minimal standards of practice.

It's the Relationship

Barry Duncan insists that it doesn't take rocket science to tell the best therapists from those who are mediocre: It's all about their ability to form solid therapeutic alliances with those they help. We hear over and over again how it is the quality of the relationship more than any other single factor that best predicts a productive and satisfying experience. Interestingly, this alliance can be structured in all kinds of different ways, depending on the particular approach. It can be structured as a collaborative partnership, holding environment, working alliance, corrective experience, authentic engagement, or any number of other permutations that have similar features that include mutual respect; a sense of safety, trust, and intimacy; and some degree of negotiated goal attainment.

"In the '80s and '90s," Duncan remembers, "I used to direct a training institute that also housed a big group practice. I was very fortunate to witness the work of several very talented therapists. We took turns being the therapist in the room with the client while the team and the primary therapist watched behind a one-way mirror. It was the most enriching learning experience of my career and one that I will always look back on with great fondness. There was one therapist, Greg, who stood out because of his remarkable ability to engage clients from all walks of life, facing all kinds of despair and destitution."

Duncan recalls Peg, a client who came to the agency on maximum doses of two different antidepressants, plus strong pain medication because of an injury she had suffered years earlier. The staff had recommended hospitalization and shock treatment because of the severity and apparent intractability of her depression and suicidal ideation.

As soon as the therapist escorted Peg and her husband into his office, he had already begun to connect with each of them about common interests, commenting about their strengths, resources, and remarkable ability to deal with some very difficult challenges. The therapist shared how much he admired them and then, within the next few minutes, invited them to talk about ways they might improve their situation, beginning with the appropriateness of all the medications.

Duncan could only shake his head in awe at how skillfully this therapist was able to build a relationship so quickly, even with a supposed hopeless case: "He engaged people, even those who seemed impossible to engage, in meaningful conversations about how their lives could be better."

Duncan acknowledges that most of the clients who come to see us present relatively easy opportunities to connect with them and get down to business. "But what about everyone else? What about the folks who are mandated by the courts or protective services or who just plain don't want to be? What about people who have been abused or traumatized? What about folks who never seem to get a break or have lost hope? What about the adolescent who starts off the session by telling you to go screw yourself?"

These are the clients who challenge us and who present the clearest opportunities for extraordinary practitioners to "engage people who don't want to be engaged. *This* is what separates the best from the rest." And this is the hardest work that we do, even though it receives significantly less attention than all the models and fancy interventions that become the rage at popular workshops. According to Duncan, the relationship is usually treated as merely an appetizer—first, you gain rapport, and *then* you do something really useful and meaningful. "The alliance is not the anesthesia to surgery, the stuff you do until you get to the real therapy. We don't just offer Rogerian reflections to lull clients into complacency so we can stick the real intervention to them! Intervention is not therapy. In fact, there is a far better empirical case for the alliance being the therapy. It certainly is the aspect of the work that makes some therapists stand head and shoulders above their peers."

Wondering What Things Mean

Experts in almost any field are relentlessly curious, always trying to figure out better and different ways to be more efficient and effective. Among therapists, in particular, our main job is to make sense of others' behavior and figure why they do the things they do. We are curious about how to help people find their best selves. In that sense, we are architects and artists who help sketch a new plan out of seeming disasters and disappointments. We do this by creating an environment in sessions that is not only hopeful and safe, but also one that inspires deep exploration.

Diana Fosha, creator of accelerated experiential-dynamic therapy, attributes her sense of competence to her deep passion to understand herself, others, and what makes things work. "I am blessed (or cursed) with an impossibly low threshold for detecting authenticity—which has kept me searching and searching to get better and better, and understand more and more because of my intolerance for things that don't *feel* right."

It is this search to make sense of things, not only within sessions or helping relationships, but in larger life, that also inspires feminist theorist Laura Brown to try so hard to make a difference. "I embrace the utter ambiguity and out-of-control nature of the process. I truly believe that our clients are the ones with the inner wisdom and they are the ones in charge. When I temporarily forget this, I discover once again that I'm not the one driving the train!"

Talking to the Masters

You will have noticed that what is missing in this simplistic summary is exactly what we search for most in books like this: interventions that are "proven" to be most effective. Yet meta-analyses and reviews of research related to positive outcomes consistently demonstrate that such techniques account for a small fraction (sometimes cited as less than 10%) of the results.

If you were to survey your own clients systematically and conduct follow-up studies to determine what they believe made the most difference to them, we would seriously doubt that you would hear reports that it was a particular metaphor you weaved, or a single confrontation or interpretation, or that role-play you initiated. More often than not, clients talk about how they felt heard and understood, or how they were pushed to do things that seemed beyond their capability, or that they were helped to understand some things about themselves, or the way the world works, that changed forever the way they operate.

If one definition of a master therapist (but not the one we are using in this book) is someone who has attained fame and notoriety as a major contributor to the field's advancement of knowledge, then we have been privileged to have access to these esteemed professionals on a number of occasions in which we interviewed them. In a series of books during the past decade we have asked a "who's who" list of distinguished thinkers a number of very interesting questions. Our list of eminent theoreticians and practitioners includes those who represent a variety of disciplines, orientations, settings, backgrounds, and clinical specialties (see Table 2.1). We even included several healers outside the traditional boundaries of contemporary Western psychotherapy, including those within spiritual and indigenous traditions.

Table 2.1 Master Therapists Interviewed for This Project

Patricia Arredondo	Gay Hendricks	Bill O'Hanlon
Fred Bemak	Harville Hendrix	Parker Palmer
Insoo Kim Berg	Michael Hoyt	Peggy Papp
Joel Bergman	Susan Johnson	Paul Pedersen
Laura Brown	Judy Jordan	Frank Pittman
Scott Browning	Bradford Keeney	Terry Real
Jim Bugental	Howard Kirschenbaum	Domeena Renshaw
David Cain	John Krumboltz	Howard Rosenthal
Jose Cervantes	Steve Lankton	Ernest Rossi
Raymond Corsini	Arnold Lazarus	David Scharff
Nick Cummings	Michael Lerner	Kirk Schneider
His Holiness the	Pat Love	Richard Schwartz
Dalai Lama	Cloe Madanes	Jhampa Shaneman
Keith Dobson	Steve Madigan	Francine Shapiro
William Doherty	Michael Mahoney	Len Sperry
Barry Duncan	Alvin Mahrer	Richard Stuart
Loren Eisler	Allan Marlatt	Melba Vasquez
Albert Ellis	Leigh McCullough	Frances Vaughan
Diana Fosha	Nancy McWilliams	Lenore Walker
Art Freeman	Scott Miller	Roger Walsh
Arun Gandhi	Dan Millman	Bruce Wampold
Sam Gladding	Alfonso Montuori	Gordon Wheeler
William Glasser	Thomas Moore	Robert Wubbolding
John Gray	John Murphy	Michael Yapko
Les Greenberg	Robert Neimeyer	Jeff Zeig
Jay Haley	John Norcross	
Ken Hardy	Violet Oaklander	

During our interviews, we asked these professionals a number of different questions, depending on the particular project:

- In our study of failures and bad therapy, we queried: "Tell us about your worst mistake and failure as a therapist."
- Exploring the nature of reciprocal changes that occur in therapeutic relationships, we asked: "Tell us about the client who changed you the most."
- Cataloguing greatest success stories, we asked: "What was your finest hour as a therapist in which you did your best work?"
- Digging into the fringes of human behavior, we asked: "As you look back on your distinguished career, tell us about your most unusual case."
- Looking at seminal cases that may have been the basis for their innovative theories, we asked: "What was your most creative breakthrough while working as a therapist?"
- Delving into the realm of spiritual leaders and healers, we asked: "Tell us about how you ended up following a spiritual path."
- Expanding our interest to therapists involved in social justice projects, we asked: "What led you to start such a project, and what lessons have you learned that might be helpful to others who are interested in more direct advocacy work?"
- Investigating the nature of deception and dishonesty in therapy, we asked: "Tell us about a time in which you were duped or lied to by a client over a long period of time."

JC Almost every Wednesday and Thursday for the past 18 years the television studio at my university was transformed into a therapy office. Overstuffed chairs, thick carpet, and background walls were created as a stage, complete with even a window opening onto a lush garden setting replacing the institutional curtains and grey backdrop. Technicians scurry around to adjust lighting and sound, carefully arranging microphones and cameras in optimal positions. It is on this stage that I have had the unique privilege to host over 300 different therapists and 3 times as many clients, who have come together to let others see what actually happens in the private world of psychotherapy.

I have been pleased at the level of honesty and disclosure that the courageous volunteer clients provided as they opened up their inner selves, not only to the therapist, who was basically a stranger they were meeting for the first time, but also all the technical staff and studio audience. The clients shared lifelong secrets, tales of abuse, incest, neglect, mistrust, and physical violence. The participants collaboratively explored the inner workings of depression, panic attacks, bulimia, hoarding, cutting, addictions, suicide, parenting issues, and just about every other problem imaginable.

I was able to study the writings of the expert therapists and to do advance preparation for what each participant was going to bring to the simulated consulting room. It was surprising to me how many of the invitees, known for their sterile reputations and public confidence, felt so much trepidation and doubt demonstrating their skills in action. Many worried that they might not be able to perform as advertised or that they might freeze on stage. I remember Jeffrey told me, when it was his turn many years ago when we first met, that he wondered if on this given day of filming he might have lost his magic.

It turns out that Jeffrey, and many others, had no reason to worry, even in these stressful circumstances. Each theorist usually sees three different clients during a visit to make sure we obtain an exemplary session that demonstrates their salient ideas. Most of the time, things go quite smoothly, and I have learned a lot from these amazing practitioners who are truly masters of their craft. Yet, on occasion, I have also been shocked by how awkwardly and inarticulately some of these notable figures have presented themselves; in some cases, we had a difficult time finding one session that was salvageable even after inviting them back a second time to see more clients. This, of course, is the exception, but it nevertheless highlights the idea that we don't really know who is really great at what they do based on their self-reports and writing.

Over the years, I found myself anticipating with great relish the opportunity to meet and talk to individuals whom I have long admired. Sometimes I would even start new video projects focused on parenting or addiction because I wanted to learn more about those specialties. In some cases, I was terribly disappointed, not only by the theorists' less than stellar demonstrations of their ideas but also because of their arrogance. One famous theorist even demanded that before she would agree to be filmed seeing a client there had to be a teleprompter available so she could read a script because she was so insecure about her clinical skills when others are watching (and it was still a pretty awful session). There were even a few times with certain individuals when I seriously thought about yelling "cut" in the middle of the filming to rescue the client from what I perceived as pretty miserable work. I must also mention that I have been surprised in the other direction as well. There were some theorists whose writing I found tedious and inscrutable and yet they turned out to be incredibly talented clinicians; their written volumes failed to capture the power of their wizardry.

Even though the hundreds of therapists we've recorded represented many different kinds of therapy and approaches to helping people, I've been struck by what so many of them have in common.

What Famous Therapists Appear to Have in Common

Qualitative data analysis often leads to both "vertical" themes that emerge, those *within* the interview, and "horizontal" themes, those that stand out *across* interviews. Since we are interested primarily in those variables that are salient among most, if not all, of our informants, we will review those that struck us as most revealing.

They Aspire to Greatness

It's probably not surprising to learn that these are a bunch of highly ambitious, driven, and achievement-oriented individuals who feel it's important that they leave behind some kind of legacy. They feel a strong personal investment in their professional ideas, which have become their "children," their offspring. They show a certain possessiveness and attachment to their theories, sometimes threatened by perceived attacks. Yet, over time, those whose ideas have endured have learned to embrace critical inquiry. It is similar to the qualitative methodology of grounded theory in which the researcher who has developed a new conceptual framework grounded in the data then begins "theoretical sampling" in the latter stages, deliberately looking for outliers and those who might represent exceptions to the emerging paradigm.

They Work Harder Than Others

Perhaps more than any other single factor, masters of their craft flat out work harder than others. They try harder, persist longer, and practice more "deeply." This is consistent with what Scott Miller, Mark Hubble, and Barry Duncan found in their studies of "supershrinks," what Malcolm Gladwell described in his book *The Outliers*, what Michael Rønnestad and Thomas Slovholt described in their book on therapist development, and what Daniel Coyle observed in *The Talent Code*. If you look carefully at the lifestyles and daily schedules of many notables in our field, you'll find that they commit themselves to improving their effectiveness with a dedication and rigor that is extraordinary. They are really, really good at what they do, in part, not because of some natural talent but rather due to establishing and maintaining a "culture of excellence" that drives them to continually improve.

Failures and Mistakes Provide Valuable Feedback to
Improve Performance

They learned as much from their mistakes and failures as their successes and breakthroughs. Those who are not in denial (and there were a few) are very forgiving of their lapses and limitations. Frank Pittman's classic admonishment was that if you're not doing bad therapy, you can't possibly be doing good therapy, meaning that being an exceptional therapist involves experimentation, taking constructive risks, and venturing *way* outside the bounds of what's already familiar. Many of those we interviewed don't even subscribe to the language of "failure" and instead prefer to think in terms of relative success. Arnold Lazarus said it best by pointing out that his job is not necessarily to help his clients score "touchdowns" but rather more modestly to help them move further along the field to attain "first downs."

Passion Reigns Supreme

Even after so many decades of practice, most of the theorists still absolutely *love* their work. They have discovered ways to keep themselves fully engaged and energized. This is all the more impressive when you consider how many years they've been in practice (some over 60 years!). Yet being famous gives someone career and lifestyle options that are not necessarily available to therapists in the trenches. They can choose their clients more carefully, balance their practices with more varied work assignments, and also enjoy a degree of reverence from other professionals. Also there is certainly a "halo effect" operating in that many of their clients feel fortunate that they have managed to secure an audience with such a notable figure.

Flexibility and Innovation Define Their Thinking and Their Work

In spite of their reputations for being associated with particular theoretical or conceptual orientations, we mentioned earlier that being a master means demonstrating a high degree of pragmatism and flexibility, employing a variety of methods and strategies, depending on the situation and client, as well as their moods. Even though they make a living (in a sense) "selling" a branded ideology, when behind closed doors they employ a wide range of other strategies that they've learned from "competing" orientations and diverse colleagues.

One of the things that surprised us the most during our conversations with theorists over the years is that often what they do in sessions is very different from what they are known for in their writing. Whereas many of them have a branding associated with a particular model they have created, they actually employ a variety of different approaches, depending on what may be best indicated. When William Glasser, founder of reality therapy, described one of his most successful cases that essentially relied on relational factors to produce a breakthrough, we asked him what happened to his favored "choice theory" interventions that involve confronting clients to accept responsibility for their behavior. Glasser just shrugged and confessed he stopped using a lot of that stuff years ago. We mention this not as an example of inconsistency, but rather to debunk the myth that great therapists only follow their own theories.

They Found Their Own Voice

From the very beginning of our training, we are molded by instructors, mentors, and supervisors to choose an approach that best fits us, usually one that they endorse. This isn't necessarily ill advised as a way to learn the basics, but it often leads to stifling many of our own ideas.

We tend to idealize the notables in our field—put them on a pedestal and worship them. When attending a national conference recently, we observed there was an hour wait in line to obtain the autograph of the keynote speaker who has written several classic books in our field. Now we admire this person's writing as much as anyone else, but can you imagine this happening at a dentistry or engineering conference?

The major theorists in our field have found a way to make therapy their own. Whereas at one time they may have followed mentors, each of them discovered a way to adapt, develop, and invent a style that reflects their individual personalities, values, interests, and goals. It is more than a little ironic that these mavericks who rebelled against their own mentors and entrenched theories sometimes struggle with their own followers who wish to depart from orthodoxy and launch their own variations.

What made it possible for them to develop their own therapeutic approach was challenging conventional wisdom and the status quo. They questioned why things were done a particular way. They are provocative and enjoy stirring things up in sessions, as well as their writing, supervision, and dialogues with colleagues. They broke the rules in a sense, without jeopardizing the welfare of their clients. Yet they also risked disapproval and censure by going outside the bounds of accepted standards of practice at the time. Although we may now routinely accept some of the contributions of our most influential theorists, they were often subjected to considerable criticism, if not ridicule, for their rather unorthodox methods.

Their Ideas Evolved Over Time, Followed by Their Developing Practice

Even with their relatively simplistic theories (no theory could possibly capture the essence of experience or the complexity of human change), most of the theorists appreciate the unique individual and cultural differences they encounter. Their influence continues because they were willing to evolve in their thinking and change according to the times, setting, context, and client needs, as well as their own personal and professional development. Most are (or were) voracious readers. Many of them systematically review and study videos of their own work, as well as that of esteemed colleagues. They are involved in active research programs. And they are always looking for ways to improve/alter/upgrade their approach in light of new discoveries.

Their Clients Were Their Greatest Teachers

That's not to say they didn't learn things from their instructors, colleagues, mentors, supervisors, research investigations, and favored books, but rather that many of them traced the birth of their seminal ideas to a particular client or clients who forced them to go *way* beyond what they thought they understood. Theorists such as Robert Neimeyer, Lenore Walker, and David Scharff were challenged to invent something altogether new because their current repertoire was insufficient to address needed issues with a particular client. In that sense, their clients became coauthors of a new or revised approach. In the cases of Violet Oaklander, Steve Lankton, Pat Love, and Frank Pittman, they experienced a kind of extraordinary empathic transcendence with a particular client that led them to revise their thinking about the power of relationships.

In addition, many were profoundly influenced *personally* by their clients that went far beyond professional development. They were touched deeply by those they helped and by the intimacy of the relationships. Some initiated major life changes as a result of contact with particular clients who pushed them or who were following a parallel process. Still others were affected deeply by the changes they witnessed in their clients. According to a study by David Orlinsky and Michael Rønnestad on how therapists develop over time, 97% say that one of the most significant sources of learning for them occurs as a result of what their clients teach them.

From the very beginning of our careers we have been curious, and a bit dumbfounded, by the reciprocal influence that takes place during helping encounters. We are not talking at all about therapists meeting their own needs in sessions but rather the kind of incidental learning and "gifts" our clients offer as part of the parallel process that occurs. One of our first supervisors once commented to us that he felt most psychologically healthy during those days when he was talking to clients about issues that he had yet to resolve. Our own reaction to this disclosure is that such unfinished business only

made us feel ashamed and hypocritical that we were helping someone deal with something that we had yet to work through.

Ever since then, we've tried to reflect on our own personal
growth and learning that occurs after each session we conduct.
Sometimes we're lazy and "forget" to do so, but at least a few times
each week we find ourselves reeling from some new revelation that
cropped up in a session. Our clients (or students) hardly ever realize this, and we rarely talk about it to them, but we attribute much
of the precious stability of our life to what we've learned from our
clients as much as the times we've been in therapy as clients or under
supervision.

When we look back all the years with our greatest teachers, we'd
certainly acknowledge the influence of several charismatic mentors,
but just as prominent in our memory are a handful of clients who
really taught us most of what we know and understand about how
change occurs. And this process continues to this day. As a matter
of fact, as we write these words, we are both struck by something
that happened in a session this very week that we'd each never encountered before. This leads to a certain amount of confusion and
uncertainty but also is responsible for stretching us in new ways.

Master therapists begin with a "calling" or deep desire to help
others and to use themselves to make a difference in the world.
This desire will become important as the numerous challenges to
mastery appear, including inevitable failures and disappointments.
Master therapists learn from these setbacks just as they do from
the best teachers they can find, acquiring depth of knowledge
and experience. Yet excellence in our profession, or any other that
involves close relationships, is not just what we know, what we
understand, or what we can do that makes all the difference: As we
will see in the next chapter, superlative clinicians are, above all else,
the embodiment of caring and compassion.

CHAPTER 3

DEEP COMPASSION
AND CARING

In this first in a series of explorations of how master therapists become who they are, and what they are able to do so extraordinarily well, we examine what we consider the single most salient quality of such experts: Beyond all else, they demonstrate deep compassion toward those they help. They may reveal their caring in all kinds of direct and implicit ways, sometimes through authentic and genuine human engagement, and other times by setting clear, consistent boundaries. Master therapists can be either (or both!) demonstrably affectionate or express their caring in other ways that match their personality, style, and particular client needs.

Some of the most kind, caring, and loving people we know are therapists. However, there are other practitioners, remarkably effective in their own right, who appear downright withholding, if not overly critical. They appear to have the interpersonal skills of a toad, croaking in an annoying tone, demanding, self-justifying, and sometimes rude. Yet we'd like to think that in their own way these professionals have a rather unique way of expressing their caring to their clients, one that is no less effective. Even among those who don't explicitly acknowledge that caring is an integral part of their work, and that it may even lead to nonproductive pity, they still leak their compassion in other ways that their clients would recognize.

Compassion can be described as the deep understanding of another's experience in such a way that the corresponding responses communicate kindness beyond mere empathy. Compassion is what unifies most of the world's religions (at least in theory), as well as most approaches to helping. Whether embedded in the so-called treatment alliance or more directly in the identified core conditions of any therapeutic relationship, compassion is among the strongest instinctual human drives. Its close cousins, sympathy and kindness, are among the strongest components of mate selection, more important than status, power, or appearance.

Creating Connections

We express our compassion toward clients through our reassurance and caring words, but also through our actions. This often includes three distinct features: (1) "I feel for you," (2) "I understand you," and (3) "I want to help you." Interestingly, the critical point is not whether we truly feel for someone and understand him or her but rather that others *perceive* our actions that way.

Russ is a 24-year-old man who has been in therapy for 3 years struggling with addictions to alcohol, drugs, and gambling that have all but ruined his life. He has consulted several different therapists in the past as well as attended inpatient treatment programs, all with limited results that ended in relapses.

Russ has been able to get by most of his life because of his extraordinary physical stature and athletic abilities, standing 6 feet 4 inches. He has enjoyed other advantages, not the least of which were his physical attractiveness, charm, and Ivy League education. Even with a troubled childhood, conflicted family, and unstable relationships with his parents, he was destined for greatness, at least until his addictions took over his life during college.

Knowing his background and previous failed attempts to respond to treatment, his therapist attempted a variety of interventions, including structured exercise programs, support groups, family sessions, job change, and so on, all without putting much of a dent in his continued drinking, drugging, and gambling. Most recently, Russ had experienced blackouts, spent several months in jail, and suffered injuries falling off his bike (his driver's license had been revoked).

The most surprising thing is that Russ attended his therapy sessions voluntarily, never missing an appointment or showing up late. He actually seemed to enjoy the conversations and especially appreciated the relationship with his male therapist, considering the life-long difficulties he experienced with his father. These feelings were in marked contrast to those of his therapist, who was feeling increasingly helpless and frustrated by the apparent lack of visible progress.

"I know you seem to like coming here," the therapist confessed to Russ one time, "but I wonder what it is actually doing for you? I mean you may show up and say the right things, but not much has really changed for you out there." As he said this, he pointed to the door.

Russ nodded. "I guess that's true. But I look at you right now, that expression you have on your face. I know I drive you a little crazy and you must feel disappointed. . . ."

"Russ, it's not that. It's . . ."

"Wait, let me finish. I feel so badly that I'm letting you down. It's not like my parents at all, who always seem to have their own agenda for me, who tell me constantly that I'm wasting my life and shaming the family name. I know they love me and all and want what's best for me, but it's different with you. Sure, I lie to you sometimes. . . ."

"You do? You mean you haven't been completely truthful in everything you've told me?" They both laughed.

"Well, maybe just a few little things. But I'm being serious for a change right now. I want you to know how much I appreciate your caring for me. It could be my imagination, but it seems like that when I'm hurting you seem to be actually feeling my pain. It's like I'm hurting you when I hurt myself."

"I appreciate your saying that. It's true that I do care about you, quite a lot actually, but I wouldn't exactly say that you are hurting me or even disappointing me. But I do feel somewhat helpless sometimes trying to get through to you."

"Hey, there's only so much you can do for me. You've made that clear. It's up to me to make the changes I need to make and, until I do that, all you can do is hold my hand." Russ laughed again, but it caught in his throat. Tears began to form in his eyes, which he quickly wiped away with his sleeve.

The therapist waited, nodding in agreement.

"I guess what I'm saying," Russ continued in a hoarse voice, "is that I just appreciate your hanging in there with me when it seems like everyone else has jumped ship and given up. I know that eventually I'm going to work this out, but it's just taking more time than both of us prefer."

What Russ is describing, of course, is what all of us recognize as such a critical part of our work that goes beyond our techniques and interventions. Whether you prefer to call it empathy, compassion, a holding environment, therapeutic alliance, or anything else, master therapists excel at creating connections with their clients that appear intrinsically healing. We may subscribe to the belief that our favorite techniques provide what clients need most, but they are almost always powered by the compassion and caring that are communicated.

JK When I was a graduate student eons ago, one of my heroes was Albert Ellis, who had just reached the status of superstar on the workshop circuit. I showed up at one of his "performances" and found a room filled with over 300 participants; the only seats left were in the front row, so I was delighted to have the best view. I had been learning and practicing Rational Emotive Therapy (as it was then called), so I was eager to see the master demonstrate these techniques that had already been so useful to me.

Boy, was I surprised to learn that the front-row seats were reserved for volunteers who were going to come on stage as clients! I watched in awe as Ellis plowed through the sessions, one after another, "fixing" each client with a wave of his magic disputing of irrational beliefs. The thing that surprised me, though, is that he looked mostly bored with the routine, as if he had been through this procedure thousands of times (and he had!) and it was just a matter of reciting the script. It seemed to work well enough, but it seemed like something else was going on, which I tried to figure out as I waited nervously for my turn on stage.

Ellis talked about his theory, his assumptions, his technique, the research that supported this approach, and it was really all about following the regimented steps—describe the activating event, list the emotional consequences, identify the irrational beliefs, and so on. It seemed like a recipe that was fairly easy to memorize and not that difficult to put into practice. Perfect for a beginner like me.

Finally, it was my turn and I slinked up on stage absolutely terrified. Here I was, a lowly graduate student, in the presence of the great master, surrounded by hundreds of professionals. But I tried to block out all those distracting thoughts, using what I already understood about his theory, and it wasn't that difficult to do. As it turned out, I was smack in the middle of a major crisis: My mother was dying. But here's the thing: Rather than feeling terrible anticipatory grief and loss, I was actually relieved that she would be gone soon. My mother had always been a burden in my life, a depressed alcoholic who was often suicidal. She was dying of cancer, and I was less than grief-stricken—a condition that led me to feel extremely guilty that I was such a terrible son. I assumed there was something wrong with me and that guilt was the punishment for my uncaring attitude.

I'm sure you can guess the kind of thing that Ellis would have said to me—challenging my beliefs about what constitutes a "good" son, disputing my irrational thoughts regarding "appropriate" behavior, and so on. I went along with the program—after all, we were on stage in front of all these people. Ellis was talking to me in that screechy voice. I was more than a little intimidated by him, especially considering that he began the day by addressing a group of nuns sitting in the back of the room, scolding them that if they were going to be offended by his "fucking" language, they might as well leave now. They solemnly filed out.

There is nobody else in the audience who could really see or feel what was happening during my session on stage. When they were asked to comment afterward, members of the audience identified all kinds of different techniques and interventions that Ellis used with me—and it really was a pretty stunning conversation that forever changed the way I thought and felt about my mother's death and my relationship with her. But when I was asked afterward what it was that Ellis did that was most helpful, my response was simple and straightforward: "Nothing in particular."

When I later reviewed the tape that was made of our session, I became more convinced than ever that it really wasn't the RET that helped me; it was Ellis—as a person. I don't think there was anyone else present that day who could sense and feel how much he seemed to care about me during the brief time we were together. We were sitting close together, our knees almost touching, and I felt truly heard by him. I felt his compassion for me. I felt that he really knew me in those moments.

This was an absolute breakthrough for me, not only as someone who was suffering from the impending death of a parent, but as a beginner who was learning to be a therapist. I realized after that experience that as important as I imagined technique might be, it was really this feeling of caring, of compassion, that was so incredibly powerful.

During the ensuing years, I completely reconceptualized my work. Granted that much of what I do no longer takes place in a therapy office, but rather in the field, so to speak, whatever interventions, techniques, strategies, and methods that I have learned over the years have now become assimilated into who I am. Whether I am doing a home visit in a remote village; volunteering in a school or orphanage; or leading a service trip to a disadvantaged community, teaching, coaching, supervising, or conducting a therapy session, much of what I'm trying to do is communicate my caring and compassion to those I am assisting. This is caring without pity, without reciprocal demands, without (mostly) meeting my own needs. I inserted *mostly* because I reluctantly acknowledge that what I do isn't just about helping others but also fortifying myself. I need to feel wanted, so to speak. Although I prefer to have my efforts appreciated and explicitly expressed, sometimes that feels like a need as well: I'm frustrated a lot of the time because I can't really tell whether my work is doing what it was intended to do.

Looking back, most of my own teachers, supervisors, therapists, and influential mentors, taught me "stuff," meaning that I learned certain skills, knowledge, content, and wisdom from them, but I also felt loved—or at least respected—by them. This wasn't always the case, of course. I can think of a few who not only didn't love or respect me much, but they didn't even seem to like me. But that taught me some important lessons as well, painful ones that also shaped what I've become.

I would be remiss if I didn't mention that there are exceptions to almost everything, including the rather obvious supposition that compassion is a significant part of therapeutic work. We have all encountered clients who could care less if we care about them or even like them. This is business for them, and they just want some answers—or action. Some are completely oblivious to relational issues, either because they were born that way or trained from childhood. When we might try to demonstrate some modicum of empathy for their predicament, they just shrug as if to ask, "That is great you feel that way, but how is that relevant to what we're doing right now?" And they genuinely believe that.

There was a time when I was in private practice full time and was feeling frustrated, maybe even burned out, by the futility of my work. I was questioning whether what I was doing made any kind of important difference in the world, given that most of my clients at the time were among the "worried well," relatively middle-class working professionals struggling with adjustments to all the stress in their lives. I felt replaceable, that so many others could do what I was doing. I also had some serious doubts about whether my work even had much lasting value. How did I know my clients were really changing? Among those who were truly suffering, what could I possibly do for them for 50 minutes each week? I had lost my therapeutic "faith." I had also somehow misplaced my compassion, more often seeing my clients as noncompliant and resistant. It was during this time that I had this great idea for a new book that would be called "Clients From Hell," in which each chapter would be about a different kind of client who tortures us with their manipulative games, noncompliance, or stubborn obstructiveness. Admit it: Wouldn't this be a fun, validating book to read? Anyway, upon completion, the book was sent out for review and one reviewer hit me pretty hard with the observation that it seemed like I had lost my compassion, feeling like clients were being sent from hell to make my life miserable (I swear—they were!). That single comment helped me to change my perspective, and the title of the book, to *Compassionate Therapy: Working With Difficult Clients*.

By the way, you'd never guess who the reviewer was who made the comment that I'd lost my compassion and love for my clients.

Albert Ellis.

Commitment and Investment

As we will discuss in a later chapter, *love* has been the forbidden word in our profession, largely because of its associations with exploitation, sexual improprieties, countertransference, codependence, and personal indulgence on the part of the therapist. Instead, we use terms like *alliance, unconditional positive regard,* and *empathy* to describe the relational connections that develop with our clients. And certainly, there are some people we see whom we don't much like at all; in fact, they work pretty diligently at making themselves as unlikeable as possible. Nevertheless, we have long believed—and kept this pretty much to ourselves—that it is love that drives a lot of our therapeutic work.

When the Dalai Lama was asked to define what love means, he hesitated for just a moment before breaking out in his trademark smile. He spends a lot of his time entertaining visitors who like to stump him with challenging questions that may appear to be deceptively simple. Sometimes he will stall for time and wait for his translator to repeat the question in his native Tibetan language, but this time he just shrugged and answered immediately in English. "Love," His Holiness answered, "is the wish to make someone else happy."

At first we were disappointed by the response that seemed both trite and oversimplified. Like many pilgrims who traveled so far for this audience, there had been a distinct hope for some surprising insight that had previously escaped us. It was only with time, and a lot of reflection, that we finally appreciated the depth and profundity of this comment. We realize that therapy isn't always about making our clients happy, but it is nevertheless our wish to do so, sometimes quite desperately.

We are often called upon to do and say things that, at least in the short run, are hardly perceived as loving or even designed to promote immediate happiness. In fact, one could say that some of our best work is actually designed to make people feel worse about themselves the way they are.

When working with couples, for example, we rarely ask a couple if they love one another because we already assume that is the case. The problem is usually not about an absence of love but rather about how it is expressed or withheld. Most people understand this distinction, yet when they are asked to describe their respective role in maintaining such an unsatisfying relationship, they show acute sadness and disappointment.

"You don't understand," one partner will soon interject with great exasperation. "I'm not the problem, he/she is!"

"At least you both agree with that position," might be one response. "You are each blaming the other for your problems, refusing to accept any responsibility, and as long as that continues, there is little chance you will work together toward your stated common goal—which is to have a more fulfilling, loving relationship."

Such confrontations are hardly appreciated at the time, nor are they felt as particularly loving and compassionate. But when such conversations lead people to make significant changes in the ways they relate to one another, their initial discomfort and misery are soon converted into their desired outcomes. As such, love in therapy is all about communicating to clients how much we want them to have a satisfying and more fulfilling life.

We don't mean to become ethereal and deliberately obtuse and mystical about what makes a therapist truly great. We love our favorite stories, techniques, and interventions as much as the next person. Yet we recognize that there is a preoccupation—even an obsession—with techniques and interventions in our field, as if memorizing some incantation, hypnotic induction, metaphor, or procedure will consistently produce miraculous results if we simply follow the instructions. There is an eternal search for the Holy Grail of manualized treatments, one that is foolproof and easy to learn and will produce guaranteed results. Each year it goes by a different acronym—EMDR, EFT, CBT, DBT, ACT, RCT, MBCT. Following a parallel course, researchers continue looking for the singular operating variable that produces positive outcomes.

As much as we hope for the quest to end with a prize, what has kept us most energized, excited, creative, enthusiastic, and wildly passionate about our work has little to do with any particular approach or technique; it is about caring and even about loving people in a nondemanding, nonexploitive, nonromantic way that represents genuine, authentic, and deep commitment toward those we help. Person-centered therapist David Cain, a colleague of Carl Rogers, talks about what he considers to be among the most important qualities for any helper—dedicated investment in others' welfare. "Investment, in its essence, represents the therapist's unwavering personal and professional commitment to alleviating client distress and promoting well-being. It embodies a combination of a caring attitude, a 'being-for' the client, and a dedication to the client's hope for a more effective manner of living. Invested therapists are accessible and available, feel genuinely concerned, and can be relied on to support and assist in any way that seems promising. The therapist's attitude is that he or she will stay the course, will accompany the client through the worst of times and situations, and will not give up. The invested therapist's attitude is fundamentally altruistic in nature since his or her major concern is the client's well-being and progress toward the client's goals."

What David Cain speaks about as commitment, we ordinarily might consider as a form of love, a subject that we take up again in Chapter 12. This is the origin of our dedication to helping others, and it is what sustains us. We'd like to think that beyond anything we offer to our clients, students, and supervisees in the way of constructive advice, input, feedback, insights, and content, many of them also felt loved by us.

JC As you may recall from the introduction to the book, I received a (temporary) stay of execution with regard to the cancer that has polluted my blood and snapped the vertebrae along my spine. It appears after all that I will live long enough to see the publication of this work, even if it means learning to live with crippling pain. Stem cell transplants purged the cancer from my blood, but at a dear cost that makes each day both a gift and a plague. Every system of my body is purified, yet also in chaos. It takes teams of doctors to regulate my blood pressure, internal organs, immune system, and heart (did I mention that I had to undergo cardiac surgery right before the transplants?). This requires frequent, lengthy stays in the hospital in which I am subjected to all kinds of drugs with awful side effects, painful procedures, and worst of all, the uncertainty about my recovery.

Of course, I am grateful to the surgeons, oncologists, and other doctors who literally saved my life with a miracle cure. I was fortunate to live close to a teaching hospital with experimental treatments, but it also resembles a factory with its impersonal, antiseptic atmosphere. Doctors I've never seen before visit me in my drug-induced stupor. Residents stream in all day long with their medical students in tow, showing me off like a prize-winning steer. Nurses, physical therapists, speech therapists, occupational therapists, and technicians make the rounds, nodding hello, then making notes in their electronic scanning devices. They are choreographed in their shifts, color-coded in their scrubs, each cued to keep things running efficiently and profitably. Most of the time I don't feel human; I'm just a part in this huge machine, taking up temporary warehouse space. They draw their blood, analyze my urine, run me through their CAT scans, X-rays, and other diagnostic screenings, all to fix what they consider just an annoying problem that happens to reside in my body. During moments of my greatest despair, it all struck me as a grand scam in which they were just trying to run up the medical bills as high as possible before I expire.

Each time a staff person would enter my room, I'd ask in exasperation, "Is this really necessary? Why do I need this? Who ordered this?" I wondered why they wouldn't allow me to die in peace with some dignity. I was so out of it most of the time that I was terrified they'd do something to me while I was unconscious, cut off a piece of me that they felt was getting in the way. It started to become a game for me, and, in some ways, it helped to save my life because I was determined to remain as awake and aware as possible so I could fight them back—and at times it really did feel like they were the enemy, not the cancer. I could accept that for the cancer it was nothing personal, it was just doing its job, but these people in this medical factory seemed like I was only a body and not a person.

But then something changed for me, and it had nothing to do with their medical procedures. Of course, I remain grateful for the incredible brilliance and expertise of the staff that worked on me, but it was a few of the nurses who gave me hope and the will to live (along with my family). I must admit that I was a miserable patient—demanding at times, confusing and out of it other times, angry, impatient, frustrated, ornery, argumentative, and sometimes without hope. What helped me most was the soothing love and caring I felt from a few nurses who stayed with me, sometimes all day long, just holding my hand and whispering words of reassurance. I know I was "just" a patient occupying a bed in their intensive care unit, but it felt like so much more than that to me. One doctor, who seldom talked but always showed great interest in my well-being, brought me a bobble-head doll of a major league baseball pitcher who was known as a "closer," someone who comes into a game right near the end and saves the victory. She told me to finish up this cancer treatment with a victory and get back into the game of life. I know that sounds trite, but it made such a difference to me.

It was Pamela, the head nurse, who "cured" my soul and psyche as much as the cancer treatments cured my body. She truly understood the agony and the helplessness I was experiencing and decided to make me her special project. Even though her main job was administrative duties, she made it a point to spend a part of each day with me, feeding me, massaging my aching back, talking to me, listening to me. She "joined" my family in the same sense that we attempt such interventions with our own therapeutic work. She spent time with me "off the clock" and gave of herself in a multitude of ways, including sharing part of her own life with her husband and children. To this day it's hard for me to think about her without tears in my eyes, without feeling such incredible gratitude for who she is as a person as well as a professional. I try to think about what it is that she did that made such a difference in my life, and my recovery, but all I can do is feel soothed by her love.

What Pamela did for me is what I believe any master helper or healer does for those they help. What Pamela taught me, or rather what she reminded me, is never to underestimate the power of caring in what we do.

The Growth Edge

Traditionally, some of our most complex systems of helping, whether psychoanalytic or existential in origin, have now embraced the overriding value of caring and compassion beyond any interpretative technique. Nancy McWilliams, a psychoanalytic theorist, mentions the importance of humility and curiosity in her work that leads her to keep compassion at the forefront of her work, regardless of the direction that conversations are going: "I suspect that the most important quality I bring to the work is a genuine interest in other people, their individual subjective differences in the ways they make meaning of their experiences. I was never shamed as a child, and so I have very little tendency to shame others. My curiosity is great, and my respect for others is pretty automatic. I'm kind of a junkie for learning about people and for experiencing the widest possible range of emotions. I'd rather be surprised by a patient—and by my own prior ignorance—than go into a session assuming I know what is going on."

Although she speaks about this caring, respect, and humility as a natural condition we suspect that Nancy invested a lot of hard work in her own personal and professional development to make it possible for her to remain open to others' experience with a complete absence of judgment. Most of us talk a good game about how empathic and accepting we are with clients, but the reality is that there is often a fair amount of critical chatter bouncing around inside our heads when clients say or do things that strike us as spectacularly stupid.

Nancy reports that she doesn't need to fake or simulate understanding her client's experiences: She really feels that most of the time she is able to be there with them without concern for "my own immediate comfort or narcissistic satisfaction."

Each of us is working on our skills and competencies as a therapist, a helper, and a healer. We attend workshops and accumulate continuing education credits, obtain advanced degrees, accrue licenses, and read books such as this one, in order to upgrade our therapeutic options, increase our wisdom, and provide additional guidance. We are continuously searching for alternative ways to become more effective. Whereas those discoveries certainly include new and better ways to *do* therapy, an often neglected but critical piece has to do with growing our compassion for others.

Anyone who has been in this field for a while understands the challenges of keeping ourselves fresh, energized, and passionate about what we do. It is very easy to function on autopilot, to listen to our clients with partial attention, repeat the same well-worn stories and anecdotes, and use the same time-tested techniques that have (or have not) worked previously. It takes considerable commitment and energy to truly remain engaged in sessions, to co-create individually designed, unique therapeutic masterpieces that not only promote lasting changes but inspire clients to maintain the momentum long after the work ends. We all have to find our own path to doing so, pursuing our growth edge, one that helps us keep things fresh. For us, that has been about accessing and expressing love in what we do, love for the people we help, love for the work that we do, and love for the gratitude we feel in what we've been privileged to learn from our clients and students over the years.

CHAPTER 4

SOPHISTICATED INTERPERSONAL SKILLS: REALLY, *REALLY* LISTENING

The ability to focus on another's life is a skill (and attitude) that is acquired and developed with practice. Beginners learn the rudimentary components of listening that involve all the appropriate attending and reflecting skills. What distinguishes an extraordinary clinician is not only the ability to listen well, applying the requisite skills, but the commitment to do so in such a way that clients feel they have been understood at the deepest level.

What is it that distinguishes a beginning therapist who has learned the basics of active listening from a master who has internalized those skills in such a way that they have become an integrated and personalized way of being?

It is one of the gifts of our profession that we have these amazing opportunities to continually develop and enhance our ability to relate to others in more caring and responsive ways. Beginners in the field have been drilled in the mechanics of active listening, reflecting content and underlying affect to demonstrate that they have been attending (and understanding) adequately what clients have expressed. They learn the basics of core listening and responding skills, each of them broken down into their component, sequential parts. They are evaluated on the accuracy of their reflections and often the clarity of their statements.

Over time, and with sufficient practice, many practitioners move *way* beyond these basics to develop a unique style of relating to others, one that consistently communicates intense focus and engagement with the other. Frances Vaughan, a transpersonal psychologist, shared that what she practices as deep listening doesn't only involve what she hears from people: "I can actually *feel* my client's experience. I listen as much for what is missing, what is not said, what is avoided."

In some circumstances, certain professionals have even discovered the means by which they incorporate this "way of being" into their daily lives: They make it a priority to demonstrate "deep" listening in all (or most) of their relationships. In many different ways, we will return to this theme throughout the book—that true masters practice in their personal lives that which they value most in their helping encounters. That's why we chose to highlight this theme in the subtitle of the book, emphasizing that truly master therapists practice in their own lives what they preach to their clients in sessions.

JK "It's all kind of hopeless when I think about it," Abbie stated almost casually.

I shrugged, not sure what to say to that.

"I mean, what's the point?" she said, raising her voice at the end, turning everything into a question.

Again, I just waited.

"Sometimes," she started, then stopped thoughtfully, "sometimes . . . I don't know . . . sometimes I wonder if it's worth it. You know what I mean?"

I nodded but didn't have a clue what she meant quite yet. We'd been talking for only a few minutes, but already it was clear that this young woman was profoundly, devastatingly depressed. She was so depressed I could feel her despair settle on top of me to the extent that I kept involuntarily shrugging my shoulders, as if to lift off the added weight.

"Is it always going to be like this?" she asked me. "Is this what I've got to deal with my whole life?"

I immediately thought to myself, "This girl definitely needs some meds." Here she is, 19 years old and already feeling like her life is over. She's been to I-don't-know-how-many other therapists, none of whom have been all that helpful. What could I possibly do that others hadn't tried?

Abbie had already recited the long list of mental health professionals she'd consulted since childhood. She'd been practically weaned on psychoanalytic therapy. She'd been to see cognitive therapists. She'd tried group therapy. Family therapy. I think she said she'd been Rolfed, too. Now she was trying me as a last resort, as if I had some magic tricks, but I was already thinking about pawning her off on a psychiatrist for a medication review.

Deep breath. Time to start over.

"Abbie, let's back up again," I said in a voice so soft I couldn't be sure she even heard me. "Before we get into all this stuff about what's wrong with you, and what your other doctors have tried, and all the other ways you are suffering, could you just tell me about you?"

Abbie cocked her head. "What do you mean?"

I wasn't exactly sure myself. "Just tell me who you are. I don't want to know quite yet about all your problems and failures and frustrations and your messed-up family and all that. I just want to hear more about *you*—as a person, not some screwed-up patient."

She looked thoughtful but I couldn't tell if she understood what I was asking or not. Even I wasn't sure what I was asking.

Abbie was looking at me as if deciding something. I don't know what. Should she trust me? Was I playing some game with her? Where should she start?

"Look Abbie," I broke the silence. "I'm interested. I just want to hear about who you are. I really do."

And I did. I really did.

During the ensuing months, I mostly just listened. That's one thing I love about adolescent or college-age girls rather than most guys I see: They will actually verbalize what they're thinking and feeling. And once Abbie got started, it was like something broke loose. I know she'd had plenty of training with her other therapists, but it seemed to me that she was telling a story that was relatively unrehearsed. It wasn't a smooth or chronological or even coherent narrative. It wasn't scattered, either. Just raw.

I mostly just listened to Abbie during our sessions together. And I must say I was riveted, not because her story was so interesting, but rather because it was so obvious that she desperately wanted—needed—someone to hear what she had to say without trying to correct or fix her.

It struck me at the time that this was one of the easiest cases I could imagine; after all, she was doing all the work; all I had to do was just sit there and listen to her. But that's really hard to do, especially to do it well. And once we add into the picture the almost universal necessity that we not only have to listen really carefully to our clients but also make some semblance of meaning from what they are saying, things get a lot more challenging.

It is when I walk away from such encounters, those in which I have listened so carefully, so attentively, so deeply, that I can actually feel the other person's experience, that I marvel at the kind of transcendent empathy that can be possible with sufficient commitment. Here's the problem that makes me feel more than a little uncomfortable: I rarely demonstrate such focused attention outside of sessions. I get as distracted as anyone else by the chatter inside my head; the plans, wishes, and desires for what comes next; the interruptions from various mobile devices; the intrusions of various sights, sounds, and other disturbances that capture my attention—all the while nodding my head and pretending to listen.

It is such awareness of hypocrisy that motivates me most to strive for greater congruence in all my relationships, especially those that matter the most. It isn't just listening that is so critical for deeper connections, but also trying really, really hard to understand what is being said. I mention this with the full awareness that actually understanding another's experience is impossible most of the time. I am fully aware that it is the client's perception that she or he is understood that matters most. Nevertheless, most of us got into this work in the first place because we have such a strong interest in understanding what is going on around us and within us.

"I don't know."

That probably *is* the most honest answer we might offer when a client (or beginning therapist) asks how it is that you managed to literally read between the lines and hear some underlying feeling or message that had been hidden or disguised.

Sometimes we really have no idea what people are saying or what they really mean. We entertain the illusion that with sufficient skill and practice, we can learn to decode the deeper meanings of speech, accurately read nonverbal cues, identify implicit and symbolic messages embedded in the surface messages, recognize metaphoric illusions, and generally *understand* what is being communicated. In theory, anyway, it is supposed to be our job to *attend* to the client(s) with full and complete focus; *listen* carefully to what is being communicated; *hear* nuances that have previously gone unrecognized or unacknowledged; *deconstruct* the narrative; *analyze* the contextual basis for what was said—or not said; *make interpretations* about the interaction; and so on. In other words, we get paid to really, *really* listen to people.

We do try to listen as best we can. But our attention constantly wanders. Even this moment, as you are reading these words, figuring out where this sentence might be going, you may be thinking about other things: "I'm hungry. My shoulders feel tight. I must remember to do some stretching. Where did I put my keys? I know this stuff already; should I move on to the next chapter?"

All of us have struggled with a limited attention span ever since we can remember, even with the disciplined training we've received. With that said, we do hear things that others often miss. It is a plague as much as a gift: In many cases, we'd rather *not* become aware of why people seem to do the things they do.

We try not to fool ourselves into thinking that we really do understand what people mean, or what they are *really* saying. We've got our hunches, even hypotheses supported by evidence, but we're also wrong at times. And that's humbling.

Now that we've offered this disclaimer, we believe what we do, what *any* good therapist can do, is listen very carefully. We're not just talking about *pretending* to listen with all those little tricks we have to nod our heads, employ laser-like eye contact, and throw in a few "uh-huhs" as needed. We mean that any master therapist can listen with an intensity and focus that is beyond the capacity of "civilians." It is really quite amazing, when you think about it, that we can enter that place of transcendent attention, an altered state of consciousness in which we feel encapsulated in a bubble. Extraneous sounds disappear. Time ceases altogether or at least becomes elastic—a single minute can seem to last a second or an hour, depending on the client or the session.

Of course, it isn't enough just to listen unless, first, we can *communicate* this interest and, second, *do* something useful with what we hear. We think it's more than a little interesting that so much of our training, and subsequent continuing education and supervision, is all about how to do new stuff rather than how to listen better. It's just assumed that we already know how to listen to clients well enough, but what we need a lot more of is what else to *do* with them. It is presumed that what separates a run-of-the-mill, average therapist from one who is extraordinary is that the latter has mastered more advanced and elaborate techniques. Yet we've become more and more convinced that along the way one thing we often forget is how critical it is to help people to tell their stories and feel like they are deeply heard, perhaps more so than ever before in their lives.

It isn't as if once we've reached that state of almost-perfect attunement we can maintain it consistently without considerable vigilance. We see certain clients with whom it seems we can barely stay awake, much less listen carefully. There are even whole days we feel listless and disengaged, struggling to listen to ourselves, much less anyone else. We are preoccupied with unresolved issues in our own lives. We remain worried about a previous client and find it challenging to switch channels. This is all consistent with what has been reported in various studies that document how rarely we listen fully to our clients, and when we do so, most of the time we don't really understand what has been communicated.

We've conducted our own research over the years, asking practitioners to estimate what percentage of the time they are actually giving their full attention to their clients and listening to them with unwavering focus. Stop for a moment and consider approximating your own pattern: In a typical session, how much of the time are you really and truly focused on the client, without distractions, without indulging in internal fantasy, without leaving the room and going somewhere else in your head? Before you answer, try monitoring how much you actually listen to what *anyone* is saying to you during a conversation. We've heard estimates ranging from 20% (probably those who are burned out) to 75% (probably unduly optimistic), with an average of about 50%. That means that roughly half the time we are in session with a client, pretending interest, we are actually somewhere else in our heads, not listening much at all.

Master therapists seem to have the ability—or the self-discipline—to listen more carefully, for longer periods of time, without the frequent self-indulgent lapses that are triggered by boredom or pushing our buttons. Of course, our clients can often sense when we aren't really with them no matter how sly we think we are being disguising yawns and disinterest. The only reason they might not call us on our lapses of concentration is that they are so used to being ignored or devalued. That is one reason why this particular aspect of our work is so critical, and why over time we might lose focus because of what we believe is overfamiliarity with what we are hearing.

Little Things Make a Huge Difference

The differences between novice practitioners and those who are considered exceptional may often seem quite subtle, especially related to such "basic" skills as listening. Master therapists might appear to listen, just as anyone might attend to a conversation, but they would hear, see, and sense more information, decode communications in deeper ways, find patterns that are invisible to others, and focus on client strengths and resources with acute accuracy. This is something that Jeffrey Zeig has been teaching and practicing for decades after launching the Evolution of Psychotherapy Conferences and studying the work of Milton Erickson. Erickson might have been best known for his wizardry as an innovator of hypnotic technique, but he was first and foremost a deep listener who first noticed the ways that little things that are done and said can make a big difference in promoting change.

Even when therapists hone in on aspects of the conversation that almost anyone else might notice, they respond with greater style and panache. Their professional behavior can be described as *compleat* in the archaic sense of that term, referring to the ultimate level of attainment, the ultimate goal to be attained for any professional.

It is precisely the little things that compleat therapists have mastered, permitting them to "hold" the complexity and confusion of an interaction in such a way that behavior becomes more comprehensible. It is also such experience that allows them to decode actions that might escape less attentive practitioners.

Imagine, for example, that Margo sits in your office during a first session, positively exuberant about how well her life is going. You nod your head waiting for the rest of things to unfold; after all, she was referred for help because somebody believed she had a serious problem.

"Seriously," Margo repeats to you for the third time, "things couldn't be any better."

"So," you respond, buying some time, "you really sound pleased with how you've been able to stay so upbeat even when you have to face some difficult challenges." That last part is a bit of a stretch because, so far, all she's done is recite a litany of satisfactions and successes. Unfortunately, she doesn't take the bait.

"Yeah," she says with a huge grin. "I've got tons of friends. School is going well. Getting good grades and all. Like my classes. You know, couldn't be better."

You are listening carefully, very carefully, not just to the over-enthusiastic presentation, but noticing the facial expressions that don't quite fit the words. You also remember that when she was first referred to you by her parents, she was described as "acting weird" lately. Weird, indeed.

You study her carefully as she continues to talk about how great her life is going, and that makes you even more suspicious considering that you can't recall the last time you talked to an adolescent who didn't have *some* drama going on. It is then that you notice the ways she gingerly rests her wrists on her lap. You don't know exactly how the idea pops in your head, but immediately you picture her arms covered in cuts or burns or some kind of self-mutilation. If someone asked you how you came up with that idea, all you could do is shrug, but you can't get that picture out of your mind. As you've been listening to her for the previous half hour, you can't help but feel like something is terribly wrong even if you can't pin her down to admit it.

You decide it's way too early to confront her, or even ask her about your hunch. Considering she won't admit to any problems and insists that everything is "awesome," you think to yourself how almost any other therapist would simply dismiss her from treatment and ask her to return when she's got something to work on. You feel tempted to do just that, sensing Margo's reluctance, and feeling quite certain that asking her to roll up her sleeves would earn an immediate denial and loss of trust. You decide to skip that step and go deeper.

"Margo, if I might interrupt you for a moment, I do hear you saying that there are many things in your life about which you feel a lot of pride and accomplishment—and with good reason. You have so much going for you and seem really on top of many things."

Margo nods, but you notice her acknowledging smile is down-turned at the corners, hesitant and insincere.

"But I wonder . . ." You hesitate for a moment, giving her a chance to prepare herself for what comes next. "I wonder when exactly it happened that you started hating yourself."

"Excuse me?" she replies, a flash of anger, quickly gone, replaced by confusion, then a slight nod. Tears puddle in the corners of her eyes.

You just wait, listening now not to her words, which have been so deceptive and inaccurate, but to her behavior.

"You won't understand," Margo says finally after a full minute of uncomfortable silence. "Nobody understands."

"And you think it's a waste of time to try to tell me as well. How could I possibly understand either?"

Margo nods. She is crying now in earnest. "It's just, you know, everyone thinks my life is so great, that I couldn't possibly have any problems, that I always have to pretend that I'm happy. I guess I do have a lot people who say they're my friends, but I just feel so alone. My best friend, Kara, is always busy at school. My boyfriend never has time for me. My parents just treat me like I'm some kind of trophy or something to show their friends. Sometimes it hurts so much it feels like the pain won't ever go away. And I guess I deserve it because I just can't be what everyone wants me to be."

"And that's why you cut yourself and make yourself bleed?" This is a guess, of course, but immediately you can see it hit home. Margo looks shocked that her secret has been uncovered so quickly. And with that admission, everything changes.

Listening Differently

Several researchers such as John Gottman and Paul Ekman have been developing training programs to teach clinicians (and law enforcement personnel) how to listen and observe more carefully to identify nonverbal and verbal microclues in facial expressions, body movements, word selection, and intonation, in order to recognize deception, contempt, or other hidden feelings. Clinical experience also teaches us innumerable ways to hear and observe the most subtle and disguised messages that are beyond the client's awareness. That is why we are often suspected of reading minds—because of the ability to hone in on tiny nuances of communication that reveal deeper messages. All of this is predicated, of course, on our willingness to listen very, very carefully.

As closely as we try to focus on what the client is communicating, we are simultaneously listening to the internal voice(s) inside us. Much of this is "noise" or distraction, especially when it is largely triggered by our own unresolved personal issues. But we also find this internal voice instructive when it sparks intuition and creativity, checking out our level of deep understanding, linking remarks to what has been said earlier, and identifying significant themes for further exploration. Finally, we are often flooded with so much information flowing in that we must suspend focused listening in order to make sense of what we hear. That is one of the greatest challenges we face while listening, in that there is hardly a dearth of information coming through but rather more than we can handle comfortably.

It is also interesting the way exceptional therapists listen differently than others to the stories they hear. Long before positive psychology was "invented" or became popular, skilled practitioners learned to listen to dimensions of clients' strengths and resources rather than merely hearing the problems and diagnosing the psychopathology. Since we often guide the trajectory of therapeutic conversations, prompts are frequently designed to highlight what is going right rather than wrong, as well as fleshing out the client's inner emotional climate. After all, what we actually hear when we listen to someone is guided by our beliefs about what is most salient and meaningful.

Family therapist Scott Browning finds that what distinguishes truly exceptional clinicians from their brethren is that they have an extensive range of therapeutic options available to them, including a variety of techniques from an assortment of different approaches, depending on the particular needs of the client. They are also not afraid to take an active and directive role when it is necessary: Sometimes listening alone is not nearly enough. "This is not to suggest a domineering attitude in the session," Browning explains, "but rather a clear emphasis on comforting the client to know that they are in the hands of someone who will not let them replicate dynamics that happen all the time at home. The skilled therapist knows how to shift the topic in such a manner that all voices are heard, unhelpful attacks are rerouted, and appropriate teaching can be provided. Masters of treatment seem to have the uncanny skill to speak actively, listen completely, and know how to switch between both positions."

JC As I reflect on the ways I listen to clients, I am struck by how differently I view them than they see themselves. Clients who are struggling seem to understand themselves and their world in an unhealthy and hopeless manner. I try to help them interpret their situations in a more constructive and hopeful light. When relaying stories of working with clients, there is often a "gasp" from others who believe that is just amazing how this can be done or where these insights came from. It is not magical and something that only masters can accomplish, but rather comes from practice and listening deeply to all that the client says—and means to say.

Jimmy came to see me because he was unemployed and experiencing dissatisfaction in his 2-year-old second marriage. His first marriage ended on friendly terms, and he and his ex-wife do not seem to have any problems co-parenting their children. He was the youngest of four children and the only boy. He saw himself as intelligent, lazy, rebellious, spoiled, and someone who generally did not try to please others.

He indicated that his wife was upset because he did not "pull his weight" in the marriage and that he expected her to do everything. He believed that he really did not have the time to help her, as he was busy trying to find a job. He had a good resume, with an MBA from a prestigious school, and had received regular promotions at his prior corporate job, from which he was released when the company moved its headquarters to Mexico.

He thought that many of the things his wife expected him to do were things that were not really his responsibility. He didn't do them in his first marriage and never saw his father do any of the things she thought he ought to do. Jimmy was convinced that he was correct in his views and felt that if he could only get another "good" job, his wife would back off.

Jimmy liked coming to therapy because he felt that it was an opportunity to be challenged and to dialogue with another intelligent person. As we talked, Jimmy talked with confidence and seemed to always have a pleasant, if not smiling, face. He dressed in comfortable clothes that seemed to be stylish. He appeared to be in good health, with a tanned and ruddy complexion. He appeared open to learning and genuinely wanting to make his marriage work. He was not too worried about finding a job, as he was confident in his abilities and his employability.

"So, Jimmy," I began, "if I understand things correctly, you are someone who knows what he wants and is used to getting it. When your wife places these unrealistic requests on you, it is really frustrating. What you would like is a partner who did her job and focused on being there for you."

"Wow, Doc, you nailed it! That is exactly how it looks to me. When I talk to others, they tell me that this is the age of equality and I should step up like she wants if I want the marriage to work better than my first one."

"What stops you from doing what your wife and others think is the right thing to do?"

"I guess because I've never done it before."

"It seems to me that you do most things pretty well and with little effort."

"That has been my history. There is not much I can't do and not much I can't do well."

"What would it mean to you if you went along with your wife's request?"

"I guess it would mean that I am a good partner and she might start treating me in a more loving manner."

"Isn't that what you want to have happen?"

After a little further discussion, Jimmy realized that he could very easily be a better partner and improve his marriage. Although we did not talk about Jimmy's other problem—that he was unemployed—he did not feel that this was a problem that was not going to work out on it's own.

By listening carefully to Jimmy and focusing on his strengths, he was motivated to change in a short two-session treatment. Previous therapists had identified him as a narcissistic personality who needed to be less self-centered. This message was one that Jimmy could not hear, as it didn't fit the person he thought he was.

Being in the Moment

We might have gotten a little ahead of ourselves. As important as listening is to everything else we might do with clients, we wish to broaden this perspective in the next chapter to include a discussion of what it means to be fully present with others in *all* capacities— not just through hearing but through all our felt senses.

Whereas ordinarily we might think of experts or masters as those who have at their disposal an assortment of varied interventions and strategies to solve problems and attain desired outcomes (and we agree that is important), in another sense such professionals are able to put aside all the chatter and analysis inside their heads in order to become attuned to what is going on with the other, with oneself, and the interaction between them. Listening is a big part of this process, but so, too, is the stillness that comes with being in the moment.

CHAPTER 5

BEING FULLY PRESENT WHILE FOCUSING ON THE OTHER

Effective therapy involves keeping the focus on clients while remaining fully present and tuned into their felt experience. In a contemporary world of distractions, conflicting priorities, and multitasking, and beeping mobile devices, the ability to be present is a skill that requires commitment and regular practice. Master therapists have developed extraordinary abilities to be mindful, not only during their sessions but also applying what they have learned to do professionally in their personal lives.

One of the things that is most remarkable about our work is that every day is an adventure into the unknown—at least it can feel that way if we remain fully engaged in the process. Of course, that is not nearly as easy as it sounds to beginners, who can't imagine that any therapist's attention could wander or that it is possible that we would ever turn things over to autopilot. Any activity that feels repetitive becomes habituated over time, whether it is commuting to work, assembling an object, telling a story, or conducting surgery. For those therapists who have taught themselves to meet each new client as a unique individual rather than a familiar diagnosis, or who view each session as an exceptional interaction rather than as an incremental step in a treatment regimen, there are opportunities each day to venture into novel territory. In that sense, every meeting is a special collaboration in which something altogether new is created—in theory, anyway.

The reality, of course, is that some clients are incredibly repetitive, uncooperative, or annoying, and some sessions are tedious beyond imagination. We can't possibly remain fully attentive to any conversation more than half of the time, and even that's doing pretty well. There are lulls throughout the day, especially in the middle of the afternoon, when most mammals take naps and most industrial accidents occur. And, for a variety of reasons, there are some clients with whom we find it challenging to remain fully present.

JK I've been sitting with a client absolutely bored out of my mind. Not only has Trent been repeating the same story that he's told me at least twice previously, but I swear I've heard variations of this exact scenario at least a dozen times from other clients. Granted, I haven't been listening very carefully, but the gist of the long monologue is that (a) nobody really appreciates Trent the way he deserves, (b) it's because they don't really understand all the incredible things he has to offer, and (c) if his wife hadn't given up on him because he wasn't making enough money. . . . This is the point where I lost the thread of what he was saying because I had lapsed into the most incredible fantasy of . . . well, never mind. Suffice it to say I wasn't listening to Trent, and, even worse, he didn't seem to care. I suppose that was part of his problem in that his self-esteem was so awful that he had become accustomed to people not listening to him—even me!

I wish I could say that this was an anomaly, but sometimes it feels like I have the attention span of a hamster (I looked it up and they have the briefest focus of any animal). I know I'm not the only one who loses focus at times or who pretends to listen when I'm busy planning what I'm going to do next. There are other instances when I become distracted or triggered by some statement that sends me way off into my own personal reverie.

Learning to be fully present has been my life's greatest ambition. Or at least that's what I settled for after I surrendered my dream to fly after I injured myself jumping off the dining room table wearing a towel around my neck as a cape (give me a break—I was only 7 years old). I definitely have trouble sitting still. I have tried yoga (hurts my back), tai chi (can't remember the form), visualization (trouble focusing), and meditation (did I mention I can't sit still?). I still marvel at how someone like me with an attention deficit and speech issues as a child ever ended up as a therapist. It's no wonder that my preferred methods of relaxation and stress reduction involve running, cycling, skiing, and traveling—staying in motion. My mind is always wandering, generating new ideas for books and articles, new places to visit, new projects to begin, lists of things to remember, and also reminders about what I should try and forget.

I know that my best work, including what I'm writing now, comes from complete focus on the moment. I pause for a second, hear distracting sounds outside, a grumbling stomach, a flash of a thought about what I'll make for dinner, and then refocus to complete this sentence. And that is exactly what happens for me in a session, including the conversation with Trent I described earlier.

Once I become aware that I've left the room, or lapsed into fantasy . . . which, by the way, reminds me of the interesting choices we make regarding where we go in our minds. I used to think about stuff I wanted to buy, then felt terribly guilty about my materialistic yearnings that I so despised in my affluent clients. When I was younger, much younger, controlling sexual fantasies was a challenge because they were so distracting and inappropriate. Most recently, I can't stop new book ideas from intruding at inopportune moments. Lately when I'm teaching, I keep a notebook nearby because I sometimes become bored listening to myself give a lecture, so I keep myself engaged by taking notes on the parallel conversation going on inside my head.

I think this makes me just about the worst Buddhist in the world. It also makes me more determined than ever to practice full engagement in the moment. What cycling and skiing and writing have taught me is that I can easily lose myself in four consecutive hours of activity without a single conscious thought. I sometimes lose whole days when immersed in a project, forgetting to eat or even stretch. Then there are those clients that I find so interesting, and their stories so riveting, that time flies by and I have no interest whatsoever in leaving the room for a second. There are times when I become so over-involved in the conversation, so completely engaged with a client, that it feels like we have merged into one being. I can finish the sentences that the client begins. It feels like we can read one another's minds. When it is time to stop, it's then that I notice that my heart feels so full that my chest aches.

If I am disqualified as a master therapist, it is primarily because of my lapses of concentration and limited focus. I suppose I've convinced myself all these years that operating at half capacity is more than good enough, but I surely know better. If I am to believe some of my colleagues, a few have convinced me that their experiences during sessions, even a half-dozen in a row, completely command their full attention. I believe them because I've learned to do the same thing when leading groups—which is why I love doing group therapy so much. There is so much going on in the room, so many different things to track and monitor, so many dynamics operating, coalitions and alliances playing out, potential conflicts simmering, nonverbal behavior to read and decode, and loose ends to follow up, that I feel absolutely overwhelmed most of the time. Every group is different; in fact, I get in trouble most often when I convince myself that something going on is familiar, stopping me from seeing things the way they really are in the moment. I have no trouble remaining utterly and absolutely in the zone. I don't exist except as a vehicle to process everything that is happening. It feels exhausting and yet effortless. When the group sessions are over, I look around and remember that there is a world outside the room, that I actually have a body that I inhabit. Oh my gosh, I'm salivating just thinking about the rush!

I think each of us has found a way, at least those among us who still thrive in their work, to structure their sessions in such a manner that stimulation, challenges, and the demands of the tasks require total concentration. I'm not saying that we don't have our occasional lapses of laziness or distraction, but the goal to which we all aspire is one of transcendent focus on whatever is at hand.

Altered States of Being

We are aware that the best therapy sessions are those in which *all* participants are in an altered state of consciousness or "flow" state, in which time, as we know it, ceases, when we are transported to another reality. It is when we seem to be able to read each other's minds—and hearts. It is when we become more fully aware of things inside us, and between us, but at the same time we become less aware of everything else outside the room. It happens with those altogether rare sessions when we are startled "awake" by the realization that the session has ended, time's up, time to move back into the other world that awaits. It is when we feel transported *together* to a different place in which we feel more open to new possibilities, new options, to being influenced by one another in ways that wouldn't be otherwise possible. It is when there is either a sense of peace and centeredness or profound agitation and emotional arousal, each of which can spark new learning and potential growth. It is when walls collapse and boundaries become temporarily invisible or blurred. It is when words can't begin to describe what happened, much less explain why. In fact, it is when we try to make sense of the experience and demystify it that it may lose its magic.

Being present is synonymous with being aware and in deep focus. It involves being open and receptive to another. The idea of being mindful is very popular today because so few people do it. Jack Kornfield has remarked that one reason we are so lousy at staying present is that there is so little in our schooling to prepare us for this significant life skill. Whereas once, as children, we could easily stay completely immersed in a task as if in a hypnotic trance, we are taught to surrender this single-minded devotion unless propped up in front of a television or computer screen. With the increased presence of mobile devices in our lives, we are now even less inclined to stay focused on any one thing for more than a few minutes.

"With the past, I have nothing to do, nor with the future," observed Ralph Waldo Emerson, commenting on the fact that the only things we can ever control occur in the present moment. Nevertheless, we remain obsessed with what has already happened or what may occur next. Our minds race with plans, next steps, dreams, desires, hopes—unless we are ruminating over past mistakes, reliving failures or triumphs.

While we are supposedly listening to clients, we are making connections in our head—tracking what they are saying and comparing it to what we've heard previously; resonating with parallel processes in which we are personalizing the issues; and, most often, simply taking little "trips" in which something that was said sparked an idea that we follow until we lose the thread. Yet it is only when fully and completely present that we truly feel deep connections to our clients. We enter an altered state of consciousness in which we lose ourselves in the process, a kind of mindfulness that focuses all of our faculties. In this transcendent state, we notice things that would be invisible to anyone else. We are not only hyperaware of what is going on with the client but also what we are experiencing as response, all the while remaining fully present.

It is such mindfulness that gives us access to a much greater spectrum of experience by reducing our need to avoid and hide from our mental and emotional life.

Mind Chatter

Our lives are only becoming more hurried and fast-paced. We are now expected to be available and accessible almost every minute of the day. During those rare moments when we are alone, perhaps driving in the car, we are still doing several things at the same time—tracking the GPS for directions, listening to the radio, drinking coffee, talking on the phone, glancing at incoming text messages, planning what comes next. This behavior has become so habitual that we can't help but bring all this mind chatter into sessions, eroding our ability to stay in the moment.

During sessions, there is often a lot of second-guessing: Should I have really said that? Why didn't I pick up on that cue that seems so obvious? What is he thinking about me now? What's my supervisor going to say when I tell her what happened? I wonder if I should go back and pick up on what he said earlier? What should I do now?

While the client is talking, our minds are racing with questions about the proper diagnosis, a revision of the treatment plan, what will be recorded in progress notes, and how to best word and rehearse what we want to say next. No wonder there are times when we just check out in order to give ourselves a brief respite from all the chatter.

Those we think of as master therapists have trained themselves (and it definitely involved loads of practice and commitment) to be as attentive as possible. Just as in a meditative exercise, each time they catch themselves drifting away, even for a moment, they gently pull themselves back. They use their breathing to enhance the mindfulness just as a monk might do during meditative incantations. Under such conditions, trained disciples aren't even the least bit distracted by a loud gunshot—there is no visible flinch, blink, or physiological marker signaling anything other than continued focus and presence in the moment. It leads us to wonder whether we should be altering our training programs to include more attention to improving focused concentration rather than all the other things that we do. This would only empower and fortify all our other interventions and skills as we learn to improve our ability to block distractions unrelated to what is going on in the moment. It is under those conditions that we are not only more effective but also enjoy more passionately what we are doing.

"When you eat, just eat" is a Zen saying—that can be applied to any aspect of our lives. The best meal we could ever experience is one in which the flavors, aromas, textures, colors, and sensations become so present that there is nothing else except the bite that is in your mouth, with no anticipation of the next one. And so it is with the practice of therapy: We are sponges that simply absorb what we take in.

JC In the past few weeks, while working on this chapter, I have tried really hard at being present, completely present, in different aspects of my life. After reading Jeffrey's story earlier I also felt a bit like a hypocrite because I have been studying Buddhism and meditation most of my adult life and still struggle to stay in the moment. My friends and family tease me that I have a library of Buddhist books that could rival any monastery. As much and as long as I have studied the literature and practiced meditation in my daily life, I am still very much a work-in-progress.

I spent the past few weeks trying harder than ever (in the way a Buddhist tries, which means to not try and allow effortless energy to take over) to practice mindfulness in my therapy sessions. I have concentrated on breathing slowly and deeply to begin the sponge-like process of being present. I found myself not so much watching my clients as using "soft eyes" to open myself up to all that was occurring in the room. It was a very interesting experiment because as I remained more fully in the present moment, I noticed that the clients followed my lead. The content of the sessions shifted to far more meaningful areas, especially those based on what clients were experiencing in the here and now. Since I often use an Adlerian approach in my work, one that integrates all kinds of other interventions, it was intriguing to hone in on full engagement in the moment.

This process struck me as similar to what has been happening over the past year of medical care when doctors bombarded me with test results, treatments, and prognoses. In order to manage my anxiety, I would breathe during these conversations so I could take in most of what they were telling me. I would initially feel flooded with apprehension, anxiety, despair, depression, hopelessness, and helplessness—until I would breathe and watch these feelings pass as I returned to the present. Just imagine how distracted you would become when waiting for a death sentence to be pronounced.

My breathing and mindfulness exercises helped me to keep the panic and fear at bay, at least enough that I could continue with whatever is left of my life.

I was fortunate in that I had 40-plus years of being a therapist and daily meditator to prepare me for this crisis. Staying in the present was not a new concept for me; however, I realized that the context was the most difficult one I have ever experienced.

The nurses were concerned that I didn't seem upset or worried at each day's grim news, even when my chances of survival were minuscule. "It's okay to cry if you want," the nurses would tell me over and over. "Isn't there something you'd like to talk about before, you know, before it's too late?"

The truth (or at least my truth) is that I was living as much as I possibly could in the moment. I knew I was getting the best medical care available, that I happened to luck out and end up in the facility where the first stem cell transplants were perfected. My family was around me. I had everything I needed. There was nothing else to be done—except to breathe. And I did that exceptionally well.

I was breathing deeply, aware of where I was and what was happening and, with the help of various pain medications, feeling pretty comfortable. I chose to be present, even with pain that was so horrific that the tumors cracked the vertebrae in my spine. While breathing and meditating, I did not panic. I chose not to deny what was happening in my body, but since there was nothing else I could do, I relied on a lifetime of experience as a mindful therapist to stay as present as possible during what might be my last days.

I realize that death may still be around the next corner. The cancer cells that have been evicted might be busy reproducing themselves. This realization makes it even easier for me to stay in the moment because it may be all that I have. I am noticing that I can listen better and be present at a higher level when I'm with my clients (yes, friends, I'm still seeing some clients during this cancer journey). More than ever, my clients seem to be willing to go deeper than ever before, in part I think, because I've never been more present with them. It might be my imagination or wishful thinking, but it seems to me that I'm now doing the best work of my life, all the while struggling with staying alive.

A Way of Being

We have both long admired Carl Rogers as a historical figure in our field because of his emphasis on presence in helping relationships. He was an early influence on our development because we both shared the same doctoral advisor, who was a student of Rogers. Yet like most contemporary practitioners, we have long since moved on to other approaches that are more contemporary and responsive to the realities of today's needs. New schools of thought that emphasize the therapeutic alliance have advanced his work; many of Rogers's seminal ideas related to the power of the relationship have since been empirically validated. But it is his focus on *presence* that we still find so useful as a healing force.

It is interesting to consider all the ways that presence can be manifested in helping relationships. We have already talked about it in the context of Buddhist mindfulness, as well as Rogers's conception that included strong threads of genuineness and authenticity. Yet there are many other ways that therapists of different persuasions and conceptual backgrounds practice presence in their relationships with clients—as a holding environment, attachment, reciprocal influence, working alliance, co-constructed partnership, social exchange, transference object, and so on. In each of these manifestations, the goal is for the therapist to become as attentive as possible to the client's needs at any moment in time. Whereas it is an admirable goal of Rogers to be nonjudgmental, we know that is virtually impossible without lapses because we make all kinds of critical judgments about what we believe is good and bad for our clients.

Over time, a master therapist learns to brush away this intrusive critical voice and replace it with only concern and caring. When the mind wanders (as it does constantly), a cleansing breath returns focus to the present. As the client talks, thoughts fly through the therapist's mind. The therapist watches these thoughts, withholding judgment, just taking in what is happening in the moment. Therapeutic presence makes it possible to know when we are tuned in or have lost focus. Many experts believe that being present is the most important element of helping others heal. This allows us to bring our full and receptive self into and remain in engagement with others. Cultivating a mindful presence provides a state in which we attend to our inner life as we remain focused on others. This inner subjective world has often been neglected, as the therapeutic community focuses on the external objective world of self and other.

A therapist steps into the waiting room to greet a new couple referred by a local minister. As she opens the door and surveys her clients, it is as if she has entered a new level of consciousness. She can almost feel her eyes dilate, her ears attuning themselves, all her senses intensifying to a point that she is quivering with sensitivity like an insect's antennae. She notices some things about this couple consciously: their position and postures, their appearance and non-verbal behavior, and that one of them frowns while the other smiles. She observes their mutual anxiety and much, much more that she can't put into words—but there are things she feels. She takes a deep breath and says their names, Carolyn and Jake, as if a mantra.

Once settled in their seats, Carolyn immediately begins. "I'll do anything to save our marriage. Anything. I just want another chance." She looks at her husband, who is not meeting her eyes. "Please. Please just give us a chance. I know I hadn't wanted to come here, but I'm here now, aren't I?"

Without looking at his wife, Jake addresses the therapist in a calm, dispassionate voice. "Five months ago I might have welcomed this conversation, but it's too late now. It's over." He crossed his arms as he made this final pronouncement. He looked ready to leave now that he'd said what he had prepared.

"What he means," Carolyn clarified, "is that he met someone else. He's done with me." She stops to compose herself and wipe away tears that smear her eyeliner. "He's dumping me for a younger model, leaving our kids too."

The therapist listened to this initial exchange in a trance. She was nodding appropriately, communicating all the appropriate non-verbal signals that she was tracking carefully what each was saying. She was also working hard to resist any impulse to interpret what was happening and, at this early stage, except to notice there was a familiar distance-pursuer dance going on. "Pardon me," she said after a long pause, "but I'm a bit confused. If you are planning on a divorce, I wonder why you are here instead of consulting an attorney?"

"But I don't want a divorce," Carolyn said, this time looking directly at her husband. "I keep telling you that I can change and be whatever you want me to be."

Jake shook his head. "It's too late for that. I asked you so many times to go to counseling with me and you always said no."

The therapist tried her best to ignore the conflict and what it might mean, asking them instead if they had told their families of their plans. They both replied no, which the therapist found interesting. If they were really planning on ending things, wouldn't they have announced their intentions? This kind of obvious realization was possible precisely because the therapist was doing her level best to stay focused on the present and not (yet) get sucked into rehashing prior dissatisfactions.

The therapist explains her approach: "I don't work with couples when one of them is involved in another relationship. I told them that I was willing to see them individually but not work on their marriage unless Jake was prepared to end his other relationship first. I also told them, unequivocally, that it is *never* one person's fault—the failure of their marriage belonged to both of them. I invited each of them to talk about their role in the problems, opening up space for a shared responsibility. This may sound like it is a standard procedure, but I assure you that idea arose from a deep sense that both of them really wanted to stay together and that Jake was feeling neglected and using leverage to get some attention. Although I'm explaining this now, or perhaps making this up to explain it, I was not conscious of these choices. All I remember is my breathing to stay present with them."

Regardless of the particular outcome with this case, the therapist's way of being in the session illustrates her own unique way of being fully present with her clients. This is the way she has learned to absorb the flood of information during a first session, when emotions are high and she feels a lot of anxiety about wanting to know what's really going on (as if that's possible).

Staying Present With Ourselves

Returning to the case of Trent that began this chapter, we want to close by commenting on Jeffrey's confession about his own struggles with boredom. As hard as he is on himself, we'd suggest that it is the willingness to closely monitor our reactions to what's going on in the moment that permits us to alter their flow. All the things mentioned, the repetitive nature of client concerns, the way that some people repeat themselves, the chatter inside our minds, the distractions, the ways our buttons are pushed, this is all so familiar and, dare we say, normal. We are trying to be honest and transparent in disclosing the struggle that is common to all of us who see clients like Trent.

When we are distracted or inattentive, the key is to explore our internal sensations of boredom or disengagement. Trent was pushing his therapist away just as he does everyone else in his life, and Jeffrey was doing his best to make sense of his own reactions. Why was it so difficult for him to remain in the room? Would he rather be doing something else, or was he escaping from something that was uncomfortable for him? These are precisely the questions that lead each of us to become more masterful at being fully present, not only with those we are paid to help, but also with those we love the most.

CHAPTER 6

KNOWING WHAT
MAYBE/PROBABLY/MOSTLY
MAKES A DIFFERENCE

Let's be honest: We don't really understand how and why change takes place, whether within therapy or in the outside world. Of course, there are hundreds of theories and tens of thousands of studies on the subject, but the bottom line, after everything is said and done, is that we can often describe what happened in sessions but have a difficult time explaining how and why the changes occurred. The situation is compounded by the extreme discrepancies, not only between what different experts believe, but also the varied reports from clients that so contradict what their therapists think was most helpful.

One distinction between beginning therapists and those who have attained some degree of mastery in the field is that the latter have mostly shattered illusions that they will ever understand what is going on in sessions. Most of the time we sit in awe—or confusion—trying to make sense of all that is happening in the room, within the client, within ourselves, and between the two of us. In the case of group or family therapy, the complexity is magnified by a factor of 10, or 100, or 10,000!

With that said, it isn't as if we don't have rather strong opinions on the matter. Read the progress notes of any clinician and there will be a neat set of descriptions regarding (a) the presenting problem, (b) related symptomatology, (c) treatment interventions, (d) client responses to treatment, and (e) ongoing prognosis, all demonstrating an apparent logical connection to the original diagnostic summary and treatment plan. The reality is that most of what we write is pure fiction, or at least exaggerated confidence meant to appease the powers that control permission to continue treatment.

A completely honest progress note might more realistically resemble something like the following:

Client reported that he is still feeling "incredibly weird" and "disoriented," conditions that even when pressed he can't quite explain. I can't figure out whether he's more depressed or anxious, so I split the difference and revised my diagnosis to "Adjustment Reaction With Mixed Emotional Features." That about covers most anything.

When client was asked about progress thus far, he shrugged and said he wasn't sure. I'm not either. But we both agreed we'd keep at it even though we are not certain where this is going.

I attempted several different interventions to reduce the "weird feelings," whatever form they might take that can't yet be described. Responses to reframing his condition resulted in an uncertain and confusing result: He answered, "I don't know," to any question posed. This may indicate underlying resistance and defensiveness or, on the other hand, it just might mean he really doesn't know. I don't know either. I'd describe the prognosis as "guarded," meaning that we are both closely guarding whatever the hell is going on.

Okay, perhaps we are exaggerating. But the fact remains that the process of psychotherapy is so complicated, the change processes so convoluted, and involves so many different variables, the interactions between a client and therapist occurring on so many levels, the number of extraneous and intervening variables in operation almost limitless, that true understanding is beyond what is possible. When you add to the equation the amount of distortion, denial, and deceit that takes place in client self-reports, multiply that by a similar level of self-deception on the part of the therapist, who exaggerates what is really understood, and we have a real puzzle.

JK Most of my life, I assumed that true master therapists were those who knew what was really going on in their sessions. That has rarely been my experience, which I suppose is why I have tried to write so much about the phenomenon in order to come to terms with my uncertainty and doubts. There have been times when I was absolutely certain what produced a particular outcome and eventually learned that I wasn't even close, at least if I believe what a client reported. There are other times when it feels like I don't have a clue what is really going on, and it doesn't seem to matter that I can't put it into words: The apparent progress is both startling and still gaining momentum.

Over time, I've learned to feel less certain about what I'm doing. That doesn't mean that I'm not confident in my healing powers; rather, that I feel humbled and awed by all the mysterious and amazing things that seem to occur without the need to explain them.

It always seemed unduly arrogant to me when I'd watch colleagues on stage, or read expert authors, who speak with such perfect assurance that psychotherapy works in a particular way. There are many different theories that appear to directly contradict one another. Yet one thing I figured out a while ago is that maybe great therapists are really all doing basically the same things. Maybe they have different names for their most favored strategies or seminal ideas. What might be most useful is to look critically at the apparently different conceptions, the conflicting claims, the most well-regarded studies, and especially clients' perceptions of what helped them the most, and distill them into a reasonably comprehensive list of operative variables.

What Makes a Difference?

If you were to make a list of those factors that you believe are most instrumental in facilitating lasting change in clients, what would you nominate as most significant?

We are talking about "big" changes, not insignificant ones, those that have been described as major transformations, quantum changes, or major shifts in the construction of reality or self-identity. We are also most interested in changes that "stick," meaning that the progress gains momentum and continues once sessions have ended.

Between us, we've accumulated decades of clinical practice, studied the research and literature as it continues to evolve over time, read widely on related subjects as well as those far afield, interviewed hundreds of therapists and thousands of clients and ex-clients, and written so many books on the subjects of change and learning. Based on this experience, here are some factors that we consider worthy of mention. We don't claim our list is exhaustive, or even that all/many/most of these items are absolutely necessary conditions, but they do represent those that are most often mentioned by clients as important to them.

Hitting Bottom

We often find it frustrating, if not discouraging, that people wait so darn long before they decide to consult us. We lament how much easier things would be if we had been able to intervene much earlier, before things became completely out of control. Nevertheless, we often do our best work when clients are most desperate. After all, they have nothing to lose. They can't stand living within their skin for another minute. And they will try most anything to reduce the suffering.

When clients have hit bottom, when they feel like they've lost everything, with little hope of ever changing things, *that* is when they are most open to what we have to offer. Over time, experience teaches us *not* to take away a client's pain just because we feel so helpless and uncomfortable. It is precisely that suffering that acts as a powerful force to motivate necessary changes, and it is the prospect of its return that keeps progress moving along. Even beginners understand that in theory, but it takes true masters to put this realization into practice—meaning that it is often as important that we *don't* act during times when clients are in the throes of excruciating agony. The challenge, of course, is reading accurately just how much discomfort a client may tolerate before doing something self-destructive or bailing completely from therapy.

Confront Pain and Suffering

There is a Buddhist saying that pain is inevitable, while suffering is optional. Pain is simply a signal that something is wrong or in need of attention. Unfortunately, too many clients manage to turn their pain into suffering instead of relief. Most of the time, this occurs when the pain messages are ignored. The problem is compounded by novice therapists who see their job as removing the pain without necessarily attending to its particular meaning. Master therapists, however, help clients to change their relationship with pain, learning how to focus on it rather than just making it go away. This is particularly important, considering that sometimes the goal isn't to make the pain go away as much as learn to live with it, such as the case with life circumstances that can't be escaped or chronic illness. Of course, it takes patience and training to learn to sit (or stand) with pain, observing the experience without altering or judging it as anything other than a different reality.

JC I was a sickly child and learned early in life about pain. Unfortunately, I learned to view pain as something that happened to me and that I had little, if any, control over the situation. My parents would take me from doctor to doctor to try and find a new miracle cure for my numerous health problems. Like so many of us, my training as a therapist better prepared me to deal with pain through my chosen interpretations and responses. It also helped that I had been a competitive athlete, a long-distance runner, so I had developed inner resources to think of pain merely as a minor annoyance.

Over the years, I devoted many hours of study to learning and practicing meditation, which is just a way to focus the mind on one thing, diverting its attention from others. Whereas initially my interest was primarily to develop skills to help my clients, I couldn't help but internalize these lessons in my own life.

All these years I have been teaching others to live with emotional and physical pain, and now I have the opportunity to practice what I've been preaching. I truly believe this is what saved my life as much as any of the medical treatments. If I hadn't had such a high tolerance for pain, I never could have survived the chemotherapy, surgery, radiation, drugs, and other assaults to my body.

What I've been trying to do this year is the same thing I've tried to do with my clients: teach them to change their relationship with pain. Since it wasn't going to diminish any time soon, I chose to make it my companion, if not my friend. After all, it is just another part of me. When I think this way, when I breathe mindfully, I notice the intensity subsides to the point that I can ignore it altogether if I choose. I know there are drugs that will do something similar—and there are times when I've needed them—but I take tremendous personal satisfaction in doing what is within my power to manage myself.

Creating Hope and Optimism

The ability to help the client see that the glass is half full is seldom taught in training, although certainly positive psychology is making some inroads. It is something every therapist is just supposed to know. It is an important part of helping others through difficult times and seems to be at the heart of most pastoral interventions. Martin Seligman refers to this as *learned optimism*, as he realized that this ability to see situations as hopeful, or at least more hopeful than the client sees it, is cultivated with experience. Hope and optimism create motivation to hang in there and keep trying.

We frequently find ourselves being cheerleaders with our clients, helping them to increase their motivation, access their resilience when things get really tough, and follow through on their stated intentions. In other situations, we attempt to "sell" particular ideas that we believe are useful, persuading clients to do those things that are most challenging.

Whether you prefer to associate optimism and hope with the placebo effect or view it as the engine that motivates constructive action, our passion and enthusiasm (plus wisdom and skills) inspires clients to have faith in us, in the therapy process, and most of all in themselves.

Creating a Safe Relationship

We keep circling back to the point that, more than any other single factor mentioned by clients, it is the relationship that heals them. They may feel grateful for all kinds of other things offered by their therapists' advice, favored techniques, wisdom, interpretations, and so on, but without a caring and constructive alliance, much of that falls on deaf ears. We find it especially interesting that although research consistently shows that techniques and favored theoretical approach are not nearly as important as other variables like client characteristics, therapist characteristics, and the quality of the relationship, many practitioners remain obsessed with learning the next best faddish method that is supposed to render everything else we've learned obsolete.

Extraordinary clinicians seem to recognize that they are far better off developing themselves and their ability to create strong connections with others, rather than clamoring to jump on the latest bandwagon that has yet to be empirically supported. Just as important, they work hard to apply these same skills and intentionality to their own most cherished relationships with family, friends, and colleagues. In that sense, the therapist serves as a model for his or her clients, as well as a coach, instructor, confidante, and cheerleader.

In a project that we worked on a few years ago, interviewing notable master therapists about their most creative breakthroughs, we found the gender split among our participants to be more than a little interesting. We had asked for heroic efforts, so it wasn't surprising that most of the distinguished therapists provided spectacularly successful stories in which they did all kinds of amazing things that most of us would never dream of considering. We are talking about interventions so outrageous and provocative that perhaps only a famous figure could get away with such a thing. Some theorists we interviewed described taking a client to a bar to learn to meet women, or asking clients to complete all sorts of very peculiar tasks that appeared to have nothing to do with their presenting complaints, or assembling a whole community together to offer support to a client. They were indeed remarkable cases and instructive lessons in the ways that we can reach *way* beyond what we think we know and understand about how change takes place. Yet as groundbreaking as these stories were, we were especially struck by how two of the well-known women theorists responded very differently to the invitation, insisting that they were not very creative at all but just had creative clients.

Laura Brown, distinguished feminist theorist, and Judy Jordan, cofounder of relational cultural therapy, were among the women in our study who absolutely insisted that what makes them good at what they do is essentially empowering their clients to do the work and take the credit for the successes. They see their roles as facilitators rather than as instruments of change and view the essence of therapist mastery as putting the clients in charge. Perhaps they are unduly modest, but Laura Brown's observations also cover an acknowledgment that, more than anything else, she is quite skilled and committed in relationship engagement: "I can be pretty genuinely present as a witness to people's pain." She also considers that truly exceptional therapists feel a lack of ownership to the outcome since it is the client's success or failure.

Given the emphasis in her approach on egalitarian collaboration, it's not surprising that Judy Jordan considers the relationship to be at the core of what makes any of us most effective. "I believe being able to establish a relationship with the client that promises a safe place to fully represent herself, a relationship that assists the client in taking the appropriate risks involved in moving from isolation to connection, is key to helping rework dysfunctional neuronal pathways.

Developing Compassion and Caring

Deeply caring about others and having compassion for their welfare is at the heart of most religious traditions. It is, hopefully, what led most of us to this field (along with healing ourselves). We feel a strong commitment to make a difference in other people's lives, not only by what we do, but how we exude such caring for others. It is a kind of love that is nonexploitive and nondemanding, a deep feeling of engagement with others that we hope supports them. We "hold" their sadness at times, respecting the client's pace and needs at any moment of time. We offer reassurance and essential kindness. We communicate the utmost respect, especially to those who have suffered neglect or abuse.

Compassion and caring become a way of life far beyond the arena of therapy. Adlerian psychotherapy refers to this as "social interest" and advocates this as an important component of mental health and life satisfaction. Most clients feel low levels of social interest and tend to become too focused on their own problems, losing perspective on what really matters. This is another area where we walk our talk, helping them to follow our lead in expressing more love and compassion for others. It is our hope that, beyond anything else clients might learn in therapy that is relevant to their original presenting complaints, they also learn some important lessons related to more complete engagement with others and the world.

Honoring Secrets

Even the most dedicated behaviorist or brief therapist would now acknowledge that it is sometimes useful to provide time for clients to share aspects of their lives they may never have admitted to themselves. It isn't necessary to believe in conventional catharsis to accept that people feel better when they can unload forbidden thoughts, frightening ideas, and disturbing feelings.

Except for rare occasions when disclosures may be potentially harmful to others, we hold the secrets of the world. We invite clients to talk about their experiences in the most honest and forthright way they can manage at the time. Beyond mere confidentiality, we offer safety without (mostly) critical judgment. We do our best to persuade people that we don't keep them on probation, that they can tell us most anything and we will listen with an objective, if not accepting, ear.

Reframing or Restorying the Problem

Clients often feel trapped and helpless, not so much by their circumstances but by their perspective. Almost every therapeutic approach has its own language and method for helping people to "reinterpret," "reframe," "reconstruct," "restory," or simply reconceptualize things in a more helpful way. We do this as much for our own sense of helplessness as we do for the client's well-being. After all, it is nearly impossible to fix someone's bad luck, poor genes, tragic past, physical characteristics, family members, or other factors *way* outside of one's control. Beyond anything else we do, we often begin by persuading clients to redefine what it is that is actually causing the difficulties, hopefully something that is much easier to address.

Vin feels embarrassed because when he invites friends over to his house to hang out, his father acts rude and withdrawn. "My dad is such a self-centered jerk. I don't think he even wants me to have any friends."

It is during one session that Vin comes to realize that his father never had a father himself, so he is somewhat clueless about how to serve best in this role. Vin began to change his view of the situation in such a way that his father was really doing the best he could in a confusing situation. He appeared withdrawn and quiet because he most likely didn't want to say or do the wrong thing. Vin started to feel more compassion for his father and stopped blaming him and feeling resentful. Naturally, this reduced the tension and discomfort between them and made it much easier for Vin's father to begin reaching out without fear of alienating his son further.

Almost every situation or problem can be examined from many different points of view, each of them offering alternative outcomes. "Everything can be something else" becomes the mantra to open new possibilities.

Challenging Beliefs and Assumptions

Regardless of the particular theoretical approach, whether based on cognitive, psychodynamic, feminist, constructivist, Adlerian, or any other model, superlative practitioners see their job as helping clients to confront their dysfunctional thinking, self-defeating behavior, and less-than-constructive choices. Moreover, they can do so in such a way that their clients are willing to examine these issues without undue defensiveness or denial. And if you think about it, there are few therapeutic skills that require more diplomacy and deftness than encouraging people to look at aspects of themselves that are most threatening.

Michele Weiner-Davis, one of the originators of brief therapy, describes herself as 95% successful helping couples to put their differences aside and reconcile, even when one partner stubbornly insists that he or she is done with the marriage. How does she exert such extraordinary influence? "I really believe that I have a strength in being able to join with whoever is in my office. They feel heard, validated, honored, and when that happens, I begin, little by little, to challenge unhelpful perspectives and actions. There really is an art to being able to challenge someone who already thinks you might have an agenda and to not create resistance. But because I so fully 'get them,' my advice and suggestions are heard and heeded." Michele makes a big distinction between challenging clients and criticizing them. She also considers timing to be crucial: "I can always tell when the time is right to try to say something a bit riskier. I use the fact that I am warm and people seem to like and trust me as a means to nudge them proactively. Relationship is not everything, but it's nearly everything."

Of course, without a trusting and safe relationship, clients are not going to be very amenable to examining the difficult issues that are brought to the forefront, nor are they going to be open to facing confrontations that will mean a whole new way of seeing themselves and others. Perhaps more than any other skill, master therapists have developed ways to challenge people by minimizing perceived threats.

Growth (Versus Deficit) Orientation

It takes us a long time to "unlearn" our original training that so emphasized identifying symptoms, diagnosing disorders, assessing dysfunctions, classifying mental illness, and thinking in terms of what's wrong with people. Many years before the positive psychology movement became popular, Abraham Maslow, Carl Rogers, Alfred Adler, and others urged clinicians to look at people's resources and strengths rather than just their problems. Although this growth orientation has now become a part of many therapeutic approaches, master therapists have long embraced a philosophy that explores the best in their clients, as well as their personal struggles.

Recently, we have seen increasing interest in posttraumatic *growth* instead of just seeking to restore "survivors" of posttraumatic stress disorder to previous baseline functioning. Other influences from mindfulness-based treatments, quantum change, and developmentally focused strategies have further encouraged us to help clients access their inner resources rather than pathologizing their behavior.

We have all seen how many people actually improve and grow when they are placed in difficult situations. Hardship and tragedies allow people to develop resilience and strengths that they were unaware of possessing. Asking clients what they learned, or how they grew, as a result of what happened might allow them to be more aware of what they have rather than what is missing.

We are not talking about "emphasizing the positive" or "accessing resources" as a *technique* to be employed in certain clinical situations but rather presenting a *way of being* that is adopted by master therapists in which they consistently look at the best in people and help them to see more clearly those parts of themselves. We would again mention that this is another aspect of personal functioning that master therapists are able to apply in their own lives.

Rehearsal and Task Facilitation

Let's face it—there are limits to insight, self-awareness, and understanding. We all know people who have been in therapy their whole lives and articulate all kinds of brilliant analyses about the nature of their problems, but still haven't changed their behavior in any significant way. They are still highly anxious, depressed, self-destructive, lonely, dysfunctional, or addicted. They can even talk a good game during sessions but hardly ever follow through on commitments they say are so important to them.

Excellent therapists from all orientations and approaches are quite skilled at getting their clients to take action. This is formulated in all kinds of ways—as homework, therapeutic tasks, rituals, experiential activities, role-plays in session, enactments, practice dialogue, or behavioral rehearsal. Clients are gently nudged, pushed, cajoled, or persuaded to get up off their butts and do something constructive and meaningful—a little bit every day. Just as important, they are held accountable for their commitments and expected to accept responsibility for their behavior.

Group and Family Support

If it's the therapeutic alliance that forms the glue that holds everything else we do together, then it is the other relationships in a client's life that maintain and support the changes made. For better or worse, it is peer support and group pressure that enable ongoing destructive behavior, as well as lead to recovery and continued growth.

In moments of brutal honesty, we often feel unable to help people change lifelong patterns or intractable, chronic problems when we talk to them for a few minutes each week. Anything they appear to understand, anything they commit to doing, often loses its momentum when they're barely out of the office. Once they return home and slip back into the same environment, begin interacting with the same people in the same ways, it's no wonder that setbacks are so common.

Master therapists well understand that what they do in therapy is not nearly as important as what happens between sessions. Unless ways have been structured to help clients make healthy social connections and functional family interactions, any gains are going to be lost.

Constructive Feedback

One of the things that distinguishes master therapists from ordinary clinicians is their interest and responsiveness to feedback. The way we get better at anything is to constantly identify weaknesses and strengthen them. We attempt to search for new, more effective ways of helping, refine our skills, add to our repertoire, and adapt what we do according to the context and circumstances. This process occurs both generally and situationally. With regard to the former, we do what we can to keep ourselves in top physical, emotional, intellectual, and interpersonal condition. We may read books like this one, view videos, attend workshops, study for advanced degrees, attend therapy and supervision, review our sessions critically, recruit mentors, consult with peers, and apply in our own lives what we teach to others. Yet just as important is the contextual feedback we actively solicit from our clients.

Feedback flows in both directions. One of our most useful functions is to provide clients with honest, direct input about their choices and behavior. There are times when we are the ones whose job it is to tell clients what they are doing is really unsafe, misguided, or counterproductive. In some cases, we are the *only* ones who will tell them the truth about what they are doing and its consequences. Throughout their lives they have been pushing people away or sabotaging themselves by engaging in repetitive patterns that we have clearly identified and pointed out. We also offer constructive advice about more effective ways to get their needs met.

However, clients are experts on their own experience. They know what it is that we do that is helpful to them and what feels like a waste of time. They are well aware when they are disengaged in sessions or even shut down. They know when they are only pretending to listen with no intention whatsoever of taking in what we are offering. As such, they hold deep wisdom about their own process (they also hold lots of illusions, distortions, deceptions, and biases, but we'll cover that later).

In any given session, we make dozens of mistakes, miscalculations, and misinterpretations. Even with a lifetime of experience, we sometimes push too hard, become self-indulgent, miss important clues, mismanage the pace, or otherwise do or say things that are less than elegant or sensitive. In order to make necessary adjustments or even repair damage, we've *got* to have accurate and honest feedback from clients about what is working for them and what is not. That means that we must continually and systematically invite clients to tell us how they are responding to what's happening and what we could do together to make things better.

Preparation for Setbacks and Relapses

It's one of the dirty little secrets of our profession that we may often measure the effects of therapy but all too rarely follow up to see how the changes have endured over time. Once clients leave our care, we rarely hear about what happened in the months or years afterward. Did they revert back to old patterns? Were they able to keep the momentum going?

Relapse rates for certain presenting problems like addictions, impulse disorders, and other chronic conditions are discouraging, with perhaps as many as half the supposed successes eventually dissipating. Even with the most common complaints that are treated in relatively brief, efficient treatment programs, we don't often have accurate data about what happens after the sessions end. There are all kinds of good reasons for this, most notably that it is time consuming to follow up with ex-clients and often difficult to reach them.

Realistically, it may not even be all that practical for therapists in the trenches to conduct their own research on long-term outcomes. That's why master therapists, even when they can't (or won't) follow up, spend considerable time in the latter sessions preparing clients for inevitable setbacks. This often means anticipating likely traps, identifying triggers that may lead to difficulties, rehearsing recovery responses, even deliberately choosing to relapse just so supervised practice can demonstrate successful recovery. After all, the main problem is not encountering failures, mistakes, lapses, or setbacks, but not having the skills and wherewithal to recover from them.

Flexibility to Reduce Stress and Demands

Sometimes clients are so overwhelmed with the demands of life that all they can do is struggle to keep their heads above water. Teaching them strategies that help them to reduce their external stresses, as well as manage the internal ones, is one of the most important goals in therapy. It isn't always possible to eliminate the stress, but it is usually possible to help them manage things better.

Laura and Bob were the parents of four children, all under the age of 5. They sought counseling to help them improve their marriage. Predictably, each one of them complained that the other one was not making the relationship much of a priority but only cared about the massive energy and time required to manage their herd of young children.

"You're probably right," the therapist said. "You've certainly got your hands full."

Both of them smiled and looked relieved. "So you're saying we're not supposed to have a great marriage now?" Laura asked.

"I'm not saying you shouldn't take better care of yourselves, and shouldn't try to make that a priority, but you also have to be realistic about what you can do with four kids so young. There is some interesting research that for couples that have kids under age 5, the relationship is at its lowest level of satisfaction. It's a time to tread water."

There are times when the situation calls for damage control, or at least maintaining a holding pattern, when stress is unrelenting and overwhelming. This flexibility is a hallmark of experts, knowing when and how to abandon their own agendas and preferences in order to meet clients where they currently reside. Many therapists become overattached to their preferred theory, which, while providing comfort and structure for the clinician, can lead to losing a degree of flexibility and preceding with a plan without concern for readiness levels to change. This can lead to overgeneralizing and making people fit into existing paradigms instead of seeing each client as a unique individual.

Above all else, Michael Hoyt tries to be as kind and loving as he can, conveying that there is always hope. He is less interested in a particular method than trying to be an advocate for his clients. "People tell me that I'm smart and on their side." Although he is certainly fond of using a variety of interventions in sessions, borrowed from many approaches, Hoyt believes it is the sheer variety of options available to him that makes it possible to deal with whatever occurs in the room. In his view, master therapists are, above all else, flexible, and able to anticipate potential pitfalls before they become major problems.

Consistent with Hoyt's observations, John Norcross and Bruce Wampold have devoted years to reviewing all the meta-analytic studies on treatment outcomes and concluded that the best predictor of success has to do with optimal matching between client needs/ characteristics and the chosen therapeutic strategies. Depending on the client's coping style, personality traits, cultural and family background, spiritual beliefs, reactance levels, and stage of readiness to change, truly exceptional clinicians are able—and willing—to adapt and adjust the treatment to fit these unique and special variables. And we repeat once again: They are not only *able* to do this (which most of us are) but actually *willing* to invest the hard work of inventing a completely individualized treatment for each person they help. Let's be honest: Many times it is just easier to go with what we already know, to follow the prescribed treatment regimen, rather than to venture into new territory.

Make It Meaningful

The master therapist knows the more meaningful an idea is to clients the more likely they are going to make it a reality. Helping clients to see how a change will be useful, important, or have a purpose will increase the likelihood of its happening. When the therapist can connect or relate the change to the client's values, it is far more likely that it will be internalized and personalized.

A therapist was meeting with a woman who was trying to decide whether to continue an affair and divorce her husband of 20 years or break it off and work on her marriage in therapy. She couldn't decide until the therapist said to her, "Which of those choices seems most like you?"

The woman paused thoughtfully for some time, stretching into several minutes while the therapist waited. Finally, she nodded her head, as much to herself as the therapist. "I have spent my entire life doing what is right. I even preach this at church, where I lead the youth group."

"Okay," the therapist responded, "so what does this mean to you?"

The therapist helped her to see that even though the affair seemed fun and pleasurable in the short run, in the long run she might have a problem living with herself afterward. If a change provides opportunities for people to pursue values they regard as important, they will be more receptive to cooperating and collaborating to find ways to bring about the changes they say are most important.

Passion and Enthusiasm

Helping clients to find or create meaning from their experiences, as well as from the therapeutic interactions, is among the most daunting of tasks for those who are relative beginners to the field. Such an endeavor requires a certain amount of experience and deep reflection, yet we wish to reassure those who are just starting their careers that what you may lack in a breadth of knowledge can sometimes be compensated for in other areas that are unique to novices.

Thomas Skovholt makes a case that, in at least a few areas, beginners actually enjoy some advantages over veterans. Novices have the edge in terms of demographics in that they are likely younger, have greater familiarity with popular culture and technology, and more recent direct experiences related to life struggles. They will often be more enthusiastic, passionate, and intense about the work, given its novelty and freshness. They have a "beginner's mind" in that they are seeing things for the first time and are hesitant to make assumptions that are not actually supported with behavioral evidence. This may lead them to be cautious, perhaps to make mistakes, but this attitude also helps them to see and hear clients individually and uniquely instead of making comparisons to others. Finally, new therapists often have more cutting-edge knowledge and are likely more familiar with the newest research and evidence-based practices. A number of studies over the years have supported the idea that the longer therapists have been out of school, the less likely they are to stay current on empirically based practices.

When we compare our own training to that of our current students, we are struck by how different programs are today. Whereas now most graduate programs require 3 years of intensive training, our master's degrees were composed of only 11 classes! Certainly, formal training programs do not necessarily teach all (or even most) of what is needed to operate at the highest levels, but they do form a significant running start. We, therefore, want to reassure beginners that although your enthusiasm and passion can sometimes get you (and your clients) in trouble by acting impulsively or naïvely, this excitement for the work, often tempered over the years, is one of your greatest strengths that should be valued and honored.

Beyond Understanding: Honoring Magic and Mystery

Bradford Keeney, previously known as a cybernetic family systems theorist, and more recently an expert in indigenous healing practices, identifies one ingredient of mastery that is never spoken about by Western therapists. "Among the Kalahari Bushmen it is called *n/om,* and among flamenco dancers it is called *duende.* There is no equivalent word in German, English, and many other languages. It refers to the vitality of the therapist, perhaps close to what we sometimes too lazily call the vital life force. The Japanese word *seiki* is also a way of pointing to this vitality of presence. Carl Whitaker hinted at it when he said therapy was as good as the goodness of the therapist. Though his words are easy to misunderstand, they imply a truth: "I found *seiki* at the heart of most healing traditions."

Keeney is referring to his decade-long journey around the world, studying with the most accomplished healers in southern Africa, Latin America, South Asia, among the aborigines of Australia, and to many other far-flung places that hold ancient practices. He finds it more than a little amusing that in the culture of therapy we are so obsessed with things that matter so little to others around the world. "I have learned that one's model or protocols matter not at all and that evidence-based therapy is a gambler's way of pulling the authority card. If you have *seiki,* or a powerful life force, then any model will come to life. Without it, the session will be dead and incapable of transformation."

Keeney finds it challenging, if not frustrating, to try to explain this idea to those who don't speak this language. "I guess if you have *seiki* or *n/om,* you feel what I am talking about; if you don't, no words will matter. The extent to which you feel, smell, taste, hear, and see this vitality is a measure of how much mastery there is in your practice and everyday life."

We believe it is an illusion that master therapists truly understand what therapy is all about and how it works. The reality is that the process has many different dimensions and nuances that we never really grasp. There are aspects that appear both mysterious and magical.

The fact that we don't completely understand something doesn't mean that we can't operate effectively. We don't understand how electricity works, but we can turn on the lights. We don't understand how a steel object as big as a building can float on water or fly in the air, but we still willingly board ships and airplanes. We don't even understand how engines work, but we still drive cars.

We trust the process of therapy when certain conditions are established. We may not understand as much as we would prefer about how it all works, but we also honor the mystery of what happens. This belief is in marked contrast to some of our colleagues, identified as master therapists as a function of their publications or notoriety, who present seemingly perfect confidence that they know *exactly* how therapy works, especially if you follow their approach. On some level, we envy this assurance, even if we are suspicious of its validity.

We don't think it is necessary to understand everything about how change occurs in order to put into place the healing ingredients that will likely make it happen. Most of the time when clients leave with successful results, we *think* we have some rough ideas of what may have happened to help them, but we also willingly acknowledge that a lot of things will remain a mystery.

CHAPTER 7

SPEAKING THE TRUTH

Master therapists practice transparent honesty with as much tact and diplomacy as appropriate, given a client's willingness and openness to handle useful feedback. The important message in effective therapy is that you can count on me to always tell you the truth, or at least one semblance of it. It may be uncomfortable, and difficult, but that's why you're here—because I will tell you things that nobody else would say.

Imagine you are sitting at dinner with a group of strangers, waiting for the next course to be delivered. You look across the table and see that one of your tablemates has a smudge of creamy garlic dressing on her nose, a remnant from the salad that has just been served. Do you say anything to her?

The essence of what we do is create an environment that makes it safe to tell clients our perceptions of them, presumably related to helping them function more effectively. This most often involves helping them to speak their truth, to tell their story in the most honest, unvarnished way, with all the accompanying shameful, uncomfortable parts. The other half of the contract we make with clients is the promise to speak the truth to them, as we know it.

Often, what brings clients to therapy in the first place is that their level of self-deception sabotages any attempt to achieve what they say is most important: intimate, loving, authentic relationships. They lie to themselves, in part, so they can hide from things that are painful and disturbing. They also lie to themselves so they can more convincingly lie to others. To complicate matters further, distorted memories lead to fraudulent narratives and personal myths that have little basis in so-called objective reality.

Lies in Therapy

It is a bit ironic, if not paradoxical, that people would come to us for help and then be less than forthcoming about why they're there or what they really want. People lie to their doctors and dentists (sure, I floss every day) for the same reasons—to avoid embarrassment and look good. They want our approval and feel desperately afraid that if we knew the real them, we would kick them out of our offices in disgust. Clients lie to us to bide time until trust is earned. They lie because it feels good to fool someone with power and authority. They lie because it's fun and interesting. They lie because it's part of who they are.

Our job is to ferret out some approximation of truth, at least that has some basis in reality rather than fantasy. We are being paid to help people to become more fully functioning, and often that involves confronting hard truths that nobody has been willing— or able—to communicate previously. Almost everyone we see has creamy garlic dressing on their nose; everyone else knows it except them. When they look in the mirror, they see a perfect, unsullied profile and have no idea why people react to them the ways they do.

A client tells you that things are going pretty well in his life. He's got a good job, a stable marriage, and a decent relationship with his kids; he only wants help with a "little" problem he's having feeling a bit "blue." The problem is that you've also been seeing his wife for several sessions and you happen to know that his marriage is on the rocks, on the verge of divorce; his kids barely speak to him; and he feels so depressed about the prospect of going to work in the morning he can barely get out of bed.

Robert Wubbolding, a major proponent of reality therapy, sees an important part of his job as helping clients like this to face the disowned parts of themselves and their lives. As attractive as the idea might sound, he thinks it is rather naïve to believe that people naturally tend toward self-actualization and our main job is simply to remove blocks to further growth. There is too much evidence to support the counterpoint, that people also have the potential to be supremely self-sabotaging. "I believe it helps a therapist to see clients as trending toward either self-actualization *or* self-destruction. Our job is to help them take responsibility for this direction and, furthermore, to choose a humane path. Similarly, suspending judgment has its place, but it is not an all-pervasive worldview." In other words, sometimes it is necessary to confront clients vigorously when they engage in behavior that is patently hurtful to themselves or others—or when they lie to themselves in such a way that prevents them from reaching what they say is most important.

Although a strong advocate of the practical dimensions of William Glasser's choice theory and reality therapy, Wubbolding also values an existential philosophy focused on helping clients to make sense of their behavior and life journey. "I believe a master therapist rejects and does not participate in an unintended facilitation of people as permanent victims, but rather sees clients as searching for meaning and purpose and capable of change." This process begins with an honest assessment of what is working and what is not.

Confronting Deception

It is one thing to "know" things about our clients that they don't seem to realize about themselves; it is quite another to tell them in a way that they can hear what we are saying without shutting down or running away. Exceptional therapists seem to have mastered all three parts of speaking the truth:

1. *Knowing what is "true."* It takes extraordinary sensitivity, acute perception, and brilliant acumen to see and hear things that are hidden, disguised, buried, or otherwise inaccessible to most others. We learn to fine-tune our ability to read accurately what may be happening based on all the hard work

invested through study, observation, and paying very close attention to our daily interactions. Through this experience, knowledge, and wisdom, we recognize patterns of behavior and, just as important, can describe and name what we have observed: "It seems that your little problem of feeling blue is actually a form of depression, one that appears to run in your family based on some things you mentioned earlier about your father and sister."

2. *Communicating diplomatically and sensitively.* It is one thing to know things and quite another to tell people what you observe in a way that they can take it in without feeling threatened. There are all kinds of therapists who have very clear and perhaps accurate ideas about what is "wrong" or dysfunctional about their clients, but they may not be able to present this information as effectively as needed. Imagine, for example, a therapist says to the client introduced earlier: "You are obviously lying to yourself, and to me, when you say that everything is going well in your life. As you know, I've talked to your wife and she tells me that basically your life sucks. Your children hate you. You are on the verge of being fired at work. And the only reason your wife is still hanging around is that she believes you'll kill yourself without her there." That may all be true, but, needless to say, this client will not likely be returning for another session.

3. *Helping to do something useful with the knowledge.* It is indeed helpful to confront aspects of yourself that are less than desirable and quite another to convert that insight into constructive action that results in needed changes. A skilled clinician might approach things as follows: "I know how difficult it is for you to talk about the challenges you've been facing. I really admire the optimistic and upbeat way that you try to keep things together, even in the face of some disappointments. It's been frustrating for you to feel so unappreciated, yet you

have still managed to keep going with all the setbacks you've encountered. Given that things are much more challenging than you'd first described, it seems important to be realistic with yourself, and with me, about what we can do to make things better. I'm wondering where we might begin."

We mention this example to illustrate that there are some awfully brilliant therapists who know all kinds of wise and interesting things about people, but that doesn't necessarily translate into revealing them in such a way that it is heard, acknowledged, and acted upon. Master therapists would begin with asking themselves the particular meaning of the deception and what it may be really communicating. Is there some kind of hidden agenda? Is there a breach of trust? Is this a pattern throughout the person's life or unique to our relationship?

Given that most such confrontations will likely be denied and deflected, it helps to present some kind of supportive examples and evidence: "You say you are chronically shy and avoidant and that's why you haven't been able to meet anyone, but you have talked about a series of encounters you've had at work in which you approach people you don't know in other departments to get the information you need. It seems that you really *can* initiate conversations when you choose to, but you hold on to this vision of yourself that keeps you from taking risks."

It requires masterful skill to help the client save face when caught in more bald-faced lies. In another volume, we collected over three dozen case examples of therapists who experienced fairly extreme deceit from clients—those who faked illnesses, hid their secrets, made up stories of who they were, fabricated histories, and pretended to be suicidal, and one who even stole his therapist's identity! In each case, the therapist was left to make sense of feelings of betrayal and of being duped. Of course, there are also deep truths embedded in the lies, and that's where the therapeutic action may take place.

JK Even after so many years in practice, three or four different stints in therapy as a client, and a lifetime of journaling and self-reflection, I still struggle with one of my core issues—the desire (which feels like a need) to be liked by almost everyone all the time. Approval seeking has always been with me as long as I can remember, a constant companion that shapes my behavior and has been one primary motive behind my compulsive achievement. My parents thought I was stupid as a child; they used to tease me that I'd be lucky to get into a community college. My mediocre grades only confirmed their expectations.

I have spent most of my life trying to win my parents' approval, never feeling like I ever came close to succeeding. As far as I know, neither of my parents ever read one of my books, nor did they understand or appreciate what was most important to me. That is not to say I wasn't loved, just that I seemed to them to be more than a little strange because my interests diverged so widely from their own. I had hoped to earn their respect through education, then academic achievement, and finally professional accomplishments. Because my mother died and my father had a massive stroke when I was still a young man, I never had the opportunity to attain what I wanted most.

This theme of being—or feeling—good enough has been one of the driving forces of my life. When I was first studying to become a therapist, I was completely in awe of my mentors, teachers, supervisors, and authors, who (apparently) so effortlessly knew exactly what to do in almost any situation. They never seemed stumped by situations they faced and could speak fluently about subjects that utterly confounded me. I accepted that I would never come close to their level of expertise and confidence. I looked around at my peers and felt that I would never be as smart or skilled as they were. But still—maybe I could be of use.

It has been one of my most shameful secrets that I am fooling everyone—my clients, my students, my readers. I don't really know or understand very much; I'm just faking it. But maybe that's a lie, a kind of false modesty that I hide behind.

What I know for sure is that no matter how hard I try, I can't come close to how good I want to be. My clients and students deserve better than me. I'm pretty good—sometimes I would even admit I'm quite excellent—but I still hold my doubts, which are often confirmed because I know where to look. Because I try so hard at what I do, and prepare so well, and have so much at stake, I manage to put on a pretty good performance most of the time (if you're still with me right now, then maybe you agree). When I read the evaluations of my teaching or workshops or book reviews, they are usually quite supportive and encouraging. Yet I ignore that feedback and immediately laser in on the few reports that are critical and less than flattering. Those are the ones who have my number.

So here's the problem: If I care so deeply about what others think of me, if I am so afraid of others' disapproval, how can I risk being truly honest with others? It is the job of any therapist, especially a so-called "master," to say out loud with others think but are afraid to say. It is one of our primary tasks to provide constructive feedback to clients about the ways they are self-defeating and dysfunctional. We are the only ones who will tell them about how annoying they are, especially if we can do so in a way that they can hear what we are saying. It is part of our mission to tell them the "truth" so that they have the opportunity to face themselves in more honest ways and change those behaviors that are most getting in the way.

This is what I'm good at—and I truly know it: I am a fearless truth teller. I see my role in life as the little boy in "The Emperor's New Clothes," the one who yells out that the sanctimonious king is buck naked. In my teaching, therapy, and writing, I love talking about the forbidden, about that which is not said. I love pushing people to talk about the things that terrify them (and me!) the most. I love blurting out what others are thinking but unwilling to admit. I love pushing people (and myself) to go deeper into the unfamiliar and scary territory that has never been charted before. Okay, that last one was a bit of an exaggeration: I only like it after I've come out the other end.

The interesting question, then, is how did someone who so desperately wants others' approval learn to take such risks that are virtually guaranteed to earn a certain degree of scorn, ridicule, and sometimes censure? Ah, the complexities and paradoxes of why we do what we do!

I'm sure you can formulate your own theories to explain my behavior, but the best I can do for now is that being a therapist, especially someone who aspires to excellence, has pushed me to face my greatest fears—especially of being a hypocrite. I can tolerate a degree of ineptitude, rigidity, ignorance, ill-preparedness, disorganization, and disingenuousness, but hypocrisy makes my skin crawl—literally when I catch myself telling people to do things that I am unable or unwilling to do myself.

Hard Truths

There are some really, really difficult things we have to tell people, things that will bruise their egos, wound their hearts, and scar their souls. If we do this effectively, eventually the healing process will make them stronger and far more aware of what they do, if not more resilient. Such knowledge may not set them free, but more accurate information will often prepare them better for the challenges they face. There will be sacrifices, of course, because we all mourn the loss of our naiveté and illusions.

Monteith was a salesman so renowned within his window company that it was rumored he could convince his customers to buy products they never needed or could afford in the first place. When he shared this with his therapist, it was with a certain bravado and pride. Monteith could persuade anyone to do most anything, and he had been doing his best to sell his therapist the idea that he was a pretty affable guy. He had a bucketful of excuses why his life wasn't going well—a series of bad breaks, unappreciative friends, unsupportive family, and a run of poor luck. He actually believed all of this; it was part of his way of being.

Listening to his story, the therapist was struck by the level and depth of Monteith's self-deception. He was genuinely convinced that his bankruptcy, dissolution of his marriage, estranged relationship with his children, and social isolation were all the result of factors completely outside of his control. In spite of his success as a top salesman, he was broke and despondent. Even his cheerful, bubbly manner was deceptive; inside he felt hopelessness and despair. Or at least this was what the therapist sensed was going on.

Week after week the therapist was regaled by outlandish stories of Monteith's exploits—how he picked up a gorgeous woman in a bar; how his boss often confided in him; how his children, who never called and refused to meet with him, actually quite admired and loved him. The therapist showed remarkable patience throughout these sessions, tempering his own frustration and critical judgments. He knew, at some point, he'd have to confront his client with all the falsehoods that were standing in the way of his having the slightest chance of stabilizing his life, but such hard truths would be difficult for Monteith to hear. The therapist would have to tell him in a way that wouldn't frighten him away. And if he were honest with himself, the therapist admitted that he was more than a little appalled by his client's immorality and exploitative treatment of others. He'd have to be careful not to indulge in punitive honesty as a way to censure him for behavior that was seen as antisocial, if not hurtful.

We are in the business of telling hard truths, the kind that can be quite painful to face. Some examples of those within our repertoire might include:

- "You're not as happy as you pretend to be."
- "You are dying every single moment of your life, and there's not nearly as much time left as you think."
- "You are playing games with me and with yourself."
- "It's hard for me to be with you right now when you do that."
- "I wonder why you keep repeating the same mistakes over and over, when you know what will happen. It's as if you want to fail."

- "What do you think it means that it's hard for anyone to get close to you?"
- "You say you had a happy childhood, but it sure doesn't sound that way based on what you've told me."
- "You've got absolutely no chance of recovery unless you lose almost everything and finally hit bottom."

Therapists operate under different parameters, norms, and philosophies, depending on their setting and mode of practice. As such, we also proceed at different paces, again depending on the client, the issues, and the scope of practice, as well as a host of external pressures. Nevertheless, there's been some evidence that we can push (or lead) clients faster than we might imagine. In a provocative article, psychotherapist Jonathan Albert summarized what many researchers and brief practitioners have long discovered—that close to 90% of clients improve significantly after a single session, and that optimal progress is often accomplished in less than a dozen meetings. This isn't to denigrate the value of longer-term treatment for those who have the time and resources, as well as more severe problems, but it is a reminder that we can often challenge clients much sooner than we might imagine, as long as a solid alliance has been formed.

William Doherty, a distinguished family therapist, feels frustrated with the limits that some colleagues place on themselves by refusing to provide the structure that would lead to greater efficiency. Doherty pins down what he believes is most important in his work: "First of all, I engage quickly. I expect that clients will want to stay and work with me. Secondly, I challenge quickly, just as soon as I have a sense of engagement. Many therapists wait too long to challenge, not trusting the therapeutic alliance. Thirdly, I show clients that I get to the heart of their challenges, which is more than standard therapeutic empathy. I am also willing to talk about stuck points in our work together, collaborating on getting past those points. Finally, I pay attention to multiple levels at once: the micro steps in the therapeutic conversation, within-session strategy and flow, and longer-term strategy and flow."

Doherty concludes by saying that he sees his clients as moral agents of their lives, creating a role for him to challenge them to bring their best selves to their life responsibilities.

JC I was the youngest of four children, with my closest sibling 8 years older. I essentially grew up as a spoiled only child with five parents and could do no wrong. I always said what was on my mind, which frequently resulted in trouble with teachers who were looking for conformity. My outspoken nature did not seem to bother my fellow students since they found it entertaining. I am not sure where I learned to keep my voice and to speak up whenever I saw things that were not right, but I know I take this forthright way of speaking into my work as a psychotherapist.

I am honest and direct with clients. Some other therapists in my community have complained that I am too direct and brutally honest. The other therapists have stated that they have had to "pick up the pieces" with some of my former clients. I believe them but also reassure myself by knowing that I have had to deal with their casualties of seeing clients for months, sometimes years, without providing much feedback or results. I can live with what I do, but I wonder how they can.

Students, supervisees, and colleagues often ask, "Would you really tell somebody that?" I answer that I would and have spoken in a direct fashion. Today, I was working with a couple, for example, in which the man was aggressive and had been accused by his wife of physical abuse. She was, according to him, "always complaining and harping about something." After listening to her describe all of the things that he did that upset her, I noticed that he began to tense his muscles and his complexion was almost crimson. I asked if this is the kind of thing that they talked about as bothering them. They both nodded. I spoke to her and said that speaking to a partner like that would make even Gandhi get physical and then asked him where he learned that threatening your partner was a turn-on? They both stared at me and became silent. I then indicated that no other partner would accept them the way either of them acted and that if they wanted to have a relationship with anyone, they were both going to need to change. I told them, half-kiddingly, that they ought to stay together if only to keep two other people from being miserable.

I believe that people are able to hear and use this kind of honest feedback if it is offered in a constructive way. To withhold or beat around the bush is not ethical from my point of view. Many therapists hide behind the statement that it is important to be loving and caring to your clients. I don't disagree, but I think that being honest is just as important. I also believe that direct and honest feedback needs to be done sooner rather than later.

I recall one of my graduate school professors coming to class one day with what seemed like a chip on her shoulder. This statuesque African American woman commanded a powerful presence. When we asked her what was the matter, she told us that she had been undergoing psychoanalysis faithfully twice a week for 15 years and her analyst finally just spoke up yesterday and told her that all her problems were related to her penis envy! "What an asshole!" she blurted out. "I know Freud's theory and could have made that generalization on the first day of treatment." I remember telling myself that day that I was never going to be that kind of therapist who holds back, especially for 15 years!

I admit that there are times that I could be more tactful with my confrontations and direct statements. I work at this each time I speak and think that I have made some improvements. I also know that there are some people who come to therapy who really do not want to deal with my kind of feedback or interpretation and would prefer to enjoy the weekly (or is it weakly?) sessions with someone who just sits and reflects back positives. I have had some clients begin therapy by saying that they really want someone who is gentle. I let them know that this is probably not the right place for them.

I don't see therapy as a popularity contest. If it were, I would probably lose. I don't need to "blow smoke" or try to charm someone into liking me. Whether they like me or I like them is not really the issue. The issue is what can I do to help them to help themselves.

Taking Risks and Exploring the Unknown

We accept that there really is no objective truth, merely our own remembrances and perceptions of experiences as we believe they occurred. Yet as Jon's narrative illustrates, we have a responsibility to risk telling our clients difficult things in a way that they can hear them, in a manner that is acceptable enough to them that they will take what is said on board. We are not responsible for being 100% right all the time, merely to present our best impression of what we sense and observe. It is up to the client to do a reality check, to compare the feedback we offer to what they've heard before, or what they believe might be going on. This ongoing dialogue is not only what leads clients to make needed changes in dysfunctional behavior but also makes it possible for us to continue to refine and improve the accuracy or our "bullshit detector," in the words of Ernest Hemingway.

These can be breakthrough moments—if they are well timed, carefully framed, and presented in such a way that clients truly hear them. It is one thing to speak the truth, but a master therapist seems to have that special ability to do so with grace and caring and sensitivity.

Each of us has particular values and goals for our clients, things we believe are good not only for ourselves but for almost everyone else. We recognize that although our profession is supposed to be relatively value free, we do hold certain principles that we unabashedly "sell" to those we are paid to help. Although each of our priorities might vary a bit, there would also be some consensus that would include such things as:

- Building greater intimacy will improve the quality of life.
- We are all part of a larger community and have a responsibility for the greater good.

- Deeper self-examination is often useful to finding greater meaning and satisfaction in our lives.
- Talk without constructive action is often not that useful.
- Having more choices is better than fewer (unless we already have too many choices).
- It is often better to accept responsibility for that which is within our power to change instead of blaming external forces.

To this list we would add that it is often useful to seize the day, to live more intensely engaged with the precious, present moments of life, to take constructive risks that stretch or stimulate us, and help us explore the unknown.

We know therapists who see their work as essentially minimizing risks by developing technical proficiency. They follow protocols that have been refined by years of experience and research. They adhere to sequential steps that have been developed, rehearsed, and tested. That is just not our journey as a therapist. And we suppose that is a different kind of "mastery" than we are exploring in this book.

To us, there are tremendous risks in being a therapist—and we're not talking about jeopardizing client safety for the sake of our own experimentation. Every time we step into a room with someone in acute distress, we risk our own sanity on some level. There is only so much pain and suffering that we can hold without being affected by the experience, without shutting down that part of ourselves that is so vulnerable.

Kirk Schneider, one of the foremost leaders in humanistic therapy, draws a lot on his own experiences in therapy as a client to bolster his faith in the process. In part, this is what allows him to be more fully present during sessions.

"I was in psychoanalysis at age 5 following the tumultuous death of my 7-year-old brother, and I was in a crucial existential analysis at about 22, when I first began my graduate studies. Looking back,

I view both therapies as lifesaving in some way, the first because it was a key connection of stability that very understandably was lacking in my young life at the time. I'm sure I internalized this sensitive yet profound and supportive relationship that subsequently helped me to simply cope, and then a few years later, actually enabled me to become fascinated with the bigger questions of life. I moved from a position of abject terror to one of gradual intrigue and even wonder toward the world (never completely losing the humbling recognition of the tragic). This manifested in my increasing fascination with science fiction, creative play, and a growing capacity to love.

"By the time of my second critical therapy as a young adult, I had just suffered a kind of nervous breakdown. I was in a pretty bad way, having experienced major night terrors, early morning tremors, and a fear that I was becoming psychotic. This second major therapy was also life changing and it taught me to 'stay with myself,' no matter how scary the fears. This took a sustained period of time, of course, but it taught me tremendously about the power of presence to heal."

Schneider believes these experiences as a client taught him the most about the importance of true presence as a healing force, not only in his role as a professional but also as a human being. He believes that is what makes him most accessible to others in pain and what leads them to feel that he can truly understand them. It is also what inspires him to pursue the unknown and continue to take constructive risks in his work.

The writers and thinkers, the scientists and artists, and, yes, the therapists we have admired most were those who were willing to venture into places that others feared to tread. We have felt spellbound by biographies of those who risked such disapproval by proposing theories that were threatening to the established guardians of knowledge. Freud's story, in particular, was intriguing not just because of his controversial ideas but because of how he suffered as a result of being different. Later, when we were exposed to many others we admired, we discovered a similar pattern of their sticking their necks *way* out in order to say some things that were unpopular at the time. This suggests to us that master therapists, almost by definition, are avid truth seekers who are willing to follow their discoveries wherever they might lead and to accept responsibility for the sacrifices they make and the consequences that result.

CHAPTER 8

MAKING MISTAKES—BUT
NOT THE SAME ONES
OVER AND OVER

Master therapists are hardly perfect and make a number of mistakes; in fact, one master therapist described acknowledging failures as being absolutely critical because they mean you are experimenting and taking risks. Such practitioners learn from their miscalculations and errors of judgment and use that constructive feedback to improve their effectiveness.

The two of us once spent the better part of a year interviewing prominent therapists to tell us the stories of their worst therapy sessions, as much to make ourselves feel better about our own mistakes as to contribute to the literature. There were some wonderfully reassuring tales, among them one by solution-focused therapist Michele Weiner-Davis, who talked about a case in which she was supervising a therapist from behind a one-way mirror. She had a brainstorm in the middle of the session and so communicated with the therapist by phone in the middle of the session to suggest a brilliant intervention. As soon as the therapist began to implement the strategy, the client interrupted and looked at the mirror. "Is that Weiner-Davis lady behind there? Is she the one who just talked to you?"

The therapist nodded nervously, unsure where this was going.

"Well," the client continued, "we were in here a year ago and she tried that crap with us and it didn't work then and it sure as hell isn't going to work now either."

The lesson learned is that there is no sin in making mistakes in our work. In fact, such errors in judgment and execution are perfectly understandable considering how often we are operating in the dark without adequate information, experimenting, trying out new ideas, testing limits, trusting intuition, telling people things they'd rather not hear, confronting them before they are ready, and so on. According to Weiner-Davis, the main problem is when we are doing something that isn't working and yet we insist on continuing with the strategy even in the face of irrefutable evidence that it isn't effective.

When we talked to Weiner-Davis about this current study of mastery, she admitted that sometimes it is the fear of making mistakes that can most prevent therapists from achieving true excellence, especially if all you are after is recognition. "I don't believe I could have had the success I've had without friends and colleagues along the way: It's all about relationships. But it's also about a belief in yourself and a determination to want to help people on a grand scale. You must have passion and drive, and yet you have to be thick-skinned enough to not allow disappointments to slow you down."

Making Mistakes Isn't the Problem

One of the impediments to excellence that can so immobilize beginners in the field is their terrifying fear of making a mistake with a client. There is an irrational fantasy that if you say or do the wrong thing, the client is going to bolt out of the room, decompensate in a psychotic break, or jump out the window. In fact, what we eventually learn is that most of the time clients aren't paying that much attention to what we're saying or doing in the first place, or if they are, they are so consumed with their own stuff that they hardly notice the relative inelegance with which we offered an interpretation or introduced an idea. We're not saying that clients aren't critical consumers, but rather that most of the little mistakes we make go unnoticed, except by our own rather unforgiving internal critics.

The reality is that that we try all kinds of things in any given session that don't work the way we anticipated. We use language that is unnecessarily obtuse or incomprehensible. We miss things that we only recognize much later. We push clients to do things for which they aren't yet ready. We introduce ideas in an awkward way. We lose the thread of what is happening. We sometimes do things that are downright stupid or say things that are misinformed or inaccurate. And yet none of these blunders are necessarily a problem—unless we persist in our misguided efforts in the face of consistent evidence that what we are doing is not working.

It turns out that truly exceptional therapists can actually make *more* mistakes than others, or at least are more inclined to admit them. Bruce Wampold, one of the major researchers in the field, fully acknowledges that one of his strengths as a therapist is his willingness to look honestly at himself and his own behavior. "I am willing to recognize my own limitations and work through them, as well as the strengths of my patients. I'm ever mindful of the pain the patient feels in dealing with the world through a lens clouded by his or her problems."

In their research, Scott Miller and Mark Hubble point out that master therapists are more critical than their peers, more willing to examine honestly their limitations and lapses. Furthermore, rather than avoiding challenging cases that increase the likelihood of poorer outcomes, they are inclined to tackle them with relish. Thus, at the top of William Doherty's list of what makes extraordinary therapists is that they "never fault the client when things aren't working. Rather than being threatened by mistakes, they are intrigued by them." Because such therapists don't fear doing something "wrong," they are free to tackle the most difficult cases.

Clients usually give us plenty of latitude to try things, some of which aren't necessarily helpful right away. We are given two, three, sometimes four different tries to convey an idea or initiate an intervention in such a way that it will be most useful. Whereas we might be harshly judgmental about our awkward, inelegant, or ineffective efforts, most of the time we have other chances to get them right.

Imagine you are leading a therapy group in which there is prolonged silence that seems uncomfortable. How you intervene in this situation depends on how you read what the silence means. Your first interpretation was that the members needed more reflective time to respond, but after waiting awhile it's apparent that nobody wants to talk. Scratch that hypothesis.

Next, you figure that they are reluctant because they didn't understand what you were asking for, so you explain again what you want them to do. You try to be clear and concise but find yourself repeating much of what you said earlier. Then you wait. And wait. And wait. And still nothing much happens except shuffling feet and downcast eyes.

Hmm, you think. You missed the mark again. Maybe they are feeling some resistance because you asked them to do something that is beyond what they are prepared to do. Perhaps you should change the agenda altogether and just call on someone to respond, cuing the nonverbal behavior that seems most evident. You try that, calling on one member who seems particularly anxious, but he just mumbles that he has nothing to say.

Yikes, you are running out of options, having tried three different interventions, each of which failed miserably. Eventually, you figure out what is going on, most likely recruiting help from the members themselves, who by now feel a little sorry for your struggle. But the point we wish to make is that this kind of experimentation is not all that unusual in our work: We often try a handful of different approaches before we discover the best option that works at the time. The key to processing such situations is to: (1) carefully observe the impact of any intervention, (2) collect accurate feedback on the apparent outcomes of the attempt, (3) cease doing things that aren't working, (4) remain as flexible as possible in the ways we conceptualize and respond to what is going on, (5) try something else that might prove more helpful, and (6) continue to make adjustments as needed in light of the client reactions. All of this is predicated on the assumption that the alliance created is such that you and your clients are mutually forgiving of one another and willing to be sufficiently patient until such time that an optimal strategy is discovered.

JK When I take inventory of the biggest mistakes I've made over and over again, I'm disappointed, but hardly surprised, that similar issues remain somewhat familiar. But here goes: This is a partial list of some of my most frequent mistakes that I haven't been able to completely stop myself from repeating:

- Feeling impatient when people don't do what I prefer according to my schedule. I got into this field in the first place because I wanted to "save" and "cure" people of their suffering. When clients don't get better quickly, it triggers my own sense of inadequacy: If only I were smarter or more skilled, I could do so much better.
- *Pushing people to do things for which they aren't prepared or ready—and then pushing harder when they resist.* See above. I don't regret feeling some sense of urgency to help clients as quickly as possible, but the problem arises when I don't pay close attention to the feedback my client is giving me that he or she doesn't (yet) wish to go where I am leading/ pushing/urging. I have to remind myself repeatedly (and sometimes too late) to take a deep breath, back off, and respect the client's pace.
- *Becoming excessively self-indulgent in my self-disclosures (evident in parts of this book).* I have always found that people's life stories have been most impactful in my life. The things I remember from my best therapists and teachers are often the stories they told, many about their own lives. Those that were most memorable often involved tales of resilience and courage, but also fallibility and self-acceptance. I also recognize, however, that there is a thin line that separates effective self-disclosure from self-indulgence.

- Giving up, withdrawing, or running away when I feel unappreciated and misunderstood. I have a tendency to pout when I don't get my way. When I extend myself to others or make personal sacrifices on their behalf and such gestures are not acknowledged, I feel hurt and withdraw.
- *Allowing personal ambition to overshadow my presence in the moment.* I've long found it fascinating where therapists go when we lapse into fantasy during sessions. When we are bored, threatened, or disengaged during periodic intervals, what do we think about? I live in the future, where dreams beckon me. I plan what I'm going to do next in my life or formulate my next great enterprise. While I'm figuring out where I want to go next or some new book project I want to begin, I'm not paying attention to what's happening in the present.
- *Working harder than my clients because I never feel good enough.* I have heard myself say to students and supervisees more times than I can remember that it is the client who has to do the work. While I recognize that there's only so much that we can do to help someone who isn't willing to follow through, it often feels like a personal failing on my part when a client is noncompliant. I sometimes find myself working much harder than some clients. I recognize this in the moment but feel unable to back off.
- *I sometimes take myself way too seriously, deluding myself (and others) into thinking that I'm special.* Even as I admit this, I'm winking to myself, pretending false modesty.
- Critical judgment is the companion to the previous confessions. It must be my own insecurity that leads me to feel scorn, disrespect, and such negative reactions to others who subscribe to different beliefs or behave in ways I find incomprehensible.

While I feel a certain shame in admitting these chronic struggles, especially collecting them all in one place, I am hoping that this (excessive?) disclosure invites readers to construct their own honest catalogue of personal and professional mistakes that are made over and over again.

Practicing Self-Compassion

It is precisely because therapy is so complex that mistakes and lapses are inevitable. No matter what the situation, there are always a dozen or more options regarding what we could do. Whichever one we choose, it's hard not to second-guess ourselves and wonder if we made the optimal choice. Yet the critical point is how important it is to learn from the particular outcome and continue onward.

Scott Browning, a specialist in work with blended families, has been struck by the optimistic and resilient attitude that is favored by successful therapists. "When I consider those who are exceptional at this field, they never seem defeated by a case. This is not to say that every one is a success, but rather, the expression of defeat, the comments that suggest that the therapist sees this case as unsolvable, never appears on the face of the gifted clinician. Even in the most difficult situations, the expert finds a way to shift the focus off the insurmountable, even if it includes accepting things that can't be changed. The exceptional therapist recognizes that an impasse is often a step toward progress. Impediments are viewed as providing a clearer understanding, and are recognized as important, not defeating."

In many of the settings in which we have both worked, it often hasn't felt safe to talk about our mistakes and failures; to do so is to send a message to colleagues and supervisors that we don't know what the heck we are doing (which is sometimes the case). In schools, agencies, and organizations, staff are sometimes expected to present an image of perfect confidence and complete competence. Answering questions with "I don't know" may not be acceptable or in your best interest. As such, our doubts and uncertainties are forced underground, and we learn to live with our mistakes as secrets that must remain hidden.

This is all the more ironic considering that the growth edge and learning opportunities mostly arise when things don't unfold the way we expected or hoped. We tend to remember our failures far longer than our successes. Knowing this, master therapists are especially good at practicing self-compassion and forgiveness—with themselves. It turns out that excellence arises from taking risks, which are inevitably accompanied by mistakes—lots of them.

JC When I consider the clients who challenge me the most, I understand that I am not very different from many of my colleagues. It is probably the narcissistic clients, the ones who are always right and have all the answers even though they are hurting, that are the most difficult for me. Their responses of "yes, but" grow old pretty quickly. I clearly understand that this is part of their disorder and I'm supposed to keep things professional and not take things personally. Yet I am also human, and every once in awhile I just want to run screaming out of the room.

"Whiners" or "martyrs" would have to be a close second on my list. You know, the ones who seem to enjoy being unhappy and revel in their misery. Yesterday, I had a client call one minute before the session was to start and indicate to my secretary that he was canceling but he wanted to speak with me on the phone. I called him right away and he indicated that he didn't want to bother me but he was about as low as he could get. I indicated that he was not bothering me, as this was his time for therapy and that he was being charged for the session whether he was here or not since he did not cancel in time to allow us to schedule someone else. He indicated that didn't help him feel better and hung up in a dramatic fashion.

I struggle with dramatic clients, at least the ones who use drama to elicit the support of anyone who will listen. The man who just hung up the phone with me has been abusing his wife, and now she wants out of the marriage. He is upset because he is the victim now and can't understand why his wife wants to leave. It's hard for me to drum up much sympathy for him. I want him to accept responsibility for what he has done to his wife and himself and maybe stop this destructive pattern.

Sometimes I think that I can solve any problem. When I take this type of position, I forget that the client has the major role in the change process. I need to shape my understanding and solutions so that they have the same meaning for the client as they do for me. When I fail, it is usually when I have not helped the client clearly understand how my suggestion is meant to be in his or her best interest. Perhaps it is my choice of words or examples. They just do not seem to resonate or have meaning for some clients. I am left feeling somewhere between powerless and pissed off.

Identifying and trying to learn from our mistakes can be a painful experience. I often feel like such a fool, wondering why I didn't do something else. Even with the man who just hung up the phone, I am left wondering what else I could or should have done; after all, he came to me wanting help and I feel like I let him down. Maybe I should have listened to his tale of how he didn't do anything wrong, but I couldn't do that as I would be reinforcing his pathological response to things. Maybe I could have told him how much I missed seeing him today, but that would have been a bald-faced lie. I still feel unsure about how else I could have handled this. After much rumination, I settle on the idea that I could have pointed out that I can't help him if he doesn't show up. But that sounds punitive as well.

I remember hearing once that you can't really be a great therapist until you've made a thousand mistakes. I presume that means those we recognize and acknowledge. If that's the case, then I am truly a master because I am well beyond my allotment. With that said, these are my biggest mistakes I have made over and over again—at least those I'm aware of:

- Pushing too hard and taking clients too far out of their comfort zone.
- Moving too quickly because of my impatience.
- Misreading the situation by not listening carefully.
- Asking inappropriate questions (at least those that did not relate to what the client wanted help with).
- Triggering my own personal issues.
- Bungling the diagnosis and understanding what was happening for the client.

- Not being tactful.
- Not being tactful—same as above, as it happens twice as often as the others.

Most Common Mistakes

After our own confessions about areas in which we are most prone to repeated errors of judgment or execution, we wish to review some of the mistakes made most often by therapists in the field. Of course, the challenges faced by beginners are often different than those of more experienced practitioners. Yet, regardless of the status or context, we think that most of us tend to do too much advice giving and not enough listening. The client is sitting there begging us for guidance or specific instruction. Nobody is looking over our shoulder. Although we know it is ill advised to take the shortcut and just tell the client to quit a job, end a relationship, confront a friend, begin an exercise program, or eat brown rice, we do so anyway to relieve our own sense of helplessness. Of course, they hardly ever listen to us and almost never follow through on what we advise them, but it still feels good in the moment.

We feel pressure to perform and produce quick results from all directions. The client demands instant relief. External forces may limit the number of sessions allotted. And then there is all the internal pressure we feel to make a difference as quickly as possible. Within the first few minutes of the initial session, we are already formulating in our heads what we think might be going on and what we might do about it, even with such limited and partial information.

Understanding Trumps Truth

Quentin was an 80-year-old man who reported that he had been depressed all of his life. When asked how he knew that was the case, he said that he'd seen therapists his entire life and they all told him he was depressed. He then went on to describe his successful life as a businessman with a loving family that he helped raise. He was now retired and living in a luxury community surrounded by three golf courses. The more he described his life, past and present, the more convinced the therapist became that he sure didn't sound all that depressed. In some ways, the therapist felt envious of all that Quentin had lived and accomplished.

"I hear you saying that you are depressed," the therapist gently observed, "but I'm not sure I agree with your diagnosis."

"Ah," he answered with a shy grin, "that's just 'cause you don't know me. Once we spend more time together, I'm sure you'll see that I really am depressed." He said this like he almost felt wistful about losing the label behind.

"That may be true," the therapist agreed, "but depressed people usually don't report having lifelong friends, a wonderful family, a successful career, and their biggest problem is trying to decide which color Mercedes to buy. I don't mean to argue with you, but there's something about the way you define yourself that doesn't quite fit."

Quentin nodded, but it wasn't exactly in agreement. During the next few sessions, he shared more about his daily life. He volunteered several times each week at a local hospital. He folded towels, talked to people in the waiting room, and just made himself as useful as he could, providing assistance where it was most needed. The job seemed to give him an added sense of purpose to a life that struck the therapist as already pretty fulfilled.

Eventually, the sessions tapered off as Quentin became busier at his hospital job. Throughout the time they spent together, Quentin never showed symptoms of major depression, or for that matter, any significant signs of dysfunction. Yet he stubbornly held onto his depressive label, even in the face of alternative interpretations and repeated confrontations by his therapist. He insisted until the very end that his therapist may have been right but never really understood him. And Quentin would have been absolutely correct in his assessment of the situation: Sometimes it is so important for us to sell a particular idea that we forget that unless we help clients feel understood that the other stuff we do might not matter much.

Relieving (Our Own?) Suffering and Helplessness

One common mistake is that we want to rescue clients from their pain even though effective therapy often requires allowing them to experience their deepest feelings. It is hard for us to simply "hold" their suffering until such time that they are ready, on their own terms and pace, to let it go. There are some clients we see, perhaps the most challenging of all, who will never relinquish the anguish that seems to be part of their core identity. Survivors of the Holocaust and other catastrophic and traumatic events sometimes complain that their therapists just won't accept the possibility that there are some experiences that are so horrific that it is impossible to completely recover. We try to sell them our eternal hope and optimism, which only seems to reinforce their belief that nobody can truly understand what they have lived through.

It is one of the hardest lessons for beginners to learn that sometimes our job is not to provide immediate relief to clients or banish their pain, but rather to allow them to wallow in self-pity until such time that they feel sufficient commitment and motivation to do the hard work involved. Group therapists, for instance, find that a frequent aspect of their work involves blocking and preventing members from constantly reassuring one another that everything will be just fine: It is precisely the discomfort, and sometimes the agony (within tolerable limits), that leads to necessary change.

Illusions of Perfection

Ironically, another frequent mistake is the need to present ourselves as perfectly controlled, almost mechanical in our manner. It's all business. We are the embodiment of professionalism and objectivity.

Speaking personally, we have both found over the years that we now present ourselves as much more human, foibles and all. We've abandoned the need to project an image of perfection and control. Our wisdom may be limited, our manner far less scripted, but we are also more accessible and human.

Feminist theorist Laura Brown mentions the irony that you can't really ever become a great therapist by making that a priority. "If I had had as a goal to become known as a master clinician, I would have failed miserably. Instead, you have to show up with a beginner's mind, not just every day, but every minute of every hour of every therapy session. It takes willingness to be a fool, to fall on your face in front of clients and graciously get up, dust yourself off, and stay connected and present. This requires a healthy ego—with narcissism—so that you don't take either the praise or the anger personally."

It does take a certain confidence and courage, as well as forgiveness, to feel comfortable (or at least willing) to reveal those parts of ourselves that are less than ideal. Ultimately, you can be the judge of whether this is effective as you decide whether we have lost credibility or gained respect by sharing with you those aspects of ourselves that may be a bit shameful.

Hypocrisy and Complacency

We want to swing back to one of the central themes of this book related to practicing what we preach. Among the most common lapses, this is the most universal of all. Consider how often you ask clients to do things that you can't (or won't) do yourself. Or notice how frequently you see colleagues engaging in behavior that you would *never* wish to see in those you mentor, teach, and help. It is more than a little disconcerting that we stand for values of compassion, caring, respect, justice, and advocacy, and yet witness members of our profession acting in ways that are sometimes disrespectful, insensitive, or even cruel.

Each of us lives with aspects of our own hypocrisy. The two of us are crazed workaholics, justifying our achievements and productivity as part of a noble cause. We *say* that our first priorities are family and friends, but we follow through mostly when there is time and space available. We are not into regrets, but we are reminded once again that hardly anyone on their deathbed ever wishes that they had worked more; rather, they almost universally confess that they wished they had spent more quality time with loved ones. We are now both committed to doing just that, but it took near-death experiences or facing limited time left to finally get our attention.

It isn't so much a mistake as a lapse when therapists become complacent and stop growing. Everything we stand for is about learning and development, pushing ourselves to new areas of discovery, new challenges, different opportunities that broaden and deepen our experiences. Yet, just like our clients, we become *way* too comfortable with what we are doing. It already works fairly well, so why mess with a tried-and-true formula? There is resistance to change on multiple levels because it requires so much hard work to make the adjustments.

There are all kinds of other procedural mistakes we could mention—neglecting to process countertransference issues, failing to ask about substance abuse and forms of self-medication, excessive self-disclosure, ignorance about particular problems, neglect to maintain current standards of care, and so many others that it just makes us crazy listing them all. We often blame clients for being unmotivated or resistant, call them names like *obstructive, ornery, frustrating, noncompliant,* or *personality disordered.* We don't mean to imply that there aren't some very challenging people that we have to try to help, but it is usually a mistake to blame them for being difficult when that is what brought them into therapy in the first place. We find it interesting how therapists nominate very different kinds of clients as their "worst nightmares." Some struggle with belligerent adolescents ("Screw you and the horse you rode in on!"), or passive, withdrawn children who answer in monosyllables, while others actually enjoy the drama of working with clients who manifest multiple personalities or histrionics. In one sense, there really are very few so-called difficult clients but rather their difficult therapists who find it challenging to adjust to an interactive style that is unfamiliar or uncomfortable.

Mistakes or Just Data to Process?

One conclusion we have arrived at as a result of our conversations with notable figures in the field is that most of them have one thing in common: They are forgiving of their mistakes. Even if their readers, students, and fans have high expectations for them to be perfect, they seem very realistic about how impossible it is to live up to those ideals. We have been struck, as well, by those who prefer to avoid the language of failure and defeat altogether, reframing such experiences as an incremental learning process. They see so-called mistakes as data to be processed and acted upon, fostering greater flexibility, humility, and creativity.

It's also the case that some of these distinguished professionals are in major denial, refusing to admit that they ever fail or make mistakes, but that is by far the exception rather than the rule. Many of these esteemed individuals have had such influence in the field precisely because they are well attuned to their own limitations, constantly working to buttress their weaknesses and improve their proficiency.

CHAPTER 9

INVITING AND RESPONDING
TO CONSTRUCTIVE FEEDBACK

There are all kinds of research and anecdotal evidence that supports the idea that even when clients are critical and unsatisfied with sessions, as long as they have the opportunity to talk about their frustrations, they are more likely to report positive outcomes. As initially threatening as it might feel, master therapists process constructive criticism in ways that allow them to continue growing. In fact, superlative experts in almost all fields are most different than their brethren in that they stubbornly practice the things they don't do well rather than those that are comfortable and familiar. The feedback they solicit from colleagues, and especially their clients, helps them to become more responsive and effective, adjusting their strategies to the needs of each case.

In case you haven't guessed, writing this book with two highly opinionated and experienced therapists required a *lot* of negotiation and presented many challenges to work through. For quite some time there was some doubt whether we could ever figure out a way to reconcile our differences in style and viewpoints. There were times that we each felt misunderstood, devalued, frustrated, and confused, and wondered if compromise was possible. During this process, we each provided the other with loads of feedback—and at times it was really hard to hear—especially when we were pretty sure that one of us was right and the other wrong. Actually, we take that back: It was particularly threatening when we realized that what one of us was saying was far more on target and appropriate than what the other originally had in mind.

What makes any of us better at what we do is being able to take in information about the relative effectiveness of our behavior, and then to make adjustments according to what is needed at any given moment in time. The really hard thing about writing, as opposed to teaching or counseling, is that we can't tell how we're doing. Sure, an editor, an audience of one, makes suggestions. Add a few more reviewers to the mix and that lends assistance as well. But reviewers and editors are not really the audience for this book, and even if they were, they existed in a time and place that is wholly different from wherever *you* are right now.

We talked about learning from client feedback in a previous chapter; here, we are interested in exploring the ways that great therapists are open to feedback from others, seek it out, and are willing to do something with that they hear in such a way that it has a lasting impact on their behavior in the future. Such constructive input is what leads to what has been called progressive, refined "deliberate practice." This isn't just about the so-called 10,000-hour rule originally researched by Anders Ericsson on expert performance in many fields of art, sports, and science and subsequently popularized by authors such as Malcolm Gladwell and others. Practice, in and of itself, even decades of experience, doesn't necessarily lead to excellence unless certain other conditions are met, most notably that performance consistently improves as a result of accurate, incisive feedback from reliable sources about what works best and what is not necessarily working at all.

Discussing all the ways that talent and innate gifts are overrated when attempting to make sense of what leads to extraordinary accomplishments, Geoff Colvin has found that certain individuals simply get better and better at what they do by targeting specific areas of improvement that they work at with unimagined zeal. They not only work harder than others, but they also work much smarter. There is all kinds of evidence that experience isn't necessarily helpful, whether we are talking about auditors, surgeons, or psychotherapists, *unless* they are willing and able to focus specifically on their identified weaknesses and limitations. Of course, this is possible only with dedicated self-scrutiny, which itself has blind spots unless augmented by feedback that assists in moving beyond previous abilities. Colvin mentions golfer Tiger Woods as one example, a professional who faced a number of personal challenges related to his background, health problems, and self-destructive family problems. Nevertheless, Woods has been unrelenting in structuring deliberate practice opportunities to upgrade his skills, continually working with new caddies, coaches, and techniques. After failing at a particular stroke or situation, Woods has been known to devote himself single-mindedly to practice over and over again until he has mastered the challenge. He would, for example, drop a ball into a sand trap, grind it into the sand with his foot, and then attempt to make the virtually impossible shot until it met his satisfaction. Then he would practice it again and again.

When you examine the training regimens of world-class athletes, such as basketball players LeBron James and Kobe Bryant, you see a similar pattern. While their teammates sit on the bus or plane after a game mindlessly playing games, watching movies, or listening to music, LeBron and Kobe are watching a film of the previous game, reviewing every single mistake they made, reworking options they could have considered, and requesting input from teammates and coaches about what they could have done differently. They each also have the remarkable ability to review in their heads a visual playback of every significant moment of the game, allowing them to imagine responding in different ways to various scenarios.

It's clear that hard work is not enough to be truly great, nor is talent and aptitude. It takes much more that just desire and commitment. Truly exceptional practitioners in any field have developed the means by which to honestly and courageously look at their own behavior, as well as solicit meaningful feedback from trusted, knowledgeable others, in order to continually make improvements in their method. And then, once they know what needs to be done, they spend endless hours working to refine their techniques.

JK Here's the scene: The therapy group has been humming along for about a month, and it's been proceeding fairly well. Everyone is pretty much engaged with one another, and trust levels have clearly reached the working stage. The only thing that I'm hesitant about is one young woman, Frida, who has yet to make eye contact with me. She seems to enjoy the group and is clearly getting something out of it, but I can't read her well. Is she bored or just quiet? Do I intimidate her in some way? There's got to be some kind of transference thing going on between us because I can't think of a single thing I could have possibly done or said that would have offended her. Besides, she keeps coming back to the group, even though she has the option of dropping out if she's so uncomfortable.

I approached her after one session in which it was more obvious than usual that even when I addressed her, she wouldn't look at me. Furthermore, I observed this was not at all the case when she addressed others in the group.

"I'm just wondering," I began carefully, "if there is some way I make you uncomfortable because . . ."

Frida shook her head immediately before I could even finish my sentence.

". . . because I can't help but notice that it seems difficult for you to look at me."

Shrug.

"Even now," I continued, "I notice you won't look at me."

Frida glanced up at me for a moment, smiled, and then immediately averted her eyes back to the ground. I bent down a bit to try and catch a glimpse of her face, but she seemed to find this amusing and started laughing nervously.

"If you don't want to talk about it," I tried again, "that's okay, too. I just thought that if there's something you wanted to tell me, or if there's something going on between us, maybe we could talk it through."

With her toes pointed inward, Frida pivoted her heels, brushing the carpet. I wasn't sure if she was thinking, rehearsing what she wanted to tell me, or just waiting me out determined not to respond at all.

"I want you to know that if I did do or say something that is upsetting to you, I really apologize."

Frida shook her head again, at least I think she did.

"Okay, then, I guess you'll let me know when you're ready to talk about anything, huh?"

Frida's shoulders lifted but I couldn't tell what that meant: "Yes?" "Maybe?" or "Hell no!"

That was the last time I ever saw Frida because she never returned to the group and wouldn't return my follow-up call as to what happened.

"What the heck was that all about?" I wondered then, and for years afterward. I really have no idea. I never got the chance to make whatever adjustment was needed in order to help Frida to feel more comfortable with me. Sometimes when I think about that incident, I'm not even sure if there was a problem in the first place, except the one I created by accusing her of having difficulty with me. When I think back, I remember how much she seemed to enjoy being in the group, even with my (perhaps) imagined discomfort with me. But maybe that was misinterpreted.

We mention this one example, after which you can think of a hundred of your own, to demonstrate how common it is that something happens that we don't understand, or can't quite navigate, and how being able to solicit and hear feedback is the most critical factor in a successful outcome. Sometimes, especially among those of us who are most experienced, we think we've heard it all before, that there's really nothing new that someone could reveal to us. And yet how devastating it would be to hear someone tell you that no matter how hard you try, you still aren't good enough.

Clearly, the most direct way to get better at anything we do is to receive, accept, process, and apply input from others, particularly our clients, but also from those who are more experienced. In any profession, those who have attained a reasonable standard of excellence do so by careful observation of their own behavior, its impact on others, and ongoing feedback from others about its relative effectiveness.

Sources of Feedback

It's difficult to improve performance if you don't really know what you are doing that is unhelpful and ineffective. Rarely will people be honest enough to tell us what we are doing wrong, clients most of all. Even colleagues and trusted friends will often be politely supportive rather than truly honest and direct. Sometimes they just lie to make you feel better.

Barry Duncan, along with his colleagues, has been a major force in emphasizing from his research how important it is to obtain accurate and ongoing feedback from our clients. "I routinely measure outcome data and the quality of the alliance with every client to ensure that I don't leave either issue to chance. This allows me to deal directly and transparently with clients, involving them in all decisions that affect their care and keeping their perspectives the centerpiece of everything I do. In addition, it serves as an early warning device that identifies clients who are not benefiting so that we can chart together a different course, which in turn encourages me to step outside my therapeutic business as usual and do things I've never done before, and therefore continue to grow as a therapist. This also allows me to focus every session with every client on the alliance so that I tailor what I do to the client's expectations."

Duncan passionately insists that whereas this might sound like hyperbole, identifying clients who are not profiting as much from sessions as they could, it is actually the single most important thing that distinguishes a master therapist. "Nine randomized clinical trials now support this assertion. In our studies, 9 of 10 therapists improved their outcomes. One therapist, who was in the lowest tier of effectiveness, became the best therapist in the study when client feedback was integrated into her work!"

Clients Are the Best Teachers

It's disorienting to consider that so many people in your world know *exactly* what you do that annoys or disturbs them and yet have never found a way to tell you in a way that you could hear it. If all your clients were gathered together for a conference, they would find remarkable consensus regarding the things you say and do that push them away or compromise your effectiveness. Yet each of us blithely continues to do what we do, ignorant—if not in denial—about our hidden weaknesses.

There are many possible sources of feedback that are accessible to us. We can review recordings of our own sessions, sometimes accompanied by a trusted colleague. We can access data via a variety of methods, employing systematic collection of responses after sessions. If you are fortunate, you have a supervisor, mentor, or senior clinician who can also provide constructive suggestions.

Finally, the most important teachers and critics of our work are our clients who are experts on their own experience. They happen to know quite well the things that we do that annoy them, just as they are often aware of what is most helpful. The key is to be able to effectively solicit that honest input in a way that is most helpful.

There has been a push in our field lately to collect this data through brief assessments or reports at the end of each session. Barry Duncan, Scott Miller, and others have been tireless proponents of this strategy to improve effectiveness. We think this is an excellent idea, in theory, but often may not be as feasible or practical with some clients, in some situations, with some therapeutic styles. Regardless, whether the critical feedback is solicited in writing or as a brief inquiry at the end of the session, it is imperative that we have accurate information on what we are doing that is most and least effective. Much of the time we are operating in the dark.

Feedback That's Most Helpful

Not all input, advice, and guidance we receive is necessarily useful. People tell us things all the time that are more for their own needs and interests than a genuine desire to assist us. That's one reason why we are in such an influential and privileged position with our clients in that, at least theoretically, they don't have to wonder about a hidden agenda or that we are doing anything that is designed to meet our own needs. Presumably, that would be the case with our supervisors as well unless, of course, there really is a hidden agenda because this person is in a position of power and authority and has certain conflicts of interest within the organization or a vested interest in maintaining control.

There have been all kinds of research about what therapists find most helpful in the feedback they receive (it isn't that different from what works best with clients). It helps significantly if the input is relatively brief and targeted, if it is supported with specific examples, and especially that it is offered in a nonthreatening, sensitive way. The process does not stop with simply hearing the information; the therapist also needs to internalize and practice it in personally meaningful ways. We all understand that using a skill is different than merely accepting that it might be useful.

We routinely ask our clients to report what they learned from our work together, as well as what they intend to do to work on their issues between sessions. We also hold them accountable for their declared intentions, a crucial step to ensure that commitments are followed through. Yet one feature that distinguishes master therapists is their willingness to apply in their own lives what they ask of their clients. In this case, it means that we continually search out opportunities to hear about what we do that is most and least helpful and then make adjustments in our behavior accordingly. The one question that often echoes in our minds after every session is: "What could/should I have done differently?"

This is a difficult question to answer honestly, both because the answer may be threatening and often we just don't have an accurate picture of what happened. It is more than a little bewildering when we review studies that show the imperfect correlation between therapist and client perceptions of therapy, especially with regard to the different features that each of us point to as being most significant. As we covered earlier, therapists are in love with techniques and interventions, believing (often erroneously) that these brilliant strategies were the most instrumental in producing positive outcomes. Yet clients consistently identify factors related to the relationship while other studies point to client characteristics (especially motivation) that are most crucial. In other words, it seems important that we have multiple sources of feedback regarding our relative effectiveness rather than relying exclusively on client reports and self-assessments.

Receiving feedback is as much an art form as offering it to others. This is especially the case when what we are told is less than flattering, or even challenges some of our most sacred beliefs about ourselves, or the way we work. Can it really be true that all these years what you think has been so wonderful really hasn't mattered much? Can it also be the case that you are blind to aspects of yourself, or your style, that are actually quite potent but that you've never harnessed effectively? These are a few of the questions that disturb us, just as they ought to haunt any professional who cares deeply about getting better and better at what we do.

Processing Feedback Gratefully

Accepting negative feedback in a positive manner was not always a part of our lives. We both needed to learn how to change our relationship to the information we received, to make sense of it in a way that it could be recast in the most constructive way. Of course, it helps if it is believed that what was offered was done so in a spirit of caring rather than criticism.

We would seek support from one another during such times, but often as a way to reduce the perceived threat. The experts call this process *confirmation bias*, where we see things in ways that tend to support our own prevailing views. We are always looking for evidence to confirm what we think is going on rather than keeping an open mind to other possibilities. We had to learn not to react but to try our best to understand how this dissonant information might be accurate. We both grasped that the more we could understand, the better we would become.

It was also extraordinarily helpful to be able to talk to the field's most accomplished practitioners and theoreticians over the years, marveling at the forgiving ways that they could hear difficult things and sometimes let them go. Sometimes this might be a case of denial, so committed to a particular ideology that they wouldn't entertain perceived threats, but in many other instances there was genuine interest in taking whatever they could learn, making adjustments, and moving on.

Keith Dobson, an evidence-based cognitive therapist, reminds himself that in spite of his best efforts he realizes he can't help everyone, and there are times when it is best to let go. "It's important to recognize our own foibles and faults, and our limitations with specific people or problems. We also have to take care of ourselves and try to balance our work and home life, to develop as people, and to remain passionate about our chosen career. We need the humility to know that each person is the expert of his or her own life. I really believe that respect for each client, as an individual, is critical to the therapy process."

In Dobson's view, we often may be led astray when we fail to recognize what we might be doing wrong. "Within each case, I think we have to acknowledge that we are often simply wrong in the approach we take. I believe that part of being evidence based is collecting information from the client about the work that we do and its impact. This information can be questionnaires and forms, but it also needs to include subtle reading of the client's nonverbal and verbal feedback. Based on this feedback, we need to have the ability to stop, listen, maybe back up a bit, or completely try new directions, if the current ones are not obtaining the outcome we want or expect."

Being Accountable to Ourselves, Our Colleagues, and Our Clients

Therapy is a unique enterprise in that the process operates under a cloak of secrecy. Client confidentiality and privacy are protected at all costs. Records are kept under lock and key or password-protected. Rooms are soundproofed. There are sometimes even separate entrances and exits to preserve anonymity. And whatever is said and done in these sanctums is self-reported, sanitized, and shaped into self-serving summaries.

Who knows what *really* happens in any given therapist's piece of work when most of the time we rely on what he or she says transpired. It's not exactly that we would outright lie, but let's just say that our testimonies are somewhat limited and certainly don't cover the full spectrum. We are not inclined, for instance, to necessarily write into progress notes or disclose to supervisors a litany of all the mistakes and miscalculations we made, just as we will not readily confess to all the things that happened that we don't nearly understand.

Exceptional therapists not only try their best to be scrupulously honest and accurate in their assessments of what happened in sessions, but they also hold themselves accountable. They accept responsibility for their errors in judgment. They model openness and transparency by sharing what they don't know and understand. They apologize for their mistakes.

Pat Love, known for her work with couples, believes that holding herself accountable is one of her most cherished values, especially with regard to focusing on the client's articulated goals. "I make it a priority to get a clear understanding of what the client hopes to gain from therapy. In the past, I would impatiently listen to what clients said but then quickly jump in to suggest what I think they need most. I had to get over myself and get more into the client's frame of reference. Therapy began to be more enjoyable for me—and I feel sure for the client—when I calmed down, shut up, and tuned in."

Love believes that accountability begins with the very first session in which clients are asked directly for feedback about what exactly they got from the experience and what they can articulate is already different for them. After that, she checks in with them repeatedly, questioning the extent to which they are meeting the declared goals. "Is this the clear communication you said you wanted with your partner? I don't take it for granted; I confirm it. I think this is important so we both know we are making progress and are working toward the same outcome."

JC Each time a client leaves a session, I wonder, "Have I done them any good?" "Was I helpful?" Sometimes it is hard to tell, as clients smile on the outside but you can see them steaming on the edges. Such was the case with the couple that I had been working with for the past 3 months. They had volunteered to be filmed in the studio as a demonstration of couples therapy in action, and this was going to be their seventh and final session. During the previous meetings, the couple had made significant change and progress; they were pleased with what we had done together. The final session was going to be a recap of their progress and a discussion of what they needed to do to keep the momentum going.

As we sat down and were going through our microphone checks, I noticed that something didn't feel quite right. They were both smiling, but Rick was very tense and Sarah's skin was all blotchy, as though they had been fighting in the car on the way to the session. Sarah began the session by saying that her husband hadn't done anything for the previous 2 weeks. When I tried to clarify what she meant, Sarah couldn't supply any specific examples. Rick jumped in and said that he didn't see it that way and that he thought things had been going well. I heard Sarah muttering under her breath, and when I asked her what she was saying, she turned angry.

"This whole thing has been one big joke and a complete waste of time. We've learned nothing, and I can't see any difference from when we first came to see you." As she said these words, she looked at me defiantly, daring me to challenge her.

Feeling more than a little defensive, as well as shocked by her outburst, I did my best to summarize all the progress they had made that we had carefully documented. As I was recounting all the successes, I noticed that Rick was nodding his head in agreement while Sarah was vigorously shaking her head in the negative. This was quite a difference from any previous session in which Sarah had always been the optimistic one, whereas Rick had consistently been reluctant: It seemed they had traded roles. I felt so stunned and shell-shocked that all I could do was nod mechanically and wait for the session to end so I could get out of there as quickly as possible.

Not knowing how on earth to make sense of what happened I asked a colleague if he would interview the couple following the session to obtain feedback as to what the experience had been like for them and what impressions they had. My colleague had witnessed only this final session and was unsure as to what hornet's nest he was walking into. He began by asking the couple what number, on a scale from 1 to 10, they would assign to their sessions with me, with 1 being dissatisfied and 10 being thrilled beyond their wildest dreams. Without a moment's hesitation, Sarah shrugged and announced a "5," after which Rick gave me a measly "6."

I was watching this nightmare unfold from the studio control room. I couldn't hide my disappointment and my anger, even feeling betrayed, since after every one of the previous sessions both partners always rated the sessions a solid "10." All I could think of is that this was an indelible and permanent blot on my reputation. Even more humiliating, this whole disaster was witnessed by the film crew, who were dear friends.

My colleague attempted to save the day by asking the couple what were some of the positive things that they had noticed in their relationship over the past few months, and they gave some vague response, saying at least they hadn't yet gotten a divorce. Some compliment. They seemed to conveniently "forget" that in the months I'd been seeing them Rick had stopped gambling and found regular employment, and both of them were far more loving in their interactions with one another. Do I sound more than a little defensive? I was devastated, feeling my ineptitude was now documented on film for all eternity.

Later, after I calmed down and gained some perspective, I had to admit that I had done a lousy job. I accepted that I had become overconfident and had missed some significant cues. I had been so concerned with showing how brilliant I was on film that I had neglected to pay closer attention to the actual needs of my clients. They were appreciative of some things I had done but worried (probably more afraid) about whether or not they could maintain the gains and keep this level of happiness without my help. As I continued to miss their fears, Sarah pushed me in the only way she knew how, to lash out in a way that might wound me.

A few days later, I apprehensively invited the couple to return for another session. To my surprise, they immediately agreed. I began the session with an apology, letting the couple know that I was deeply sorry for not being there for them at such a difficult time. They perked up and said that they were also feeling much better about ending the sessions and that the past 3 weeks had gone reasonably well.

It was a painful lesson for me to learn, but I had to admit that my ego had gotten in the way. It had been more important for me to look good on camera than it was to concentrate on the needs of the couple in the room. I hadn't been listening to them as closely as needed, and as they deserved. Somehow I had lost my way and was only able to regain my bearings after facing the brutal truth of my neglect.

Life-Changing Feedback

We are very fortunate to belong to a profession in which the input, advice, and feedback we receive to improve our professional effectiveness also makes us better, more responsive and masterful people in all the other aspects of our lives. As we become more skilled and sensitive listening and responding to our clients, we (hopefully) apply that ability with others in our life who matter the most. The things we learn from workshops we attend and books like this that we read better inform our clinical work as well as our personal lives.

It is an interesting experiment to ask loved ones—a partner or spouse; a sibling, parent, or child; a best friend—what you do and have done consistently that most annoys them. Specify that they reveal something you probably don't already know. This could be a little thing, or perhaps a big one, but the point is that others know this about you, although you seem oblivious to it yourself. *This* is how we improve all relationships and increase our personal mastery the same way we would increase our professional effectiveness.

It so happens that therapists in general, and master therapists in particular, have all the skills and knowledge at our disposal to consistently transform our lives just as we do for those we help. When we are depressed or anxious, disappointed or frustrated, we have just the tools to work through these issues—if we have accurate and honest feedback about what we are doing and its effects. So we are making a case that we should not only be more proactive in seeking out feedback from clients and colleagues regarding our clinical skills and interventions but also soliciting meaningful information regarding our behavior in every other arena of our lives.

JK I remember doing an exercise in a therapy group in which each of us was providing feedback to the rest about key impressions and characteristics. To make the task less threatening and fun, the instructions were to tell a member what animal he or she reminded you of and why. In addition, it was required that the feedback contain at least one positive, constructive reason, as well as a feature that was less than attractive or off-putting.

When it was my turn, one of the group members said I reminded her of a koala bear because I seemed warm and cuddly, but if I was cornered or pushed, I had sharp claws and teeth. I smiled and thanked her but inside I felt devastated, misunderstood, and terribly wounded. Of course, you might wonder why I allowed a simple, offhand comment by a client to so hurt me (countertransference anyone?), but more to the point is that it struck me as accurate. Although I pretend to be kind, caring, and compassionate all the time, inside I sometimes feel terribly critical, judgmental, and threatened. Under those circumstances, I do lash out.

Okay, so that makes me human, and I accept that, but I also felt ashamed of myself for being seen and caught so transparently. From that moment forward, I decided that I wanted to change that pattern. I wanted to live my life, inside therapy and out, in such a way that I express as much compassion and love to others as I can. I know it's a hopeless cause to ever achieve that goal because I can never meet those or any other of my high expectations. Nevertheless, I was different after that group session.

I have never found it all that difficult to show compassion and caring and unparalleled acceptance toward my clients most of the time—I'm paid to do that. But my own hypocrisy has bothered me when I don't do this in other aspects of my life. I have been haunted by that group member's perception of me in such a way that I work every single day to become more congruent between what I say is important and what I actually do. What an amazing gift—and burden—that is!

Recruiting Master Coaches and Mentors

It is important to find a reliable source of feedback, someone we trust and value to help provide a "reality check" for our work. Early in our careers we went to former teachers and supervisors with our questions and concerns; however, as we advance in our careers and competency level we frequently outgrow these mentors and need to locate other master coaches and mentors.

Since one theme of this book is related to being able and willing to practice what we preach, that is, to live in our daily lives what we advocate for others, then we've been doing all this talk about giving and receiving honest feedback. Maybe it's time for us to model what we have been urging everyone else to do, meaning that we should discuss the ways we use each other as sounding boards to solicit input on different aspects of our functioning. This sort of peer supervision has been critical for so many experienced therapists who no longer have as many opportunities for the formal monitoring of their practices.

> **Jeffrey:** Jon, we need to talk about how important it is to recruit trusted colleagues and mentors to offer constructive feedback that helps us to become more personally and professionally effective. What do you think if we did that with one another? Right now.
>
> **Jon:** You mean that we each provide one another with things we know and have observed about one another after all these years, but may have never shared directly?
>
> **Jeffrey:** Exactly! There are few others in the world who know as much about one another, and have observed one another in so many different settings and contexts. We've written a dozen books together. We have co-presented workshops and conference programs. We have consulted on cases and provided peer supervision. We have shared students and blended our families. We co-grandparent your son's children. Your son, Matt, even has an office next to mine at the university. We have traveled together to the far ends of the Earth. I can't think of anyone in the world who is better informed and positioned to tell me what it

is that I do that is off-putting or less effective than it could be. We have been telling readers about how important it is to recruit trusted colleagues to tell them the truth about ways they could improve. What if we do that for one another?

Jon: Would it surprise you that I am often impatient with people who seem to want to suffer or struggle or just want to talk about their problems rather than fixing them? It's like they enjoy suffering. I have watched some therapists listen and reflect their clients' problems and suffering and empathically responding in a "poor baby" manner. I am much more likely to think—and maybe even say—something like, "Shit happens, get over it." Suffering is a part of life. Don't make it your career—and if you insist on doing so, don't come and whine to me about it. Some therapists actually believe that catharsis and purging is actually helpful, whereas I believe it is habit forming, and when we validate people's misery, we unwittingly reinforce the client and they feel better. Next week, they are back at your office door with this week's installment in their life of the blues. I know I'm not sounding very professional or caring. And I know, for certain, that you struggle with this even more than I do.

Jeffrey: I agree: It doesn't *sound* very compassionate, yet sometimes our job is to speak the truth or tell clients certain things that are obviously getting in their way. But what occurs to me is that if you see yourself as impatient, what does that say about *me*? Maybe it is the Buddhist in you, or the greater maturity, but sometimes you drive me crazy because of your endless patience and willingness to wait for things to unfold in their own way and time. As for me, I just keep pushing and pushing, long past the point where it is doing much good. I don't pay attention to the clear feedback being sent my way: "Thanks, but no thanks! I don't want what you are selling!"

"But it's *good* for you!" I argue. "Trust me."

I notice in our interactions that sometimes you get frustrated with me, with my speed and need to move quickly. I notice you kind of smile to yourself, nod your head, and just ignore what I'm saying or doing: One thing I've learned about you is that you can't be pushed.

But if we are after feedback, and if one thing I admire most about you is your incredible patience, then one thing that drives me crazy is all the multitasking you do, juggling so many jobs, thoughts, tasks, commitments at the same time, trying to get so much done, but sometimes not seeming to actually enjoy them as much as you could. Take this book, for instance: You had commented that you wanted to "get it out of your hair" and move on, something I certainly understand since it has been in what is left of your hair during this most trying, difficult time of your life. Yet I see this book as the child we share, as the holder of our most sacred and personal wisdom. You've forced me to slow down and reflect more than I ever have before on what it means to be a therapist, a teacher, a parent, and a friend. I know we have to complete this at some point, but maybe what I'm learning through the process is to confront my endless need for more achievement and the yearning just to get things done and move on to the next best thing.

Jon: The pace of life is so important in everything we do or don't do. It seems like that with this project, and our respect for one another, we are being forced to learn from one another at a different speed and finding that rather than getting angry and yelling "slow down, dammit" or "why can't you get moving?" we are being challenged to learn more about ourselves. Your focus and work ethic is something of amazement to many of us. The way you rise so early or respond so quickly with insight and brilliance. One moment we are talking about something, and the next you have it outlined and ready to submit. It can be intimidating if I let my mind go there, or it can be a time for me just to appreciate your amazing quickness. But I bet it really irritates others, as they find it too pushy because they have to move at a speed beyond their comfort level. Perhaps we are both learning that when our buttons are being pushed, it is a potential time of important learning. This is such an important component of mastery that is growing and reaching toward rather than just defending the status quo.

But no matter how hard I try and want to achieve mastery, I can't stand talking to critical or intolerant people who know it all or have accepted a simple path such as following a belief system that prevents them from thinking for themselves. I guess it is this black-and-white thinking that pushes my buttons as a therapist.

Mean people push my buttons, people who actually feel it is okay to hurt others, whether it is physical, emotional, financial, sexual, or what have you. I have trouble with selfish people who seem to have no empathy or compassion for others. I realize I am probably not alone, since these types of people are annoying to almost everyone, but my job is to help them, not judge them. Carl Rogers talked about unconditional positive regard, and I know that for me it is not possible with these people. What do you do? There are some people that I don't want to accept.

Jeffrey: I remember reading some research on marketing products, about how for many years companies were all about focus groups to ask people what they really want, the way we do as therapists when we ask our clients their goals and desired outcomes. But in recent years, Prego spaghetti sauce, Apple Computers, and other companies have discovered that people don't really know what they want—and their preferences are so varied that there is really no consensus. That's why there are 20 different kinds of toothpastes, shampoos, coffee products, and spaghetti sauces. And that's why Steve Jobs decided not to ask consumers what they wanted but instead gave them what he thought they needed. And that's why I wonder whether we really should be asking our clients what they want all the time. I think there are times when, as a function of our experience, training, and wisdom, we really *do* know what is best for certain people—even if we don't know what's best for ourselves. I know this is counter to all that we've stood for—honoring individual preferences, values, and needs—but there are times when we have to take a stand.

Most people genuinely believe that if only they had more of something, more love, more money, more things, more friends, a bigger house, a better job, or nicer car, that all would be well. If only they enjoyed better health, a more attractive appearance, or relocated to a more agreeable climate, then everything would turn out just great. But there is so much compelling research that our happiness and life satisfaction has little to do with these things, or what people say they want to make their lives complete. And we know this stuff: We *know* that what matters most is deeper intimacy in relationships, having a few good friends, enjoying a love relationship with a partner, and being involved in meaningful work.

Jon: This makes so much practical sense, but it is challenging with all the competing voices in my head to impress others or achieve or to excel. These nagging voices seem to take me farther and farther away from being the type of person and therapist that I want to be. At times like this, I need to remember to breathe deeply and focus on my body and see if I can change my relationship to this desire or pull toward these attractive but unrewarding dead ends. So, back to your original question: What is it that consistently trips you up?

Jeffrey: I'm not very pleased to admit this, but what immediately comes to mind is the way I sometimes behave with colleagues. I pout and withdraw when I don't feel valued. I use humor indulgently and inappropriately. I am more honest and direct than people might be ready for and ready to hear. I take on a critical voice in my head, believing that others are misguided and clueless about what really matters most.

As you mentioned earlier, I have incredibly high standards for myself—not just in quality but quantity. I don't feel good about myself if I have neglected to produce a few pages of sterling prose every day, if I don't do some kind of physical exercise, if I lapse in my disciplined eating, if I was insensitive or uncaring toward someone (even in my own mind!). It's not so much that I hold others to my standard, but, as you mentioned, people are sometimes honest enough to tell me that they feel judged or criticized, even when that's not what's going on at all. Clients and students tell me that sometimes I have this blank expression on my face that they interpret as critical evaluation when, in fact, I'm just concentrating really hard on what they are saying. I do make people uncomfortable when they feel they can't keep up. The irony is that I feel so powerless to slow down.

Conversations like this with trusted friends and colleagues can sometimes be rare. We are all so busy and overscheduled. It's hard to begin such an interaction and make sure things remain safe and supportive, especially given the potentially threatening nature of offering constructive criticism. Yet these interactions can be instrumental for us to learn so much more about the ways we come across to others, especially those parts of our style that are less inviting than we'd like to believe.

How We Know What We Know

When we look back on how we learned what we know and developed ourselves, there has been nothing more important than the ways we have assertively and selectively reached out to professionals who we thought were most in a position to teach us something useful and constructive. We've never been content to simply accept the teachers and supervisors who were *assigned* to work with us, often based on criteria that had little to do with maximizing our growth and development. There have been particular authors whom we have studied with passion and devotion. There have been instrumental figures we have sought out. There have been individuals across many disciplines whom we have contacted and asked/begged/badgered to teach us what they know. Each of us is the sum total of the gifts these esteemed professionals have offered us.

The word *consilience* refers to the theory that the unity of knowledge from unrelated, independent sources can converge to help us create some novel conclusions. That's why it's so important to access multiple sources of feedback and information, particularly from places and people outside of our own narrow discipline. Jon receives consultation from a syndicated cartoonist, a judge, a school administrator, a Jesuit priest, and a commercial airline pilot while Jeffrey often finds valuable counsel from friends who are mountain guides, lawyers, writers, and heads of charitable foundations. Both of us read *way* outside our fields. We each devour a novel every week and have stacks of volumes on our desks about a wide range of subjects. These authors, colleagues, friends, and family form our teaching faculty, who often challenge some of the most sacred assumptions about what we do and how we do it.

It turns out that native talent isn't the deciding factor in making a professional a true master, nor is commitment alone. Exceptional practitioners deliberately expose themselves to situations that will test them in novel ways. They seek out feedback and opinions, not necessarily about what they already do well but rather those aspects of their functioning that are suspect. They tend to focus on aspects of their performance that may be invisible to even accomplished professionals.

Almost any tennis pro can hit a serve close to 150 miles per hour. Likewise, most pro basketball players can hit free throws 80% of the time. And in a similar vein, most reasonably accomplished therapists can recognize when a client is decompensating and take steps to stabilize and reassure the person before things get out of hand.

But if we are talking about the best of the best, that is, practitioners who are in a category of their own because of their extraordinary effectiveness, then we have to look a lot deeper. It turns out that there are certain key factors that may remain unnoticed by 99% of professionals yet make all the difference in taking performance to the next level. A number of classic studies, described earlier by Geoff Colvin in his book on how talent in itself is overrated, indicate that exceptional performers see things that most others miss. Some radiologists are able to pick up details in MRIs or X-rays that others can't see even after they are pointed out to them. A more interesting example from tennis shows how players who are best at returning serves don't actually watch the ball but rather study their opponent's posture, which best predicts where the ball is most likely to land. They flat out see more than any of their competitors and can thus anticipate behavior before it ever plays out.

We could say this is some kind of magical inborn ability, but that is not the case at all. Exceptional performers in any field have purposefully trained themselves to notice more than others—and they learned this skill primarily through soliciting and listening/watching carefully to the critical feedback they receive.

CHAPTER 10

WHO YOU ARE IS AS IMPORTANT AS WHAT YOU DO

Who has been most influential in your life as a teacher or mentor? Whether this person was a coach, parent, teacher, supervisor, or therapist, it is likely that he or she possessed particular qualities that you admired most and wanted for yourself. Beyond any particular knowledge they held or skills they possessed that led to their extraordinary competence, it was as much their character as anything else that impressed and impacted you most.

It is both interesting and revealing how our field has recently placed so much emphasis on the "doing" of therapy. With manualized treatments, brief therapies, and empirically supported treatments taking center stage, we have moved to an era in which the specific techniques, approaches, and interventions are becoming standardized and dismantled into component parts. Increasingly, therapists are being taught the skills and strategies of helping others, with a distinct focus on reliability, accountability, and measurement of outcomes. While this has been an important contribution to the field, what is often lost in the process is neglect of the distinctly *human* features of therapeutic relationships. One thing that often distinguishes master therapists is their ability to transcend mere technique to use their distinctly personal characteristics to empower their helping efforts. Indeed, it is often who you are, and how you present yourself, that is just as important as any therapeutic techniques.

It is interesting to consider what it takes to be considered a true master of a profession. Certainly, if we are talking plumbers, electricians, or physicians, they have to be able to fix problems they are hired to address. It doesn't matter how nice they are, or how much confidence they exude, if they can't get the job done, and do it efficiently and effectively, then they aren't much good. Likewise, if therapists aren't well schooled in their craft and thoroughly competent in their behavior, then they aren't going to be very helpful to people.

We don't intend to argue that personal qualities are all that are needed to be a successful therapist, but rather that extraordinary clinicians have something far more than their skills. They exhibit characteristics that are, at once, enticing, attractive, and captivating. Whether you prefer to call this a kind of passion or charisma, or perhaps something more clearly defined, there is no doubt whatsoever that clients are strongly influenced by the unique ways we present ourselves as human beings.

Who We Are Versus What We Do

We believe that one requirement for qualification as a master therapist is that there is congruence between professionally espoused values and personally applied principles—as manifested in daily behavior. If you really *believe* what you teach your clients, then we find it difficult to understand how anyone can live with themselves when they don't apply these principles to their own lives.

Of course, we are familiar with the power of denial, self-deception, and blind spots, but still, how can we continue to delude ourselves over so many years, repeated almost every day, that we think it is absolutely critical for our clients to reach *way* outside their comfort zones to take constructive risks when we might avoid such behavior ourselves? How do we tell people that they should be nicer to others, more kind and caring to those they love, and yet practice neglect, or even cruelty, to people in our own lives? How do we advocate personal responsibility for others while we externalize our own problems and blame others for our disappointments? And the most puzzling of all: How can we be so disrespectful and unsupportive with our own colleagues?

Maybe you've been fortunate to work with professionals who really are caring toward one another. Your peers are straightforward, generally supportive, and make it a priority to build a functional community in which everyone is heard and respected. We know it is the nature of most living things to compete for limited resources, to organize themselves according to a hierarchy of power, to fight for attention, and even undermine those who might be perceived as threatening. We also realize that within any human organization, such dynamics would play out in which limited budgets, tribal affiliations, coalitions of convenience, or similar priorities would create an atmosphere that perpetuates conflict. Nevertheless, we are supposed to be experts in creating greater cooperation and relational effectiveness.

So it is still a mystery to us how we can spout the importance of values that we might violate on a regular basis. And it is even more perplexing that some might not realize that our behavior outside of sessions is just as important as what we say and do while the meter is running. This begs the question: Is it really what we *know* that is so important in our work, or what we *do* that matters most? Or perhaps it is neither of them but rather *who we are* and how we demonstrate those human qualities in our sessions and in our lives.

Qualities of Master Therapists

Obviously, knowledge and skills are critical to therapeutic success; if this were not the case, we'd skip professional training altogether and concentrate only on character building. Or we'd just find ways to identify and recruit nice, healthy people into the profession (maybe we *should* focus more on that task?). But it is also evident that exemplary practitioners display certain personal traits that lead them to be so persuasive and influential.

Barry Duncan makes the strong point that what clients bring to sessions is their motivation, expectations, and personal characteristics, just as is the case with therapists. In his own words: "The therapist is the most potent influence on outcome—not *what* model or technique he or she is wielding but rather *who* the therapist is as a person. Therapists account for most of the variance of change in any treatment delivered.

"What I bring to the therapeutic endeavor is that I am a true believer. I believe in the client. I believe in the power of relationship and psychotherapy as a vehicle for healing and change. And I believe in myself, my own ability to be present, fully immersed in the client's experience, and dedicated to making a difference. In my 30-plus years, and 17,000 hours of clinical experience, I have been privileged to witness the irrepressible ability of human beings to transcend adversity—clients troubled by self-loathing and depression, battling alcohol or drugs, struggling with intolerable marriages, terrorized by inexplicable voices, oppressed by their children's problems, traumatized by past or current life circumstances, and tormented with unwanted thoughts and anxieties—with amazing regularity. The odds for change when you combine a resourceful client, a strong alliance, and an authentic therapist who brings him/herself to the show, are worth betting on, certainly cause for hope, and responsible for my unswerving faith in psychotherapy as a healing endeavor."

Besides Duncan's nominations of authenticity, faith, and hope, which were identified by Jerome Frank so many years ago, there have been a number of attempts to identify and catalog those therapist traits that are considered to be most important, just as similar client characteristics are on the radar. We can easily spin off those that we appreciate most in those we help—a sense of optimism, flexibility, openness to new ideas, motivation to improve, resilience, hardiness, verbal and intelligent, and so on. There's also a fair degree of consensus on what therapists like in their clients—and we prefer those who are most like us in shared values and background.

It becomes a little trickier identifying therapist traits that make all the difference because there are so many possible configurations that are valued by clients, depending on their own personalities, preferences, and needs. Nevertheless, we can settle on several key personality traits that command attention and maximize influence:

1. Great therapists/teachers/leaders are honest and honorable. Trustworthiness is the gold standard from which all other traits are measured.
2. They are utterly dependable. This isn't just about enforcing boundaries but being seen and experienced as rock solid, delivering what is promised.
3. They are people of unassailable integrity and moral authority. Conforming to ethical codes and laws doesn't even begin to cover this territory. They answer to a higher standard, one that protects the rights and safety of others, even at personal cost.
4. They are incredibly flexible and tolerant of differences—unless they are hurtful. They are perceived as noncritical and (conditionally) accepting (with exceptions made when people are doing things that are obviously harmful or stupid).
5. They are self-assured, yet modest in a charming way (or else they come across as arrogant and narcissistic). Confidence is a powerful mediator to promote hope and positive outcomes.
6. They are truth seekers and truth tellers. They are honest and sincere, yet communicate with great sensitivity and diplomacy so that clients don't shut down when offered useful feedback.
7. They are spontaneous without being recklessly impulsive. They are intuitive, willing to risk sharing moments of immediacy.
8. Most of all, they are essentially kind and compassionate individuals who care deeply for others—and they communicate this in ways that are immediately recognizable. They are

empathic, authentic, congruent, and all the other wonderful things that make human beings, therapists among them, attractive and approachable and trustworthy.

You might suggest other characteristics, or prefer to replace a few, but the central point is that character does trump knowledge. Carl Rogers may have been wrong that the relational factors are a necessary and *sufficient* condition for change, but he brought increased attention to the power of such human qualities in terms of how they inspire and help others.

When you think back on who has had the most influence and impact in your own life, they were likely individuals who were charismatic in their own unique way, whether soft and understated or overtly passionate and dramatic. They were people who had particular attributes that you coveted for yourself. They became heroic figures in your life, not only because of their skills and abilities, but also because of the ways they lived their lives.

JK I was recently asked by students who my heroes are in life, and I was surprised I had no immediate response. All I could do was shrug. Have I reached an age in which I no longer have such models? Is the word *hero* no longer part of my vocabulary? I was intrigued that I couldn't answer the question, especially considering that almost everything I believe about what makes a therapist or teacher great is that they live their lives as heroes. They have courage. They live what they teach to others.

Now I recall that those mentors and heroes who have been most inspirational in my life didn't much affect me by what they said but rather by what they did. And I'm not referring to any specific actions as much as the ways they walked through the world.

My sixth-grade teacher is the only one I can recall from elementary school. I can't remember anything in particular that he taught me, but I vividly remember what he looked like. I remember his classroom and where I used to sit in the room. I can almost remember his voice. But most of all I remember that he was endearingly weird. He used to tell us stories about traveling cross-country on his motorcycle and sleeping in graveyards at night. I remember one day when we had an exam, he lifted a chair on top of his desk, perched himself on the throne, then reached into his briefcase and took out a bowl into which he poured Rice Krispies and then some milk. "Everyone quiet!" he whispered to us as we looked on aghast while trying to concentrate on the exam, "I need to hear the snap, crackle, and pop." Needless to say, such experiences forever cemented in my memory that great teachers were eccentric and unpredictable.

I had other childhood heroes, but the most influential figures in my life turned out to be those intellectual figures who were risk takers. I was spellbound not only by Charles Darwin's theories but by his voyages; not just by Sigmund Freud's writing but by the courageous way he took on the establishment; not only by Margaret Mead's books but by her immersion in adventurous field work; not only by Carl Rogers' or Albert Ellis' ideas but by the integrity they demonstrated by trying to live their most cherished principles.

My first therapy teachers instilled in me a strong belief that it wasn't only our interventions and therapeutic strategies that most impacted our clients but also our presence in the room—who we are as individuals. Because they were so charismatic, fearless, and relentless in their quest for higher level functioning, it was my greatest life's ambition to be just like them. This meant pursuing the ideal that being a therapist was far more than merely a job or even a profession—it was a quest.

Since my twenties what has sustained me in this profession is the idea that what I learn to be a better therapist makes me a better person. I may never truly resolve some of my core issues, but I'm getting closer and closer, mostly as a direct result of what I learn helping others. Don't you just hate it when you hear a client complaining about some problem that you haven't yet worked out yourself? Don't you feel awfully uneasy when you hear someone talking about an issue that still remains confusing in your own life? How about when you hear yourself give advice to a client and recognize that you can't do what you're asking of others?

Of course, we'll never come close to being the kind of person we wish we could be, or become as fully functioning as we might hope. I know there are colleagues who are blithering idiots, spineless fools, creepy, ineffectual, withdrawn, or blowhards, just the sort you would want to stay as far away from as you possibly could, and yet they seem to be reasonably good at their jobs. How do you explain that?

I can't.

I suppose they might be able to compartmentalize their personal dysfunctions and stick with business, but I still think their effectiveness is compromised by their personal presence—or lack thereof. Personally, I just could never trust a physician who is obese or smokes, or a dentist with lousy teeth, so it confuses me that some reputable therapists can be such unpleasant human beings or so unable to apply in their lives what they offer to others. But maybe they're just good at hiding their dysfunctions.

Since we are here to talk about what it means to be a "master" therapist, an extraordinary practitioner, one requirement for this lofty position is that there is congruence between professionally espoused values and personally applied principles—as manifested in daily behavior. Of course, we are familiar with the power of self-deception, but still, how can we continue to delude ourselves over so many years, repeated almost every day, that we think it is absolutely critical for our clients to take constructive risks when we might avoid such behavior ourselves?

But if our goal is to explore what it means to be a master therapist, then we think that such professionals should strive for (without ever reaching) greater congruence between espoused beliefs and behavior in the world. We should *be* what we teach to others.

Practicing Self-Compassion

It is inevitable that we are almost always going to come up short. No matter how hard we try, how much we study and practice, how committed we are to excellence, we will never reach ideal goals. If we ever hope to demonstrate real compassion with others we must first be able to apply it to ourselves.

Relational cultural theorist Judy Jordan agrees with us that the therapist's personal attributes are the key to her influence, especially those that relate to the capacity for empathic attunement and allowing herself to remain fully open to the client's experience. She sees this as a kind of "mutual empathy, a balanced and open awareness of the responsiveness of each person to the other." She believes this is attained largely as a result of our own efforts to find support and grounding in our lives that permits considerable self-compassion. Jordan accesses this largely through the regular practice of meditation but acknowledges that each of us has our own outlets that keep us grounded and humble. This view is particularly interesting considering that we often associate mastery or expertise with brimming overconfidence, if not arrogance.

JC One of our jobs is to teach clients how to create meaningful and satisfying lives. After finishing my master's degree in counseling, I was ready to learn but didn't have a real mentor. I had my university professors but no one to help me learn all that I needed to know to be successful in my chosen vocation. I was very interested in working with children since my undergraduate degree was in elementary education. For my first job, I chose to work in a particular school district because there was a noted authority who would be serving as my supervisor. He had written books on encouraging children and had just published a book on elementary school guidance and counseling. I finally had a mentor who not only knew a lot about areas I wanted to master but also cared deeply about helping me.

Don was just a regular guy, very soft-spoken and modest given all his accomplishments. Although he was committed to his work, he was just as devoted to his family. He had wide interests in sports and even coached in his spare time. I also was impressed with how close he was to his wife and sons: He seemed totally congruent in all aspects of his life.

Eventually, our friendship and collaboration grew and we became a professional team, coauthoring books and consulting on projects. Our families became close. We lived near one another. In many ways, I modeled my life after his. But far more than that, I learned so much from his honest and direct feedback. We spoke almost daily for years, sharing ideas and catching up on one another's lives.

Don certainly taught me a lot about the profession, about how to navigate the publishing and academic worlds and how to become more proficient as a therapist. He certainly instructed me, supervised me, and taught me things through his tutelage. But, looking back, I'm aware that his greatest gift to me was actually allowing me a view, and later an entrance, into his personal world. I've learned ever since then that in my own role as a mentor for other therapists and professionals, one of the best things I can possibly do is to be as transparent as possible, to reveal as honestly as I can who I am and what I stand for.

Modeling As Best We Can

There is so much emphasis in our field on maintaining competence through the accumulation of continuing education units, attending workshops, staying current on the latest research, developing new skills, and reading journals and books, but precious little about achieving excellence through personal development. John Norcross and others have highlighted how important personal therapy is for practitioners who wish to stay at peak efficiency, or reach for higher functioning. Ironically, there is considerable resistance to this in some quarters, believing that therapy is only for our clients but not for us.

Kirk Schneider believes that one thing most people don't understand about what it means to be a superlative clinician is the commitment to do "one's own down and dirty, no-holds-barred inner work, grappling with inner demons." He finds this quite at odds with most training programs that emphasize the mastery of techniques and mostly ignore the neophyte's personal development.

Consistent with his humanistic orientation, Schneider values the way that he can align himself, center himself, experience a kind of "inner home" to which he can return as a clear, healing space. "This doesn't preclude other, more visible qualities, such as intelligence, a professional and stable demeanor, and a knowledgeable skill set, but it means that those traits have become integrated in such a way as to have become 'second nature' when working with others."

Schneider recalls how one of his mentors, the existentialist theorist Rollo May, used to tell him that what was most important in therapists wasn't their accomplishments or what was on their resume but rather "how much they seemed to have struggled in their own lives, and whether they had come to a place of acceptance or appreciation for that struggle, and the courage that is needed to face it in the here and now. I think it is vitally important that a therapist has somehow 'been there' with a client—not in exactly the same place, but in a parallel place, and has found ways to work this through."

As highlighted in Jon's story mentioned earlier, one of the ways that we learn to model personal effectiveness for others is by following in the footsteps of people we admire, regardless of their particular approach to helping. Among the hundreds of notable figures we've interviewed over the years, as much as we might admire their ideas, there were several in particular who inspired us because of their way of being. Historically speaking, Sigmund Freud's courage and worth ethic; Alfred Adler's emphasis on personal and social responsibility; Carl Rogers', Carl Whitaker's, and Virginia Satir's authenticity and genuineness; and Milton Erickson's inventiveness and creativity all had a huge impact on the ways we choose to live and work. We are not just speaking about their contributions to theory and practice but rather the commitment that each of them had to apply these concepts to the ways they *lived*.

One of our personal agendas in launching our various projects has been to create opportunities to talk to the people in the field we most admire. We wanted a license to investigate and explore more deeply the ways they think about themselves and their legacies, but, most important, how they see the ways they practice what they preach to others. We remember Frank Pittman talking about self-forgiveness, Jay Haley and James Bugental struggling with their declining health, and Albert Ellis' and William Glasser's ferocious zeal to perpetuate ideas they believed would not only save the world but save themselves.

Yet, in their own ways, each of these individuals was flawed and suffered their own personal challenges. It is this personal transparency revealed that makes the ideas of mentors so much more meaningful and accessible. For many of the past years, psychotherapy has been preserved as an inscrutable mystery. During our training years, we were taught the mechanics of the process by following prescribed scripts. We weren't taught so much how to *think* as how to *perform*.

The earliest training films like the classic "Gloria" demonstration with Carl Rogers, Albert Ellis, and Fritz Perls was groundbreaking in that it supposedly presented spontaneous, unscripted sessions of what therapy was really like behind closed doors. It was only much later, while we were collecting stories for a book about lying and deception in therapy that we learned that things were not exactly as they seemed and that the producer had his own agenda that he was promoting. It turned out that Gloria was coerced by him to say things that she didn't actually believe and that she was actually traumatized by her session with Perls. Needless to say, this destroyed a lot of our innocence we still held onto about our training years.

We desperately need models who show in honest ways how they really work when nobody is watching. It doesn't help much to see scripted sessions that don't really reflect the realities that are encountered in daily practice. Our first collaboration took place largely as a result of our mutual frustration with this lack of transparency. Often, we've attended workshops in which the video clips represent very selective samples of what happens. Rarely do we see exemplary work that is also punctuated by inevitable mistakes and miscalculations. This is what led Jon to spend the past several decades producing real therapy videos showing today's best clinician's tackling real people talking about real life. And it is also what Jon attributes to his own excellence in that he has had the opportunity to watch so many models showing what they really do. Another friend and colleague, Jeff Zeig, spends part of almost every day reviewing videos of the masters he sponsors at the "Evolution of Psychotherapy," "Brief Therapy," and "Couples" conferences. It is no wonder that he has such a varied repertoire of therapeutic options with his clients.

The truth is that we don't watch each other nearly enough. We do a lot of talking about what we are *supposedly* doing with clients, what we *think* we are doing with them, but precious little critical observation. We neither watch other great therapists working very often, nor do we invite people to observe us in action.

Whereas a lot of what we have been discussing relates specifically to congruence between professional and personal lives, the effects move in *both* directions. It is the personal passion and unique configuration of personal characteristics that make what we do so special and unique. The process toward mastery will never be the same for any two professionals because we are each so different. And that is what makes it so critical that each of us finds unique ways to be more proactive in integrating what we do in our work into the other aspects of our lives that also matter so much.

Referring to the journey of becoming a master swordsman, Zen scholar D. T. Suzuki observed that the most important principle is to disavow any reliance on specific techniques or strategies. Being a master is even more than a state of mind—it is a state of *being*.

CHAPTER 11

ACKNOWLEDGING COMMONALITIES, RESPONDING TO DIFFERENCES

The master therapist knows that every client is unique, regardless of the similarities to others with comparable demographics or diagnostic codes. Such practitioners are sensitive to differences in gender, spirituality, culture, sexual orientation, age, class, and ethnic background, but also look at cultural identity as something far more broad, as well as individualized. People are just as different within particular cultural groups as they are between the groups.

Perhaps the most significant force in our field in the past several decades has been the consistent cry that we become more responsive to the needs of diverse populations, especially those outside the historical domain of the "worried well" who formed the basis for the earliest work in developing psychotherapy as a profession. When Freud and his colleagues first began their great experiment of healing through talking treatments (versus drugs, animal magnetism, or lobotomies), their subjects were primarily upper-middle-class women from the dominant culture, most of them presenting symptoms that resulted from feelings of boredom, neglect, or helplessness. Within such a backdrop, therapy evolved originally as the means by which to help fairly privileged ("chronically wealthy") individuals explore their past and find greater meaning in their lives. As such, the treatment offered fairly limited options and virtually ignored those who most desperately needed help—the disenfranchised, the marginalized, the poverty stricken, the oppressed—precisely those who would never *dream* of setting foot in a therapist's office.

In the past 30 years, therapists have been mandated by their ethical codes and professional roles to adapt their work to become responsive to clients who represent minority groups, and especially those whose cultural values are quite different from the privileged. There has thus been an overwhelming emphasis on issues related to cultural diversity and client "differentness." We are expected to adjust our roles and responsibilities, not to mention our approaches, to make them better suited to the context of each client's experience. We are required to demonstrate particular "multicultural competencies" that highlight skills and knowledge that are most appropriate for members of certain backgrounds. This has led to all kinds of impressive innovations that have finally made the helping professions accessible to a much greater number of potential clients. Although there is a long road ahead in this regard, there is still an overarching and pervasive movement to increase our sensitivity and awareness of cultural differences and how they influence client worldviews, self-narratives, and behavior. That is why most professional conferences, scholarly journals, invited papers, accreditation reviews, curricular standards, and licensing requirements now mandate that participants demonstrate clearly that they have met the standards for responding to diversity issues.

Multiple Cultural Identities

If the "average" therapist theoretically incorporates multicultural sensitivity into daily practice, continuously upgrading knowledge of cultural backgrounds, confronting unresolved issues of bias and prejudice, and adapting treatments to be more appropriate for clients of varied backgrounds, then what makes a so-called master therapist significantly different? Is it because she is more skilled at making these adjustments or even more responsive to the needs of different groups?

We would suggest that there is a balance to be struck between looking at people as unique individuals, representatives of multiple cultural identities, and common experiences that are shared by almost all of us. There has sometimes been a gross oversimplification associating people with a single cultural feature, whether that involves race, ethnicity, socioeconomic status, religion, gender, sexual orientation, or any other identity. It has been as if someone can be classified as "Black" or "Latina" or "Southern Baptist" or "gay," and that somehow captures an essence of who that person is and what is most important to them. Yet highly experienced and effective therapists recognize that culture is a *lot* more complicated than it is often presented. For one thing, each of us is made up of a dozen or more identified cultures, many of which transcend any single label.

An Individual's Multiplicity of Cultures

Lionel, a 58-year-old African American chemical engineer, presents symptoms of depression that only recently surfaced. In the first session, you learn that he is gay and involved in a long-term relationship with his partner for the past 14 years. They met during a retreat for those exploring Jehovah's Witnesses; both of them had been raised as Southern Baptists. Lionel was born in West Texas, one of the few Black families in the small town, but now lives in New York. A few more significant details are worth mentioning: (a) Lionel was in a motorcycle accident 5 years earlier and has since been confined to a wheelchair as a paraplegic; (b) he is employed by an unnamed government agency that is involved in clandestine activities; and (c) he attended the University of Nebraska earlier in life and he is an avid Cornhusker fan.

So here's the question: What is Lionel's dominant cultural identity?

a. African American
b. Jehovah's Witness

    c. Gay man
    d. New Yorker
    e. Employee of spy organization
    f. Physically handicapped
    g. Nebraska football fan
    h. All of the above
    i. None of the above

We present this example to illustrate the complexities and multi-layered cultural influences that are part of any person's identities. Is Lionel's race, religion, profession, job, college affiliation, geographic location, sexual orientation, marital status, or any one of several other cultural influences most important in his core identity? The answer, of course, is that Lionel, and each one of us, can hardly be relegated to understanding via only a single category.

In addition to the more traditional labels mentioned earlier, some people associate their dominant culture with their geographic location (Southerner, Californian, Midwesterner), profession (farmer, engineer, soldier, therapist), political affiliation (Libertarian, Republican, Democrat, independent), or avocation (gardener, stamp collector, mountain biker, blogger, owner of a Harley Davidson motorcycle), to mention a few. Interview any person, or reflect on your own experience, and it's likely you can create a "cultural genogram" with threads leading to countless identities, each with their own cultural values, norms, and rituals. We mention this as just an example of the different dimensions and levels by which we can respond to the cultural context for any client's issues and presenting problems.

Jorge is Latino but identifies proudly as Mexican American. "I was born in the United States but I see myself as Mexican in many ways." Lest we jump in too quickly with our assumptions about which therapeutic approach might be best to address the relationship issues with his partner, we also learn that he is gay. What this means to him is that he is only partially "out" since his family would never accept him if they knew his sexual orientation. Even with those two very dominant cultural identities, neither one is as important to him as that of being hearing impaired. With his unique communication style (sign language) and the values embedded within deaf culture, Jorge makes it clear that most of his friends, his partner, and those within his social group are almost all hearing impaired.

Although perhaps a dramatic example of multiple cultural identities that live within a single person, we believe that all of us are just as complex in our own ways. And master therapists go much deeper than others to explore those various dimensions that shape who and what we are.

JK There is complete chaos everywhere I look. I had tried to organize a game of "musical chairs" to engage the third graders, but they are so loud and unruly they can't hear when the music stops. Boys are climbing all over the chairs, while some of the girls are crying. A few other children refuse to get up off the chairs altogether. I've been yelling so loudly for so long that I can no longer raise my voice above a whisper. Something seems to have gotten lost in translation.

This is a lower-caste school in a remote part of Southern India. I am here with a group of students at the invitation of the school administration. This is an area of extreme poverty and neglect that was further devastated by a tsunami. We are here for only a few days as volunteers.

"Will you assess some of our students," the principal asked me, "and then make recommendations?"

I asked him what he had in mind. I was under the assumption that we were here primarily to work with the children and teachers to improve their English fluency and consult about the curriculum.

"Some of these children," he said, waving his hand in the direction of the classrooms, "they have many problems. Their fathers are fishermen." He stopped as if that explained things.

"Yes?" I prompted him, practicing the little head shake that is distinct to this part of the world.

"The fathers, they drink a lot. They drink too much alcohol and then they beat their children. Sometimes they are too sick, or as you say, too hurt, to go to school."

"And you want me to evaluate them? But it seems like you already know what is wrong."

The principal smiled sadly. "As you say."

We worked out an arrangement that instead of doing psychological evaluations, with no subsequent chance of any treatment, I would enter a few of the classrooms and interact with the children. I started with kindergarten, and things couldn't have gone any better. I introduced them to "Head, Shoulders, Knees, and Toes," progressed through my repertoire of "Duck, Duck, Goose" and "Hokey Pokey," all to enthusiastic appreciation and wild applause. I have always had a special affinity for 5-year-olds.

Brimming with confidence, the next day I took over the third graders. It seems by then I was no longer the exotic visitor but just a substitute teacher, fresh meat to chew up and spit out. Perhaps that's a poor example in a vegetarian country, but in the language of children all over the world, I was clearly a target to test every limit imaginable.

If that were the only miscalculation I made, it wouldn't have been so bad. I have been carrying an instant camera with me for years, every time I visit somewhere off the beaten track. In many cases, the people I encounter have never seen a photograph of themselves, so I like to offer them as spontaneous gifts to those I meet along the way. I have learned over the years that they become cherished objects, often placed on the mantel or taped on the wall.

When I first entered the village, I took a few photos of the first children I met, along with their parents, and ritualistically handed them over. There are few experiences more enjoyable than watching their faces when the images begin to magically appear. They start pointing and calling over the friends and neighbors, screaming and laughing, and always incredibly grateful for the gesture.

I walked away feeling the familiar giddy sensation that it takes so little to make some people happy, and this fortifies me for all the disappointments I sometimes feel when therapy takes so darn long to make a significant impact. But this time I looked back and I could see a crowd of kids starting to follow me, all shouting, "Photo!" "Photo!" I shook my head and told them that this was it, no more. Usually, this is enough to communicate that the show is over and that I only have a limited supply of film. Yet throughout the three days I worked in the school, I could never convince the children that I had no more film with me. And these third graders were making me pay big time.

I like to think that I am worldly and experienced in the ways of different cultures. I have taught in similar schools from Borneo, Nepal, and Ghana to Peru, Thailand, and Greenland. I thought I was reasonably well prepared to deal with almost any situation. Yet now, as I looked over the 8-year-olds in my charge, I began to realize that things were totally out of control and I was in so far over my head I didn't know were to begin to straighten out this mess.

That was the first step to deliverance. I had to acknowledge that I had made a series of huge mistakes, that I didn't have any idea what was going on, and had exhausted all the options at my disposal. Because of language difficulties and cultural differences, there was no way I could even figure out how to unravel the mess and regain some semblance of control.

I did the only thing I could think of: I ran out of the classroom, screaming, "Help! Help! Someone get up here quick!"

I looked down and could see two of my student volunteers in the midst of a conversation. I pointed at them and said, "You guys, quick! I need reinforcements."

It turned out that they both had some experience teaching primary school so they knew a few tricks ("if you can hear me, clap your hands"), but the children were no longer responsive to standard measures. It would take something extreme to regain their attention and respect.

Feeling lost, confused, and out of control is the default setting in my work within cultures that are foreign to me. I think that's why I seek out such experiences as often as I can—I must love that feeling of unfamiliarity even though I complain about how uncomfortable I am. I learn lessons—hard lessons that I can't seem to grasp any other way.

What We Share in Common

In one sense, every client brings a new culture into the room, one with its own unique set of rituals, norms, and customs, as well as difficult challenges to navigate. We get in trouble, as Jeffrey did, when we try to overgeneralize our preferred theory, our internalized assumptions, our previous experience, to new situations and clients who may appear similar and yet are very different. Yet it is still imperative that we work from some kind of overarching theoretical approach to guide our choices, help us figure what may be going on, and suggest clinical options. Master therapists are hardly eclectics who have collected a lifetime's armory of weapons and tools; in many cases, they are the inventors, or innovators, of new conceptual paradigms, or at least on a smaller scale, they have developed a personally adapted system that has been customized for their unique talents and skill set.

Noted Ericksonian psychologist Michael Yapko admits that although he is truly a pragmatist in that he really enjoys helping people deal with specific problems, he is also a big fan of developing some kind of organized framework that guides clinical choices—and he isn't talking about one with a lot of abstract terms and esoteric philosophical jargon that drives him up a wall. "In my judgment, there are too many practitioners who get attracted to a particular philosophy of treatment they personally find compelling for some reason, yet it has little or nothing to do with effective practice or a client's particular needs. So they remain loyal to a method, and they strive to bring the client to the method they prefer, even when the client doesn't see it that way."

More than anything else he does, Yapko tries to approach each person differently, finding ways to acknowledge and respond to their unique personalities, perspectives, and circumstances. Yet he also sees some commonalities, not only in what predisposes a client to improve rapidly but also in the ways that therapists approach their work. "A great therapist can inspire the client by co-creating a vision of what's possible and who can delineate the steps to make that vision come alive. Someone wise once said that a goal without steps is merely a wish, and I believe that. I also think that a therapist who can see people's strengths and resources more readily than their weaknesses can do much more to help. To me, therapy is about expanding wellness, not shrinking pathology."

Metabolizing Theory and Embracing Complexity

It is clear that master therapists metabolize theory differently than others. According to a study by Ephi Betan and Jeffrey Binder, superlative practitioners not only adapt and change what they learned originally from their teachers and mentors, but they also tend to develop ideas that are far more complex, comprehensive, creative, and abstract. Yapko says he doesn't have much patience for philosophical jargon, and he certainly doesn't speak that way, but that doesn't mean his conceptual framework is not extremely robust.

There is a learning curve that comes with experience and, in spite of perception, it is neither smooth nor incremental: Most of the changes are pretty chaotic and destabilizing. One reason for this is that experienced therapists—at least the truly great ones—keep expanding their theories to accommodate exceptions and anomalies. They use "nonanalytic reasoning," a kind of intuition, to find patterns that are invisible to others. They are used to making constant comparisons across a spectrum of diagnoses, situations, contexts, family configurations, individual personalities, and cultural backgrounds. In short, they conceptualize cases in such a way that they value differences rather than find them annoying or distracting. They thrive under circumstances of complexity and chaos that many others would find overwhelming.

JC Stuart is a man I have counseled for over 30 years and still see every other week. He has been married to Marta for almost 50 years, and they have four adult children. Stuart has a long history of bipolar disorder and many hospitalizations. This is complicated by an Axis II personality disorder of narcissism. Although he has several college degrees, he has never worked, and the family has lived off his disability income and Marta's work as a health aide (now retired). Marta has no presenting psychological diagnosis but is legally deaf.

Stuart's main concern over the years has been feeling lonely and that he has no friends. He has been marginalized his whole life because he is an immigrant, short in stature, never employable, and mentally ill. Recently, he has been writing a series of editorials on adult bullies and how whenever he tries to join community service groups, there is always someone who has to be in charge, leaving him feeling unappreciated and bullied and at the bottom of the pecking order again.

This week, Stuart had a counseling session and brought along Marta. He e-mailed ahead of the session indicating that he wanted to make sure the two of them were on the same page with their son moving home. He brought in a stack of books, his "therapy box," a shoebox full of medications, and several notebooks. He began the session talking about how much better he felt with his son at home because he has someone to talk to. He described that they decided (as a family) to get a new puppy. As Stuart talked, Marta watched him attentively, reading his lips and agreeing with what he was saying. This was the most connected I have seen the two of them, and I made several statements about how connected and on the "same page" they seemed to be. Several times during the session, Stuart referred to needing to finish his thesis. I assumed this was the paper on adult bullying we had been talking about. The meeting ended with handshakes, smiles, and scheduling the next session in

2 weeks. Later that day, I received a message from him telling me how angry he was with me and how "disastrous" he found the session. He vowed never to return.

It's clear that Stuart has a long history of hurting others before they hurt him, which is how manages to keep estranged from others. I know all of the many components of his life, but I also know the deep pain that he feels when he is alone and disconnected. My response needed to be honest, truthful, and direct with him. He didn't need a psychologist but rather a friend. I felt like I was able to understand the many components of his life and to respond to the essential person and not get caught up in the rage and complaints. It is important to understand what is important to the client on that day and that moment. It helped that I had formed an extensive template of various cultural/familial/biological factors that helped to shape him.

Rather than defending myself, or pointing out all the things we had accomplished in the session and all the growth he had made over the years, I just told him how much I understood his anger and disappointment. I let him know that was fine with me that he had felt that way. And I made a few connections between his feelings now and those he had experienced so many times before as part of his self-identified culture as an isolate. I pointed out that he was an example of great diversity living inside a single person, a complex person, one who was so multidimensional that nobody had ever really understood him.

We try to keep ourselves aware of complexity, not just in the multiple cultural identities of our clients, but also in the conceptual frameworks we employ to make sense of client behavior, especially when it may appear so self-sabotaging. This begins by asking the questions: "What are all the ways you identify yourself as a member of a group or culture?" Who are the people in your world who know you best, and what is it that they could tell me about you?" Rather than narrowing diagnostic categories or pigeonholing people into groups, we want to avoid seeing people solely in terms of their race, gender, sexual orientation, or mental status. Certainly, such cultural affiliations offer a kind of meaning and truth, but we are more interested in what is unique about each client. We want to accept all their multiple identities that make them singular beings and yet also connect them to the larger world.

There are many clients like Stuart who desperately want to find some acceptance, in spite of their personal difficulties. They spend their lives trying to please people that they can never please, especially when they are powerless to change features like their height, skin color, sexual orientation, or inborn traits.

We believe the goal is to see differences not as disabilities or problems but as forms of personal uniqueness. Too much of our training is geared toward identifying deficiencies, disabilities, limitations, pathological conditions, illnesses, and what is wrong with people and then fixing it. Yet master therapists have a very different viewpoint or perspective, one that cherishes hope above all else. They feel a calling that allows them to stay focused, not become discouraged, and to view life in relationship to the client's stated goals. Everything else, including preexisting conditions, diagnostic entities, presenting symptoms, and so-called personal limitations, are viewed as simply data that better informs and targets efforts to move forward in desired directions.

Stuart, in all his complexity and multidimensionality, just wanted to be seen as unique and special. Previous therapists had labeled that pathological narcissism. Yet he just wanted to be like everyone else. He wanted to be both different and the same, a follower and a leader, tall and short. He wanted to be seen and known and accepted for who and what he was, even as he desperately struggled to be someone else who was fully functional.

CHAPTER 12

LOVE IS A FOUR-LETTER
WORD IN THERAPY

When we are working with some of our clients, there is no other word to describe how we feel toward them but *love*. We know this is a peculiar word to use in this professional context, but we feel so deeply for many of the people that we help that we sometimes wonder if it really is the case that caring, respect, and affection are just as healing as anything else that we do for them.

Love has been the forbidden word in our profession, largely because of its associations with exploitation, sexual improprieties, countertransference, codependence, and personal indulgence on the part of the therapist. Instead, we usually use terms like *alliance, unconditional positive regard, compassion,* and *empathy* to describe the relational connections that develop with our clients. And, certainly, there are some people we see whom we don't much like at all, much less love them; in fact, they work pretty diligently at making themselves as unlovable as possible. Nevertheless, we have long believed—and kept this pretty much to ourselves—that it is love that drives a lot of our therapeutic work.

We have mentioned before about the preoccupation with techniques and interventions in our field, especially in the striving for mastery. There is a search for isolated variables that produce positive outcomes, especially those that can be standardized and broken down into their component parts.

Sure, we like concrete strategies and reasonably foolproof techniques as much as the next person. And yet what has kept us most energized, excited, creative, enthusiastic, and wildly passionate about the work that we do as therapists and teachers is the love that we feel toward our students, clients, and supervisees. For us, that is the origin of our commitment to helping others, and it is what sustains us. We'd like to think that beyond anything we offer to our clients, students, and supervisees in the way of constructive advice, input, feedback, insights, and content, many of them also felt loved by us.

Multiple Dimensions of Caring

Some of the most kind, caring, and loving people we know are therapists. However, there are other practitioners, remarkably effective in their own right, who appear downright withholding, if not cold. Yet we'd like to think that in their own way these professionals just have a rather unique way of expressing their caring for their clients, one that is no less powerful. Even those who don't explicitly acknowledge that caring is an integral part of their work, and who believe that it may even lead to nonproductive pity, still leak their compassion and love in other ways that their clients would describe.

In Chapter 3, Jeffrey shared his story of how it was as much the caring and love he felt from Albert Ellis as the therapeutic interventions that proved most memorable. It is interesting how we each find different ways to express our compassion, some more directly than others. Ellis may be known for the development of his cognitive-based techniques and disputing irrational beliefs, but many of his clients also felt his deep caring. It is far more well known how much he loved his work. Ellis once published in an article a detailed itinerary of a typical day; his time, from the moment he woke up until those rare times he actually slept, was scheduled with 25-minute therapy sessions, speaking engagements, meetings, writing tasks, phone conversations, and correspondence—even meals were multitasked with other commitments. It may have appeared insane to those who enjoy time for leisure, but for Ellis, work was his true love—and it showed in the passion he expressed consistently throughout his life. We have several friends and colleagues well into their 90s, like Nicholas Cummings, psychologist visionary and architect of mental health care reform, and Gestalt theorist Erving Polster, who love their therapeutic work so much that they are just as active as they have ever been in their careers, still seeing clients, presenting at conferences, conducting day-long workshops. Although approaching the century mark in age, Cummings just returned from a trip to Antarctica to interview personnel there about their experiences.

Perhaps one extreme example of this dedication was shared by Debbie Ellis in describing the way her husband, Albert Ellis, used to organize his life. It is no accident that certain individuals achieve eminence within their profession because they just work so hard at what they do. In Ellis's case, he was so conscious of the swift passing of time that he didn't want to waste a single second.

"He would usually work 16-hour days," Debbie recalled. "On planes, in doctors' waiting rooms, and elsewhere—he would never sit idly. Instead, he would engage in writing, reading, or composing songs and poems. And yet he never presented himself as someone occupying any altar of 'holier than thou' perfection. He spoke of his successful efforts as a young man in overcoming painful and debilitating shyness. He spoke often of the ongoing effort he continued to make to prevent, for example, his largely inherited tendency of impatience and low frustration tolerance. He reminded us that, for each one of us, ongoing work and practice are required for the maintenance of healthy change, sharing his example of doing so with successful results."

Debbie Ellis admitted that many people felt uneasy in her husband's presence because of his intense, all-encompassing devotion to productivity, but she insists that he never judged others for making different choices. "Al was an authentic model of what he was recommending to others. As a consequence of this, many people were less defensive and more receptive to hearing and acting upon recommendations for changing. Al did not pander to any justifications that some people presented for continuing to think and behave in their self-defeating ways. He would dispute such ideas and did not go along passively with clients or students who were hurting themselves. His no-nonsense definite manner added to the motivating energy he provided. And underneath all of that, most people felt his genuine caring and concern for their well-being."

Love for others. Love for work. Love for the things we enjoy most in life. Love for each waking moment. *This* is the passion and deep caring we are demonstrating in our daily life.

Owning Our Personal Motives

As you've no doubt noticed, both of us still struggle to make sense of what happens in that mysterious, complex, multidimensional world of psychotherapy. We have branched out far beyond our clinical offices and now spend much of our professional lives writing, working in the field, and conducting service visits with students and colleagues in remote regions of the world.

We have completely reconceptualized our work every decade or so. Whether we are doing a home visit in a remote village, volunteering in a school or orphanage, leading a service trip to a disadvantaged community, teaching, coaching, supervising, or conducting a therapy session, much of what we're trying to do is communicate our caring and compassion to those we are assisting. This is love without pity, without reciprocal demands, without (mostly) meeting our own needs. We inserted *mostly* because we reluctantly acknowledge that what we do isn't just about helping others but also fortifying ourselves. We *need* to feel wanted, so to speak. Although we prefer to have our efforts appreciated and explicitly expressed, sometimes that feels like a need as well: We're frustrated a lot of the time because we can't really tell whether our work is doing what it was intended to do.

We would also be less than honest if we didn't acknowledge that our interest and passion in the work we do, as well as our focus on love, is to fill a vacuum of intimacy that we have longed for in relationships outside of our family and friendships. We became therapists in the first place, at least in part, because we so enjoy the close connections developed with clients, especially in a context in which we get to be in charge and we're not the one who is vulnerable. Jeffrey, for example, felt pretty worthless and inept as a child—being a therapist provided just the opportunity for him to feel loved and appreciated in such a way that his own life would feel redeemed. For Jon it was more about needing to feel as though he was making a difference and leading a life that was respected by others. The therapy experiences we've most enjoyed and felt most satisfied with have been those in which not only were the clients helped significantly (and expressed gratitude for the help), but there was also mutual affection and respect and caring in the relationship.

Learning How to Love

Looking back, most of our own teachers, supervisors, therapists, and influential mentors taught us important "stuff," meaning that we learned certain skills, knowledge, content, and wisdom from them, but we also felt loved—or at least respected—by them. Both of us had the same doctoral advisor (separated by a few years) who taught us about love, caring, and support in a manner that was deeper than anything either of us had experienced. Prior to this, each of us felt like we were always on probation, in danger of being discovered as frauds, so it came as a welcome surprise that our mentor genuinely seemed not only to like us but to love us. We spent most of our time with him not sitting in his office but across his dining room table with his family, sitting in a fishing boat, or accompanying him to conferences. This was incredibly influential given our prior experiences with supervisors and instructors that felt far less than respectful, much less caring.

Bill taught us that being a professional wasn't just about what you know or what you can do, but how you can give to others, how you can love them. He modeled for us the ways that genuineness, authenticity, and positive regard can become the hallmarks for relationships.

JC I remember being in a seminar with Bill when I asked him if he really thought that career education was all that important given that it struck me at the time as being really boring. I wanted to learn the "fun" stuff that involved really engaging people on a deep, emotional level, not talking about these incomprehensible theories of career development. Bill agreed with me, saying that relationship factors and other personal aspects of a client's life were imperative as well.

"That's interesting," I responded, "because I found this article recently that says that career education is really the foundation for everything we do."

"That guy must be an idiot," Bill replied. And then he completely discredited the main thesis of the article and said that we had far outgrown those original roots.

I nodded, and then reached into my bag and pulled out the article that had actually been written by *him!* Maybe that wasn't the wisest thing I'd ever done, showing up an instructor, and the most powerful faculty member in the department, in front of the whole class.

Bill turned bright red and looked like he was going to strangle me. He stammered for minute, defended himself, accused me of ambushing him, and then declared he'd never been so insulted in his life. He promptly walked out of class and slammed the door.

The other students gathered around me to show support, some in awe, some dumbfounded why I would choose to challenge him like that. "You are in deep doo-doo, Jon. That guy's going to have your hide," one classmate said while laughing and shaking his head. I could only agree with him and figured that my stupidity and ignorance had just ended my career.

To make things even more awkward, Bill was supposed to pick me up the next day and give me a ride to campus, but there was no way I wanted to be alone with him and subject to his wrath and revenge for the humiliation. I was more than a little surprised when he actually showed up at my house. As soon as I got in his car, I started to apologize.

"Hey, don't worry," he said, holding out his hand and smiling. "If we can't be honest and even offend one another on occasion, then we don't have much of a relationship. I'm the one who needs to apologize to you for my own inappropriate behavior: I was just so caught off-guard. And I realized in that moment how far I've grown in my thinking since I first wrote that article. You actually helped me to see that."

From that experience, and so many others, Bill taught me the value and importance of an honest, open, and truthful relationship, one built on mutual caring, respect, and, yes, love.

Love Is Always Possible

As therapy has become briefer, more focused on specific symptoms, better matched between conditions and treatment protocols, compassion and caring are often considered just additional variables to be moderated. How we feel about our clients, or even how we convey this concern, is sometimes considered much less important than the implementation of the treatment program. In some circumstances, and with some clients, a certain objectivity and detachment are to be preferred. Nevertheless, that doesn't fully explain how with many years of practice, our compassion can become eroded over time, replaced with a kind of distanced posture as we've seen and heard it all before.

One of our friends who worked in community mental health somehow found the means to remain inspired and energized by his work. This was particularly interesting because he worked with the most difficult population imaginable: dual-diagnosed, homeless patients who presented symptoms of schizophrenia, addictions, mental retardation, or all of the above.

"How do you manage to keep working with these people?" he was asked one day. "I mean, what can you possibly do for them?"

"What do you mean?" he said, genuinely puzzled by the question.

"Well, these people live on the streets. They are actively hallucinating. They have borderline intelligence. Most of the time, they're high, either on street drugs or Haldol they get from the clinic. They can barely focus on a conversation, much less participate actively in a meaningful therapy session. What the hell can you do for them?"

Our friend looked thoughtful for a moment. He nodded his head and, at first, Jeffrey thought he was agreeing with him. But then he said something that we'll never forget and hold dear to our hearts to this day: "My hope is that for at least one hour each week they feel like someone really cares about them."

We are haunted by these words, just as we are by the previous observation that we become most dispirited and disinterested in our work when we have lost (or misplaced) our compassion. Anyone who has been in this field for a while knows well the challenges of keeping ourselves fresh, energized, and passionate about what we do. It is very easy to function on autopilot, to listen to our clients with partial attention, to repeat the same well-worn stories and anecdotes, and to use the same time-tested techniques that have worked previously. It takes considerable commitment and energy to truly remain engaged in sessions, to co-create individually designed, unique therapeutic masterpieces that not only promote lasting changes but inspire clients to maintain the momentum long after the work ends. We all have to find our own path to doing so, one that helps us to keep things fresh. For us, that has been about accessing and expressing love in what we do, love for the people we help, love for the work that we do, and love for the gratitude we feel in what we've been privileged to learn from our clients and students over the years.

This is what the humanistic therapists like Carl Rogers, Abraham Maslow, Irv Yalom, Jim Bugental, Art Combs, and many others have been telling us, beginning with our first classes in counseling. Truly loving people is not just important to helping others but also helps sustain us over time. Those who only seem to care when they are being paid to help will never discover mastery in this part of their life.

For the famed psychoanalyst Erich Fromm, a client's symptoms are rooted in his or her inability to love. This love includes the capacity to experience concern, responsibility, respect, and understanding of another person and the intense desire for that person to grow. Often, clients are still searching for the love they never received from a mother or father or other parent figure.

Love is about moving away from ourselves and adopting a life pursuit of loving kindness, not just when we are being paid in our offices but in every aspect of our lives. It is through such love that we ease others' pain and suffering. This process of learning to love begins with loving ourselves.

JC Mike seemed like the poster boy for self-confidence as he entered my office. He was a huge guy, carefully dressed in a matching tie, sweater vest, and tweed sports jacket. He bristled with self-assurance.

Within a few minutes Mike let me know that he had attended an East Coast prep school and Ivy League university and had an MBA. He was wildly successful in terms of wealth and status. When I asked him how I could help him, he sheepishly admitted he had "lots of problems."

Mike described his lifelong struggle with "being moody," which, after elaboration, resulted in a diagnosis of bipolar disorder that led to several lengthy hospitalizations. This ran in his family, as his father, Mike Sr., also displayed these symptoms and was frequently suicidal.

Most recently, things had been going fairly well in his life when he developed premature ejaculation in his relationship with his girlfriend. Mary Anne was apparently a dominant woman who grew up "on the other side of the tracks" and, according to Mike, they were as different as night and day. He described his close family connection, while he indicated she didn't even talk to her mom or siblings and didn't even know her father. He described her as especially interested in sex and seemed to want to make love all the time and now he just couldn't keep up with her.

"If you two are so different," I asked him, "how do you manage to stay together?"

"You have no idea, Doc! If you saw her, you'd want her, too. She's a 12 on a 10-point scale. This woman is a work of art."

It seemed that Mary Anne's physical perfection echoed his own need to be as perfect as possible on the outside, given his imperfect mental disorder. It was a mystery to him why anyone would want to be with him, given his flaws. He had an incurable disease, a suicidal father, and now he couldn't even get it up in bed!

I recognized that one big problem was that Mike only saw his flaws and not his strengths, failing to recognize his achievements except those he attained earlier in life in school. And even then, he believed it was just his luck that he could associate himself with prestigious institutions but did not feel he ever earned the privilege.

We spent our time together talking a lot about seeing himself in a more balanced light, acknowledging some of his gifts while accepting some limitations. During one of our last sessions, I told him how much I admired and genuinely liked him. "Mike, you see yourself as someone who has deep flaws that must be disguised and hidden, while I see this amazing man who has created an incredible start to life despite some big handicaps. I guess I see where you are and you choose to focus on where you are not."

Mike couldn't quite hear me, insisting that he'd always struggled with his disease and now he was a sexual cripple.

"Hey," I told him, "I agree that we can't fix some things, but we can certainly manage them. And as for your problems with Mary Anne, my guess is that this is the result of not truly being yourself. Your lack of responsiveness to her in bed is your way of telling her she can't always control you. You are tired of her pushing you around."

This turned out to be a breakthrough, less as a result of this, or any other interpretation or intervention, as the accumulative love and caring he felt from me. If I could think that much of him, maybe it was time to start loving himself.

Therapists need to understand the importance and complexity of love. It seems that often without deep and honest love it's difficult for anyone to grow beyond whatever initial problem brought him or her into treatment. Likewise, it's challenging for a clinician to show deep compassion and caring to clients if they can't manage to do so with loved ones in their lives. Whether with our parents, children, siblings, friends, colleagues, neighbors, or the checkout clerk at the local grocery story, we do our best to respond with empathy. "Be kind whenever possible," advises the Dalai Lama, "and it's *always* possible."

CHAPTER 13

GETTING WILD AND A LITTLE CRAZY: PROMOTING CREATIVE BREAKTHROUGHS

Being creative in therapy is often a collaboration between a therapist and client, one in which something completely novel and unexpected arises as a result of thinking *way* outside the usual boundaries of what is expected. In other cases, being creative is more revisionist, simply figuring a way to adapt what you already know into different contexts and situations. It isn't that master therapists are necessarily more creative than others; it's just that they give themselves permission to experiment, to take constructive risks, to access parts of themselves—and their clients—that take them into the unknown.

At the most obvious level, when we think of creative therapists, what comes to mind are those practitioners who appear to offer spontaneously and impulsively the most far-out and amazing solutions to client problems, usually resulting in a cure within a few minutes. When we hear about such cases, read them in the literature, or watch them on demonstration videos, we are often left humbled and discouraged. After all, how is it ever possible that any of us would invent or try such a thing?

Consider some of the seminal cases of Milton Erickson, Carl Whitaker, Virginia Satir, or Jay Haley; we are left speechless, thinking, "Wow, I could *never* have thought of that in a million years!" We've spent years collecting hundreds of other examples of the most creative interventions we could have ever imagined and we are always left breathless. We remember Michael Yapko asking his client for a million dollars to demonstrate how absurd his goal was and Laura Brown conducting a session with her client inside a box to provide an opportunity to break loose from her self-imposed prison. William Glasser went running with his client to help wean her from an addiction to eating from garbage cans and even purposely hung his office pictures in a crooked manner to challenge a client who needed everything perfect. Brad Keeney brought indigenous healing practices into sessions. Stephen Lankton asked a depressed client to watch a sunset between the vortex of two spoons. Cloe Madanes actually told a couple to hire a new dominatrix to work through their sexual problems. Violet Oaklander conducted a session with a resistant child by talking through the pet snake that he brought into therapy. Scott Miller confronted a paranoid schizophrenic who thought he was Rambo by insisting that the guy was really the actor who played him, Sylvester Stallone. Stephen Madigan invited a whole community of family and friends to a session in order to provide support for a grief-stricken man. These legendary cases are daunting because they seem so improbable and it would never occur to us to think of something like that, much less to ever introduce it in session. Although we admire these singular efforts, we are far more interested in searching for their underlying principles that might help us to find our own way to greater creativity.

We mentioned in an earlier chapter about how we've been struck by the number of female master therapists we've interviewed who insist they aren't all that innovative—they just have creative clients! They don't "own" the creative breakthroughs that sometimes occur in sessions but rather see them as a collaborative effort. It really isn't about us coming up with some incredible new idea or technique, but only helping to create and sustain an environment where such options might emerge organically from the interaction.

When Models and Theories Limit Our Creative Options

One of the factors we've identified from our studies of the most creative therapists in the world, or at least those we've interviewed, is that most of them don't follow other people's models: They developed, invented, or adapted their own. They don't dance to others' music but have created their own. They may identify with a particular theoretical paradigm, but, if so, it is one that they have customized for their own purposes, personalities, and contexts.

Michael Yapko is puzzled why therapists seem to take the existing models so seriously, as if they are handed down by some Divine Being: "Most people don't seem to get that our therapy models are merely metaphors, one or even two steps removed from ways of trying to describe human experience with a formula or symbolic representation. Therapists get so absorbed in the metaphors as if they are real or true. There is no id, ego, or superego! Likewise, if you're not pregnant, then you don't have an 'inner child'! These are merely metaphors, but therapists argue for these and hundreds of other theoretical constructs as if they are 'the truth.' Therapists inevitably become as limited as the models they subscribe to. When therapists become more concerned with being *effective* than *right*, therapy will inevitably improve."

You have to admit that Yapko's got a point: Many of us do take our models very seriously, often to the point that they limit our options to do whatever it takes to make a difference with a client even if it means reaching *way* beyond what we previously knew, understood, and believed. Even those who are passionate advocates for a particular theoretical orientation, at least those who have been innovators, recognize how important it is for each of us to personalize the ideas and help our clients to do the same.

Judy Jordan, an enthusiastic proponent of her own developed relational-cultural model, is nevertheless aware of how oversubscribing to one theoretical orientation can limit creative opportunities. "Many people get caught up in defining methodologies or techniques as the key factors in bringing about healthy change. I fully appreciate certain "techniques" like those of cognitive-behavior therapy, in bringing about change. I agree that neuroscience is going to contribute more interesting interventions for the future." You can sense the conditional "but" that is coming, and you won't be disappointed: Unless all that is offered takes place from a position of empathy, it's not going to be very well received.

According to person-centered therapist David Cain, the best therapists he has ever known and worked with are those who are truly authentic and have developed their own unique style rather than following in the footsteps of others. This is what allows them to respond to each client as an individual and to collaborate on novel solutions to deal with issues. "Such therapists know themselves and use themselves in spontaneous and creative ways as dictated by what the immediate moment calls for in terms of what might be best for the client. When I am in this state of being, I am often using my intuitive senses to get a 'feel' for the unique person before me and how he or she relates to self and others, including me. When I'm at my best, I have a sense of my clients and how they comport themselves in their lives. I see the pattern and work to enable clients to see themselves more clearly. Implied here is that clients have implicit goals or hopes, are purposive and have a style of life. I often use spontaneous humor to help provide perspective and enable a difficult realization to be accepted. Laughing with clients also strengthens our bond."

Cain believes that the most extraordinary and creative therapists are collaborative, adaptive, and highly pragmatic. "While grounded in a cohesive belief system that guides what they do, they are flexible enough to change course as dictated by the needs of the client. They are collaborative in the sense that they form strong partnerships or alliances with their clients and view themselves as a team working together. Such therapists are keen observers of what fits and works for each client while also being receptive to seeking input about what adaptions may be needed at various times in the process. In this sense, they are not afraid to hear that what they are doing may not be effective and adjust accordingly. They are pragmatic in terms of doing what fits and what works because it is in the best interests of their clients. Said somewhat differently, they do not allow their theoretical allegiance to get in the way of doing something that is more promising. In my view, extraordinary therapists are schooled in all major approaches to therapy and draw on them when needed."

Sorting Out All the Voices in Our Heads

It isn't as if there is only one theory or conceptual model that frames what we do. Whereas this might have been the case a few decades ago when it was far more common for therapists to follow the tenets of a single allegiance, nowadays we are influenced by many different ideas, with more introduced each year. We hear the voices in our heads of all our previous instructors, supervisors, mentors, and authors, each of them whispering—sometimes screaming—directions or offering advice. And lost in all that noise is our own individual voice that is drowned out by those of others.

In the martial arts, one studies with a master to learn all that is known about a particular specialty. The mentor or *sensei* (teacher) teaches the essential skills—the blocks, kicks, punches, forms, defenses, sparring techniques, and fighting strategies—as well as the philosophy embedded in the discipline. Progress is measured by the attainment of successive belts, each designating levels of competence and rank. And yet one does not attain the status of master until the practitioner goes way beyond the basic teachings and creates his or her own novel applications. After all, martial arts, like therapy, require one to think quickly on one's feet (or chair), continually altering strategies in light of what is happening in the moment.

We will likely always hear that chorus of voices in our heads, the legacy of all our previous teachers and colleagues. It is an interesting and useful exercise to sometimes ask ourselves, "What would one of our mentors do now?" We juggle all the different advice and suggestions, sort through the myriad of options, and then try to find something that seems to fit. But what often gets lost in the shuffle is our own unique take on what works best. We have been taught our whole lives, our whole careers, to follow carefully the path set before us by others. And in so doing, we sometimes forget that each of us has something novel to offer, something that reflects our own individual style, as well as the needs of a client in any moment in time.

It is interesting how many therapists we interviewed, representing so many different theoretical orientations, basically said similar things devaluing specific interventions or even models in favor of far more human features of the process. Nancy McWilliams, for instance, often strongly identified within the psychoanalytic school, nevertheless considers that what she has to offer clients is unique to her own individual style: "Most people, even professionals, don't seem to appreciate that good therapy is much more about an attitude or overall sensibility than the application of a technique or the adherence to a particular theory. A therapeutic attitude has to be both natural to the therapist and disciplined by years of immersion in the work. Despite the fact that many techniques can be helpful in treatment, psychotherapy does not amount to a set of 'interventions' applied by interchangeable 'providers.' The person of the therapist, and the ineffable emotional chemistry between the therapist and the client, matter more than specifiable procedures."

We're sure you've heard this more than a few times before. The problem is that on some level, most of us don't actually believe this. We still tend to value the ideas of others, identified as "notable figures," far more than we do our own contributions. That's why there are such long lines to get autographs at author signings, why workshop participants grip handouts as if they contain "truth," and why each year brings some new celebrity into the forefront teaching us the next best thing that renders everything else we thought we knew obsolete.

On Being Creative

Most of the research on creativity points to the ways that individuals are able to make connections between seemingly unrelated entities or see patterns that are invisible to others. Creative therapists are able to look at problems from many different angles rather than a single viewpoint. They experiment with options that may, at first, appear to be wild and even a little crazy. When we once asked Stephen Lankton to explain the theory behind Milton Erickson's methodology, he just shook his head with a smile. He had just finished telling us another seminal story about how Erickson had sent him out into the desert to look for a particular tree from *Alice in Wonderland*. The intervention seemed to make no sense at all, and *that* was Lankton's conclusion. He believed that much of the time Erickson was thinking about the most unusual, wacky, creative things possible for his clients to do that were only tangentially related to their presenting problems. Of course, he was accessing his own intuition and felt sense of what he thought might be going on, but even that didn't seem all that important. According to Lankton, the key was getting clients to explore new territory way outside their comfort zones, to get them to do all kinds of crazy stuff, and then afterward, to make or create meaning from the experiences. Once freed from conventional thinking about what we are supposed to do, what others would tell us to do, we have many more options available to us and our clients.

Extraordinarily creative therapists are able to display high levels of originality despite the pressures to conform to the status quo. They have removed the "governors" or restrictions that were applied in their formal training and internships by professional associations and rigid instructional requirements with restrictive codes of conduct. That is not to say that they behave in ways that are inappropriate; it's just that they continually question why things are structured the way they are. Psychoanalyst Jacques Lacan, for instance, continually questioned the orthodoxy of his guild, wondering why sessions had to be 50 minutes when some clients needed much less or more time, or why appointments even had to be scheduled. Of course, he took delight in thumbing his nose at the establishment, having once pulled down his pants at a conference to show his displeasure, but nevertheless Lacan continually wondered why therapy had to follow such a rigid prescriptive structure.

We aren't interested in following what some of these famous therapists have done. It just isn't our style to sit on top of a client the way Erickson did, or take a lonely client to a bar as Arnold Lazarus did, or sing ribald songs with clients as Ellis did, or breast-feed clients on our lap as Carl Whitaker did, or chant and dance with clients as Brad Keeney did, or call together a community gathering as Stephen Madigan did, or . . . well, you get the point. While we admire these efforts and find them provocative, humorous, and engaging, it just isn't part of our way of being. Maybe we are too inhibited or cautious or lack courage. But we think it is more about each of us finding our own ways to be more creative without being self-indulgent.

As each of us accumulates more skills and internalizes the rules that govern our field, we naturally want to use this knowledge in ways that are more suited to our own inclinations. It isn't a lack of talent that will impede this creative flow of the therapist but more likely a bad attitude. Many therapists become anxious and insecure and tend to become more concerned with conformity, acceptance, and not "rocking the boat" as they tend to follow what has already "worked" in order to fit into a group of professional colleagues.

Once therapists reach the master stage, they are able to use their incredible funds of knowledge to remain open to seeing and approaching problems in unique or nonconventional ways. They use keen assessment acumen and seem to ask questions that are simpler and yet more revealing to the ongoing problem. They seem present and attentive, as they do not miss or pass over important elements to the complex life problems brought to them by their clients. They have the ability to sift through the massive amounts of information that their clients present and cull out the information that is most relevant to the presenting situation. They realize that the brain processes something like 400 billion units of information every second. It is possible to be aware of only a small fraction of what is occurring. Given that flood of data, they concentrate on relaxing and letting the hard work they have done unconsciously or intuitively guide them in the choices they make. They also possess an excitement and youthful energy that propels them forward, coupled with the rigor and discipline needed to follow investigations to the end. They are, therefore, relying on their intuition and trusting what occurs.

There are indeed some therapists who have the playfulness of a child but without the experience or the necessary discipline to coordinate the many different directions that the information can take. There are others who have vast amounts of knowledge and skill but are too rigid and lack the flexibility needed to view and implement creative problem solving. They are not able to give themselves permission to go beyond what is considered conventional and familiar. Master therapists blend the childlike spirit with discipline. They are not restricted by habits or experience as they manage to discover unseen pathways, solutions, and levels of understanding.

Master therapists often have to deal with the demands of their peers, and also their clients, to conform to the current or conventional approach to helping. Many are forced to stifle their creative spirit, only to have it return later even stronger. However, many professional therapists stop growing and become comfortable with the knowledge and skills they gained in their internships. They may feel reluctant to entertain any new ideas, especially those that might contradict others that they cherish. Master therapists are willing to live a life of uncertainty and possible ridicule as they pursue ideas that may be different from the norm. They are able to let go of their need for comfort and security for the hope or promise of the stimulation that comes from a creative breakthrough. As the old adage states, "The skillful mariner must be willing to lose sight of the shore." We would add that while this is laudable, it also must be done with the client's safety in mind, taking *constructive* risks that don't jeopardize anyone's well-being.

Seeking New Knowledge While Embracing Mystery

The master therapist possesses a deep knowledge base, not just about psychotherapy but also about the many other fields necessary to creating a satisfying life. Daniel Goleman called this *emotional intelligence,* but it represents a more global never-ending hunger to understand ourselves, others, and the world. We have both commented in other writings how one of the privileges, if not requirements, of our profession is the opportunity to apply *everything* we learn to our work—all the films and shows we see, the books we read, the conversations we enjoy, the relationships, experiences, adventures, and travels we encounter. And none of this includes what we value most—the rich experiences we enjoy, jumping as deeply into life as we can.

Although wide and varied study may produce a semblance of wisdom over time, it never comes close to providing a kind of truth. The confidence and arrogance often displayed in our field by some who claim to have cornered the market on certainty has always amazed us. They speak with utter and complete confidence that they have discovered the "one, true way" and those of us who don't follow that path are misguided, or sometimes labeled "wrong."

Most of us are annoyed, if not disgruntled, by *some* aspect of our field that we consider off the mark. It may sometimes feel as though you are the only one who sees things clearly and you can't figure out why others don't catch on. There are all kinds of issues that spark passionate debate but probably none more polarizing than the movement toward so-called evidence-based treatments as part of randomly controlled experimental studies.

Barry Duncan is bewildered by what could be interpreted as the basic assumption of this dominant professional culture: "The idea here is to make psychological interventions dummy-proof, where the users—the client and the therapist—are basically irrelevant. Just plug in the diagnosis, do the prescribed treatment, and voila, cure or symptom amelioration occurs! This product view of therapy is perhaps the most empirically vacuous aspect of this movement because the treatment itself accounts for so little of outcome variance, while the client and the therapist—and their relationship—account for so much more."

Duncan finds it more than a little amusing—and disturbing— that there is assumed to be some psychological "pill" that will provide a cure. "A treatment for a specific disorder, from this perspective, is like a silver bullet, potent and transferable from research setting to clinical practice. Any therapist need only load the silver bullet into any psychotherapy revolver and shoot the psychic werewolf stalking the client. This perspective appeals to those who believe that more structure and consistency and less clinician judgment is needed to bring about positive outcomes."

Duncan shakes his head, imagining if only it were that easy. It's not that there's anything wrong with empirically validated treatments, and they are certainly useful to learn, at least as healing rituals, but how on earth can we possibly know ahead of time what technique will work for a given client, at a particular moment? Psychotherapy, by its very nature, is filled with uncertainty, ambiguity, and mystery. And one thing that definitely gets in the way of being more creative is believing that mastery really means getting it right.

"As frightening as it feels, uncertainty is the place of unlimited possibilities for change. It is this indeterminacy that gives therapy its texture and infuses it with the excitement of discovery. This allows for the 'heretofore unsaid,' the 'aha moments,' and all the spontaneous ideas, connections, conclusions, plans, insights, resolutions, and new identities that emerge when you put two people together in a room and call it psychotherapy. Tolerance for uncertainty creates the space for new directions and insights to occur to both the client *and* you."

As a case in point, Duncan brought to mind a recent case with Rosa, a 7-year-old described as a very difficult child. Rosa was faced with all kinds of obstacles in her life—both of her parents were addicts, the father in prison, and the mother actively using drugs. Rosa had been abandoned and was in foster care. "Although much psychopathological gobbledygook accompanied her file, basically she was prone to tantrums that included kicking, biting, and throwing anything she could find."

When Duncan asked Rosa if she was willing to do some work on her situation, she crossed her arms and screamed back, "NO!" and then demonstrated one of her fabled tantrums, flailing around and kicking her therapist. Duncan looked around helplessly at the foster parents, as if to ask them what to do next. All they could do was shrug.

Duncan had never felt more helpless, having no clue what to do with this child and no idea what to offer the foster parents about how to handle her. Among the thoughts fleeting through his panicked mind, he wondered if there was an empirically validated treatment available for feeling overwhelmed and hopeless? It was then that he decided to embrace his uncertainty as he watched the foster mother begin to cry in frustration and then Rosa reach over and wipe away the tears, saying, "Don't cry. Please don't cry."

"Witnessing these actions was yet another reminder to me of how new possibilities can emerge at any moment in a seemingly hopeless session and the uncertainty of what will happen next.

"It's tough to parent a child who's been through as much as Rosa has," Duncan said in a quiet voice. "I respect your need to really think through the long-term consequences here. But I'm also impressed with how gently you handled Rosa when she was so upset, and with how you, Rosa, comforted your Auntie when you saw her crying. Clearly there's something special about the connection between you two."

The tension had dissipated, and this had been a breakthrough for the family. Although we've presented an abbreviated version of the story, it nevertheless illustrated the ways that amazing things can happen, from being meticulously systematic and well organized to capitalizing on what is going on in the moment.

"In my view, the session included that intimate space in which we connect with people and their pain in a way that somehow opens the path from what is to what can be. My heartfelt appreciation of both the despair of the circumstance and their sincere desire to help this child, combined with the fortuitous 'attachment' experience, generated new resolve for the foster parents. This session taught me, once again, that anything is possible—that even the bleakest sessions can have a positive outcome if you stay with the process. Just when things seemed the most hopeless, when both the family and I were surely down for the count and needed only to accept the inevitable, something meaningful and positive emerged that changed everything—including me."

This is but one example of how and why Duncan believes that it is uncertainty that often leads to the best outcomes. "Great therapy capitalizes on these opportunities. This tolerance for uncertainty, however, requires faith—faith in the client, faith in yourself, and faith in the process."

It is interesting that when great therapists recount the stories of their greatest creative breakthroughs, they almost always took place when they were most confused, desperate, and lost. It is under the circumstances of *not* understanding what's going on that we are most likely to experiment with new alternatives. It is mystery and uncertainty that lead us to our most innovative and courageous acts.

You've Never Heard of the Most Creative Therapists

There have been some esteemed and well-known figures in our field who consistently demonstrated curiosity, flexibility, and extraordinary ingenuity throughout their lives. They were always searching for the next best thing, always seeking more effective ways to advance their knowledge and skills, always experimenting with alternative means by which to impact their clients. Yet more often than not, some of these individuals were "one-trick ponies" who came up with one great idea that did indeed have a powerful influence on the field, yet they spent the balance of their careers stuck in the past, more committed to advancing their ideas and ensuring their legacy than truly exploring new territory.

As we mentioned previously, we believe that the most creative practitioners work in relative obscurity, uninterested in notoriety and too busy to broadcast their ideas to a larger audience. They work relentlessly and tirelessly to test the boundaries of what is known and accepted as truth. They challenge the status quo and continually ask why things are structured the way they are. Why are sessions scheduled so rigidly? Why has therapy been traditionally structured as primarily conversation when most healers from around the world incorporate movement, music, dance, prayer, and touch? Why should therapy always take place in the same locale? If indeed the purpose of the activity is to promote lasting change, wouldn't it make more sense to arrange meetings in a *different* novel environment each time so as to make the experience more memorable? And what about the ways we prepare/train/grow therapists? We talk a good game about the importance of active learning, emotional arousal, and relational engagement, while we conduct training in formal settings with all kinds of standardized formats. We even select potential students based on measures (grade point average, test scores) that aren't very predictive of success as a practitioner. And once they are admitted, we do our best to stamp out all remnants of creativity that students once valued most. We teach them not so much to write what they really think or feel or understand, but rather to make sure they conform to APA style format, use sanctioned language, and structure their ideas according to templates handed down by accrediting bodies. Beginners quickly learn that if they are to survive in the profession, much less flourish, then they better jump on the bandwagon and follow carefully and meticulously the footsteps of those before them.

JK One of my greatest fears early in my career was that I had nothing original to say. I not only believed that I could never come close to attaining the achievement and competence of my teachers, but I thought that everything worthy in the field had already been said. Like generations of students before and after me, I learned that before I could offer anything meaningful to the profession, I first had to review everything that had been done previously in the form of a literature review. My only job as a budding scholar and practitioner was perhaps to advance one small segment of knowledge related to one specific, focused area of interest that I was expected to specialize in for the rest of my life. My gosh, that is depressing and discouraging! What could I possibly add to what was already said before? I wasn't nearly smart enough, or creative enough, to think of something that hadn't occurred to the masters before me. Even though I yearned to make my mark, I knew that I was doomed to become a worker in the hive, whose main function was to serve the queen.

In the early part of my career, my voice was muted. Writing anything about my interests or work and expecting to publish it in a journal was agonizing because I had to so carefully conform to the regimented standard of what goes where, document and cite every source, complete a literature review before even beginning to undertake a study, and so on. I'm not arguing that it isn't useful, or even necessary, to follow the scientific method if our goal is to systematically advance knowledge; I'm just suggesting there are also other ways of approaching questions. And once I realized that was possible—even if it wasn't recognized and sanctioned—I turned the process around. I realized that if I ever wanted to figure out what I really know and understand, I would first start with my own beliefs and experience, and then dig down to their source. Only then, after I had already recorded what I think I know, would I then review what had been done previously related to that subject. Often, this would lead me to discard much of what I had originally thought was true, altering my beliefs and leading me to investigate the issues with a far more open—and creative—mind. But it also provided a path for me first to figure out what is in my own mind and heart. This, of course, is a signature process of some qualitative research studies when investigators begin by initially "locating themselves" relative to the question and what personal motives led them to this particular study.

It is ironic that creative therapists often follow a similar pattern. Once they learn the essential skills of one approach, they enter the real world and creatively apply what they learned to the population in their community. They complete their internship or mentorship or supervision and move into the real enjoyment of therapy. They stop wondering if they are doing it correctly and instead wonder whether they were helpful. They push themselves to discover new ways to reach clients that are difficult or challenging. They are no longer thinking about the approach they are using but more about helping the client. Or maybe we could say that differently and more accurately: They may *say* they are following a particular theory or subscribing to a particular orientation, but every study that actually investigates what therapists are actually doing in sessions isn't consistent with espoused beliefs. We are all far more eclectic, flexible, and pragmatic than we pretend to be.

Thinking Differently About Problems

We worry that over time therapists have stopped thinking for themselves. They have settled for being technicians who follow the prescribed treatment regimens and protocols. We watch them trying to do therapy just like their favorite hero or heroine, often reporting that they did just what Salvador Minuchin or Susan Johnson would have done, not realizing they are mimicking and not mastering the art of therapy. True master therapists are working at being themselves and using this self to be an instrument of change or help for the people they service. The emphasis is on "creating" movement and not on following the original model learned in their earlier black-belt schooling. They are afraid to move from the conventional approaches for fear of a lawsuit from the client and continue to do what doesn't work.

JC Even before Alyce entered my office, she began the session with a machine gun barrage of questions: "What's wrong with me? What's going on inside me that made me do something like this? I don't feel like I'm a bad person, but I did something really, really bad, so what does that make me? The policeman said I'm going to go to jail for 6 years, so what will happen to my son? I've never done anything like this before in my life. It must be really deep-seated, and I want you to tell me what it is. . . ."

Over what seemed like hours, Alyce explained that she and Bruce, her husband of 2 years, were out on a date and they'd had a few cocktails. The next thing she remembers was being in their car going home and she was beating on him, pounding his chest and face. After Bruce pulled the car over, a passerby saw the commotion and called the police, who eventually arrested Alyce for assault and put her in jail. She had blacked out and didn't remember a thing except that she was "crazy in love" with Bruce.

Alyce's son, Ryan, was in his twenties and severely disabled as a result of a careless surgeon. She had spent her life caring for Ryan and was, by all accounts, a devoted mother. Alyce spent years in court before receiving a financial settlement that would provide care for Ryan.

The authorities stated that it was obvious that Alyce had deep-seated hostility and needed extensive psychotherapy, as well as medication, to control her rage. She was charged with many different felonies and misdemeanors, including battery, domestic abuse, public intoxication, and failure to cooperate with the police. Then she was referred to me for assessment and treatment.

I was really puzzled by the situation because Alyce denied having an alcohol problem and didn't really believe that she had attacked her husband. I saw her as someone who was responsible and determined to raise her son and not put him in an institution as others had urged since his birth. This one incident of alleged violence seemed so out of character. I wondered if I was missing something behind this placid façade. It felt like it was far easier to go along with the alleged facts of the case rather than to risk my reputation on some intuitive hunch. But I have also learned that I need to trust my felt sense, even when my conclusions might run counter to conventional wisdom.

I was impressed that Alyce had never had a legal problem, anger issues, or previous incident with alcohol. I saw this single abusive event while she was intoxicated as an exception that didn't fit her lifelong patterns of behavior. The most frustrating event in her life seemed to be the injury to Ryan and the 15-year legal battle over the responsibility for his injury, which she handled logically and methodically. Even though she eventually won the court settlement, she was still really upset with the doctor, who would not take responsibility for his error. Was there something like this going on in her relationship with Bruce?

I remembered that Alyce had talked about how stubborn and closed off Bruce was. He never did anything wrong (or so he thought) and always seemed to turn things around and blame her or others. Alyce had gone to couples counseling with Bruce, but he wouldn't go back again because he didn't think he had any problems.

I rejected all kinds of obvious approaches and decided to take a stab in the dark, even though I didn't yet know Alyce very well. "Being with Bruce must have been a lot like when you worked on your lawsuit."

"What the heck are you talking about?" she responded, looking genuinely puzzled.

I wondered if I should back off but decided to try again. "It seems like neither Bruce nor your son's doctor ever admitted to making a mistake."

Alyce thought for a moment, then nodded her head very, very slowly. She admitted that she hadn't made that connection before, and I could see a flash of anger cross her face. "Well, maybe that's true. But the difference is that I love Bruce and I hate that damn doctor!"

Once Alyce recognized the similarities between the two of them, she understood the source of her anger, especially with her guard down after drinking. She decided several things in that moment. First, she would never drink again. And second, if they were going to stay in the marriage, then Bruce was going to have to begin couples counseling again to talk about their issues.

The breakthrough in this case, and so many others, is the stubborn refusal to buy into the standard ways of assessing and diagnosing the problem. This is what brief therapy innovations brought to the table when they first introduced the idea of reframing presenting issues in far more creative ways, especially those that more easily lend themselves to resolution.

When we generate descriptive adjectives to describe a master therapist, including words like *expert, wise, skilled, experienced,* and certainly *creative* would be on the list. After all, almost by definition, extraordinary practitioners have the ability to go way beyond the boundaries of those who are conventional in their approach. They see, hear, sense, and feel things that are invisible to mere mortal beings. They invent ways of connecting and influencing people that would never occur to others. And they often assess and name presenting problems using very different and creative language.

Where Has Creativity Gone?

Earlier in the chapter we mentioned what it felt like 40 years ago, when we first started out in the field, and thought that anything useful or valuable or any new creative contributions had already been discovered. We believed there was nothing that we could add, that all the seminal research had already been completed, and the major theories had already been devised. This was a time when basically there were three schools of thought fighting it out between them, when computers the size of buildings were programmed through punch cards that we had to hand through windows to technicians wearing white lab coats. It was also the Golden Years of therapy when people had insurance that paid 90% of whatever you charged, no lifetime limit. It was a time when "good" therapy took years of intensive treatment.

Needless to say, it is a very different world with regard to not only technology but also to the practice of therapy. Newcomers to the field still believe that most of whatever will be discovered about what we do has already been done, that basically we are just refining and adjusting what we already know. New researchers sometimes feel discouraged because they think their job is to merely replicate studies, review the literature already completed, and perhaps tweak a few things here and there. But we would suggest that we haven't yet scratched the surface of what is yet to come. The most creative innovations in our field are still waiting for *you* to develop or discover them.

There are all kinds of impediments to being more creative in our work and our lives. Technology is certainly a gift, but also a crutch and a distraction. Memory abilities are eroding since we no longer have to rely on our brains to hold on to critical information. Training programs are becoming more regimented, more reliant on technological aids, and more focused on behavioral skills rather than ways of thinking or being. In addition, we are more accountable than ever for what we do and where and how we do it, and are expected to document carefully the choices we made and support them with evidence.

What we have learned about creativity in the past years, talking to the most innovative practitioners on the planet, is that this ability, this process, results from curiosity—not just about what we think we already know, but what we don't know. This takes a certain amount of courage given the pressure we feel to explain ourselves to everyone—to our clients, to their parents and families, to colleagues, to supervisors and administrators, to auditors, examiners, and licensing boards. It simply isn't acceptable to admit that we don't understand what's going on even though that is usually our default position if we are really honest. It isn't that master therapists know more than everyone else; it is that they are clearer when they are delving into territory. Yes, at times that is unnerving if not terrifying, but that is when the real action takes place when we have the opportunity to create something that has never been done before.

CHAPTER 14

PROMOTING SOCIAL
INTEREST AND ADVOCACY

True master therapists commit their work and lives to causes that go far beyond the welfare of their own clients. They not only feel a greater responsibility to those who have been marginalized and neglected, but they *act* on these principles—and do so consistently over time: They don't just talk about social justice issues but devote their lives to making a difference, whether in their own communities or on a global scale.

No matter where and how we were raised, or whatever our cultural or spiritual connections, we have heard that it is better to give than to receive. There is even a mountain of empirical evidence to support that altruism and selfless giving to others increases our lifespan, prevents sickness, reduces chronic pain, provides greater meaning to life, and creates a "helper's high" from a flood of vasopressin and oxytocin. Regardless of your background, there is a universal message among most religious traditions to help those who are most disadvantaged. Many studies support that this deep concern or caring for others is at the heart of being mentally healthy. It certainly helps bond a community for common good.

There are very few people who don't agree with this life principle, at least in terms of espoused values. Some give a few dollars now and then when a fire, hurricane, or some other disaster occurs; others may selectively volunteer their time. Yet throughout most Western cultures there is a marked emphasis on *self*-esteem rather than *other*-esteem. We tend to reach out to others when it is convenient or there is some payoff, whether a tax write-off, community status, padded resume, or a ticket to heaven.

Common sense might suggest that therapists would be more involved in selfless service than the general public; after all, that was supposed to be a strong motive for getting into the field. And indeed we talk a good game. We all endorse professional codes that take a stand for social justice. We wear wristbands or badges or post messages on social media, proclaiming our support for a cause dear to our hearts. We dutifully include issues related to diversity or multiculturalism or advocacy in our conference programs. We talk a lot about the need for greater equity in the world and in our communities. But let's be honest, *really* honest: Very few among us actually practice what we preach on a daily basis. We read stories in our professional newsletters of the token efforts that a few therapists devote to some cause, without any long-term, sustained, or meaningful impact. Yet the key feature of significant social action is *follow-through*—continuing efforts over a period of time so as to build meaningful relationships, provide adequate support, and conduct evaluations to measure results and make needed adjustments that make programs even more responsive.

Who Has Time for This?

There's a whole lot of discussion about advocacy and social justice in the various fields of professional psychotherapy. Our various ethical codes mandate such service, just as our professional conferences focus on these areas as prominent themes. Journals, newsletters, social media, and Listservs discuss the importance of service and the responsibility we have to help those who are underserved or marginalized. And yet many times we've all begun service projects with the best of intentions but have eventually lost interest or momentum, diverted by other needs or responsibilities.

There are clearly realistic demands placed on our daily lives. We have to serve our own clients and take care of the business of our "day jobs," including all the paperwork, meetings, and administrative tasks. We have to earn a living and support families. In these challenging economic times, we are working harder than ever just to maintain our own standards of living. In addition, we struggle to navigate the complex problems and political conflicts of our work settings. We have to maintain our licenses and complete continuing education units, not to mention taking care of ourselves to remain vibrant and passionate about our work. We work to improve our expertise and competence, also monitoring the outcomes of our interventions. We mentor less experienced practitioners, supervise the work of others, and try as hard as we can to stay on top of the latest developments. Then we have commitments at home and within our personal lives to repair or nourish our own neglected relationships and maybe even to pursue a hobby or personal interest.

Who really has time to get involved in one other project or commitment, especially one that would require ongoing time and energy with minimal or no compensation?

Sure, we can take pro bono cases and adjust our fees to serve economically disadvantaged people who need our help, but we're talking about issues that led us into this field in the first place—to change the world, or at least a small part of it within our purview. Most of us entered the therapy profession in the first place because we wanted to make a difference, a *big* difference, especially with those who are most neglected.

Real Master Therapists in Action

It is lonely, exhausting, and frustrating being involved in service or advocacy projects on an ongoing basis. Operating in unfamiliar cultures, we often feel lost much of the time, unclear about the rules and norms, much less the effects of our effort. There are almost always political squabbles, limited resources, and organization dysfunction. For those operating in "foreign lands," there is the added strain of physical hardships and hidden agendas we will never understand.

We have been actively involved in service projects most of our professional lives. Most of the projects ran their course; some failed, but not through lack of effort. There are just so many distractions that command our time, so many commitments to honor. When we attempt to prioritize, it's easy to create excuses why our attention must be directed elsewhere. A lot of the time we feel discouraged, unappreciated, and overwhelmed.

Like most projects we undertake together, we decided that one way to sustain ourselves would be to investigate what others are doing successfully and how they manage to keep going even with all the obstacles and challenges. We thought it would be interesting, if not affirming, to identify therapists who have been involved in extraordinary service and gone *far* beyond token gestures, or even single, dramatic initiatives, to launch ongoing projects that have become major priorities in their lives. Our intention was to profile individuals, already overburdened with responsibilities and commitments, who began social justice and advocacy programs that took on a life of their own. Whether locally, or on a global scale, these professionals are models of what is possible—even with all the other responsibilities tugging at our consciences and pocketbooks.

JK I can barely catch my breath. For the past half hour we have been snaking our way up a narrow trail leading to a stupa, a Buddhist shrine, perched high over a Himalayan village. I turn and look downward, noticing with relief that I'm not the only one who stopped to rest: There are 55 girls strung out behind and ahead of me, the youngest 10 years old and the eldest in her late teens. They have all been transported here from their villages across Nepal, each of them supported by a scholarship to keep them in school.

It was never my intention to end up spending so much of my life in this part of the world. Sometimes we don't choose our paths—they choose us. It has been 15 years since I first fell into this project, identifying and supporting lower caste girls who are at greatest risk to be forced into early marriage or sex slavery. The project began by helping one academically gifted 12-year-old girl who was being kept out of school and was in danger of "disappearing." With the assistance of hundreds of colleagues, students, friends, family members, and volunteers, we now support over 250 girls in more than a dozen villages around the country. And it all began with one impulsive gesture that had far-reaching consequences and responsibilities that had never been anticipated.

I could have started a similar project anywhere, with any group of people who are being neglected, abandoned, or marginalized. There are so many people in our own community who need help, so many people around the world, it's hard to know where to begin. And it's not like I already need one more job in my life, one more obligation. Yet with all the good deeds that I attempt, all the services I provide, all the help that I offer, everything else pales in comparison to the meaning and satisfaction I derive during my volunteer work in the field. It feels challenging to take anything else in my life very seriously.

Over the years, we have spoken to dozens of therapists who have started their own projects or jumped on board organizations that are committed to service beyond their paid employment. Those in our profession may not be trained in how to run such groups with respect to budgeting, administration, political negotiations, fundraising, and so on, but what we lack in this background we more than make up in our relational skills.

So we decided we'd investigate those within our field who are not only doing good, but doing so in creative ways, using their talents as master therapists to rethink the way community activism could take place. We find so much inspiration and encouragement finding out about the work that others are doing. We feel such comfort and validation knowing that we're not the only ones who feel so over our heads, so inadequate and ill prepared, to do the kind of job that people deserve. We want to mention just a few of the stories from therapists that we collected, along with Jon's son, Matt.

Fred Bemak and Rita Chung had been sitting in a conference presentation one day with endless discussion about making a difference on a larger scale, but with almost no sustained action. They decided in that moment that they'd heard quite enough, walked out, and launched "Counselors Across Borders" in order to help with trauma issues after catastrophic events and natural disasters around the world. They have led groups to assist traumatized survivors from hurricanes, tsunamis, forest fires, floods, and civil wars. They have traveled to Myanmar, Mississippi, India, Native American reservations, towns along the Mexican border, and Uganda, to mention a few.

Cirecie West-Olatunji recruited some of her students and supervisees to begin a community engagement project in New Orleans, before Hurricane Katrina brought so much attention to the poverty and neglect in certain areas. She worked to conduct community needs assessment, improve public housing, disaster counseling after the hurricane, and substance abuse counseling. She has since expanded her efforts to global outreach projects in Haiti and Southern Africa.

Gerald Monk secured large grants to address issues of poverty in a multiethnic community in San Diego. Enlisting the help of students, faculty, and family therapy practitioners; law enforcement; school officials; community leaders; and local politicians, he put together a consortium to address issues of violence, homelessness, substance abuse, immigrant enculturation, and interethnic conflicts. Consistent with the reality-based challenges of such efforts, Gerald eventually had to turn the project over to others because of health and stress problems he developed as a result of the work.

Selma Yznaga started the Buena Vida Community Project in Brownsville, Texas, when it was brought to her attention that two thirds of the residents were living below the poverty line.

Having faced discrimination, humiliation, and abuse as a child, she was determined to improve the quality of life for a largely immigrant community that had all been ignored. She also learned how clueless she was about the culture within the inner city even though she had identified with many of the women as a fellow Latina.

Sharon Bethea has devoted a lot of her discretionary time working with families in inner-city neighborhoods, developing an "African-centered" social justice counseling model that could be applied to a variety of communities with at-risk youth. She expanded her interests to develop mother–infant care programs for female prison inmates and summer youth programs.

Jamila Codrington has specialized in working with African-descended women, focusing on issues that resonate with her own personal history growing up in a community with rampant street violence and poverty, yet also incredibly rich artistic and creative expression. She has focused, in particular, on health problems and violence in African American communities.

Kathyrn Norsworthy collaborated with a colleague in Thailand to develop the Women's Partnership for Peace and Justice, an organization that works to empower women in Thailand and Myanmar, especially refugees who have fled for political asylum. Perhaps more than any of the other interviews, this project highlights the critical nature of respectful and caring collaboration between team members, especially with such different cultural values.

The work of these professionals, and so many others, is relatively unknown within our larger professional community. The folks who get the attention are those who publish their books, appear on talk shows, and present to huge audiences. And, as we mentioned earlier, most master therapists practice in relative obscurity, uninterested in attention except to recruit more volunteers to their projects. Perhaps it leads to a new definition of a master therapist, one in which it is required that their work has gone unheralded.

JC I have been involved with a variety of professional service projects and activities, and they have sustained me throughout my career and life. I have juggled a number of different work responsibilities outside of seeing dozens of clients each week, volunteering in an elementary school, consulting on indigent cases for the court, working on projects in my local community, but nothing has been more meaningful than my work in Thailand during the past decade.

Like Jeffrey's experience in Nepal described earlier, I never intended to get so involved in this particular service project, but rather initially just accepted an invitation to do a workshop that has since expanded to a whole movement promoting parent education. I keep returning to Thailand each year, expanding the reach of our work, to include training in substance abuse, family disintegration, and working with victims of natural disasters, including the tsunami that destroyed so many lives.

While I'm doing this work to feed the urge to make a difference on a greater scale beyond my own community, I am also doing so to stretch myself in new ways. I don't speak Thai, nor do I understand many of the different cultural habits. To complicate matters, I find myself working in areas for which I've received very little training. We have created a community among my Thai colleagues to work together to deal with problems that would otherwise never be addressed.

Although we would plan all year for the next year's programs, things seldom turn out as planned. New problems take precedence over the older ones that were prepared for. I laugh at this because it so reminds me of what happens in therapy when I prepare some agenda or set of interventions for a given client and then discover that he or she has moved on to something else the next week. Likewise, it seemed the more I planned ahead of time for what I thought I'd encounter, the more I would miss the mark. I would bring films and training materials to teach a myriad of mental health skills and interventions, but they were seldom appropriate to the situation and culture at hand; there was always something lost in the translation. We would spend long hours talking, and I would show concern and caring and provide whatever I could to help the Thai people with so many incredible burdens. Most of the training sessions turned into live counseling sessions in front of crowds of professionals and citizens who wanted to learn the skills of listening. Since then, a corps of participants have taken part in these trainings every year, and it has been amazing to watch them grow in confidence and competence.

I remember one woman who appeared psychotic, hallucinating and babbling. She wanted to talk about the voices she heard inside her head and was frustrated because nobody, especially her children, would listen to her. I tried to listen to her very, very attentively, to honor her in the best way that I could. Another woman had lost her worldly possessions and was living on the street. Again, I saw my role primarily to be as present for her as possible since most of the time she felt invisible.

When I would do demonstrations, the audience would watch and ask questions about the counseling sessions, as well as volunteer to help their neighbors and friends with whatever was troubling them. I learned that the main work took place not during my conversations with the individuals but afterward, when others within the community would lend assistance and follow up. Lines of people would form as word spread in the various communities that they could get some free help.

I had no idea how to treat these problems. Many of them could not be repaired, but we could be present for them and validate their concerns while publicly identifying some of their strengths and providing hope where none existed.

One ongoing project has touched my heart. As we traveled around the country, many people described how the Thai family was disintegrating as the children were leaving their ancestral homes in the "country" and moving to Bangkok and other urban centers. The adults described the frustrations with anger, feeling abandoned by their children, as it was a mainstay of the culture to stay in the community where you were raised. This movement is not unique to Thailand; however, there was no model or method for helping parents and children to grow and launch children in a healthy fashion. Families were being torn apart as changes to transgenerational cultural patterns were taking place.

Working collaboratively with many social service experts and organizations, we developed a project that best represents sustainability. Parents and teachers from each province were solicited to teach parenting skills in their communities. These democratic parenting skills allowed parents to learn problem solving, encouragement, decision making, discipline, and communication.

Many people were involved as they learned how to lead a parent education group and then they trained others in their province in order to make it possible to reach the entire community. All of this was accomplished without funds or payment. Training, translation, and printing were completed with the social interest and concern of many people and organizations.

When I was dying in the hospital, told I had only a few months left to live, my mind and spirit continually cycled back to Thailand. It has become my second home, where I have made many dear friends whom I now include as part of my family. Talk about sustenance—one of the things that supported me most as I lay in that hospital bed were all the prayers of healing I received from so many Thai people, many of them complete strangers. For me, what goes around comes around.

Consistent Themes Related to Advocacy Efforts

Of course, we could go on and on with a list of other dedicated professionals who have taken on roles as *citizen therapists*. As we've reviewed these reports from those who have been working on projects for some time, several themes have emerged:

1. Find a cause dear to your heart, one that involves both personal passion and professional interest.
2. Recruit like-minded individuals to join the mission, providing mutual support, collaboration, and added resources.
3. Immerse yourself in the culture of the target population, bringing humility and a position of "not knowing" into the context, deferring to elders and clients as experts on their own experience just as we would do in therapy.

4. Adjust, adapt, and invent what we know as therapists to other helping contexts in local and global communities.
5. Start a project that you are willing to sustain over time, building ongoing relationships that will make the efforts endure over time.
6. Think *way* outside of the box of what is possible and the best way to do things.

Regarding the last point, so many nongovernmental organizations, charities, and service projects fail to deliver on their promises because of limited ideas about the way things should operate. They are often top-down organizations that throw money at problems, but without relationship-oriented interventions and collaborations. In Nepal, for example, 80% of the foundations and charities don't actually deliver *any* service or distribute *any* money! The staff members take salaries and expenses, spending *all* their funds on overhead. Corruption is rampant. Tribal affiliations often sabotage efforts to reach beyond one ethnic or caste group. It takes extraordinary creativity, sensitivity, and patience to navigate through this maze of difficulties. It's a good thing that therapists are so well prepared to deal with situations like this—it's what we do for a living but on a much smaller scale and different context.

One final theme that resonated with the stories we've collected about the master therapists who make advocacy and social justice a major priority in their lives: They do it for intensely personal motives, as well as for altruistic reasons. Sometimes the choice is related to opportunity, but more often it involves close connections to our own unresolved issues or early experiences.

Let's Be Honest, Really Honest

We will try to own our personal motives for giving away so much of our time, energy, money, and resources being involved in service projects. This is more than a little difficult to admit, but a lot of the motivation is completely unrelated to helping others and saving the world as much as it involves trying to save ourselves.

Perhaps like many of you, we became therapists in the first place because we suffered a lot early in life; we are doing our best to translate those experiences into something useful that might help others. We've felt worthless and incompetent during parts of our lives (why else would we work so hard for achievement?), so we've felt best about ourselves when we are doing something useful for others. This is even better when we can figure out some way to stave off death, that is, pursue immortality, by living forever in the lives of those we help.

So why don't we just remain content with the clients we help in therapy? Our hearts pound when we admit it doesn't make us feel special enough: Any decent therapist can do that. We want to reach out to those whom nobody would ever think of helping—if we don't do this work, nobody else will. We could easily work within our own community, where there are so many important things to do, but we hunger for the exotic. We thrive on new stimulation and challenges, all the while we sometimes complain about how difficult and annoying the work can be. We feel better about ourselves when we encounter people who have so much less—and we're talking about children in the Himalayas or rural Thailand who don't even have shoes! When we return from the field, we feel this ecstatic transformation, which, unfortunately, lasts only a few months before we feel our familiar materialistic, ambitious stirrings once again. We like that when we're working in such difficult, challenging, overwhelming situations, we can forget about ourselves and our own troubles.

We could go on and on about feeling smug and superior, feeling like a martyr, escaping from the mundane aspects of our lives, hiding from issues we'd rather avoid, having an excuse to travel, and having access to the forbidden or exotic that few outsiders have ever witnessed. But most of all, we so hunger for the intimacy and caring we experience with our team members, the grandparenting role we enjoy with the hundreds of children, and the close relationships that develop over time. It is so much fun to commiserate with our team members about the difficulties we faced, bitch and moan about the annoyances we encounter (squat toilets, limited food choices, armed Maoist rebels, Bangkok or Kathmandu traffic jams, fuel and electricity shortages, garbage strikes, incomprehensible cultural rituals). We love what we learn about the world—and what we learn about ourselves.

We promised to be honest, so we are obligated to take the last point back. It actually hurts like hell to learn difficult things about ourselves and confront our foibles and limitations. We actually quite hate that, as do our clients: We feel grateful only after we return to the comfort and familiarity of home.

Where were we? Oh yeah, we were talking about the most personal reasons why we remain involved in service with the sacrifices we make and dear price we pay. We like to be in charge. We like to have the freedom to make things up with our team members, invent new interventions and rituals, use what we know and understand as therapists, and apply these ideas to larger social problems. Frankly, we've sometimes been bored by the routines of doing therapy, just as we have every decade in a predictable cycle. Unless we change the way we do things—where and how we operate—we become bored with ourselves, tired of the same old stories we hear ourselves repeat. So we keep trying to reinvent ourselves, not so much to improve our effectiveness as to entertain ourselves. We just crave creative expression and opportunities to do things differently than we've ever encountered before.

Finally, we've been frustrated our whole professional lives about how challenging it is to not always see measureable results with our clients. They lie about their progress. They sometimes don't return and we don't know what happened. The clients who need help the most, with intractable, chronic problems, often take a long time to see dramatic results. We love that we can work on a project in which it takes so little money and effort to actually save and change people's lives!

So there you have it—our confession. We've spent most of our writing career, and dozens of books, writing about reciprocal influence in therapy—how our clients change us as much as we change them. We've been fascinated by the "gifts" that our clients offer us. We love the fact that we've chosen a profession that allows us to learn so much—requires us to grow so much—every day. And yet as great as those benefits are, we find them magnified tenfold when working in the field. We even like the idea that we're *not* being paid for our efforts—that it is truly an act of love.

Full Circle

Until now much of our discussion on becoming a master therapist has focused on the therapist and his or her inner characteristics— the ways they understand things, remain present, model and learn from others, and supply creative solutions to life's challenges. Like all stages of development, whether they involve social, emotional, or moral growth, the progress moves from the focus on the self to the focus on others and the larger world in which we live. Master therapists begin the journey with the focus on being the best individual, couples, family, and/or group therapists and find that when they reach that goal, they continue to use this knowledge and amazing skill toward the betterment of the world or their local community.

JK After writing this chapter, I started to feel uncomfortable, even a bit guilty, because I talk a good game and advocate so passionately about taking action within marginalized groups outside of our usual professional settings. But what have I done lately?

This started to eat away at me, especially after giving a lecture to a group of students who asked what they could do to help. I kind of shrugged and provided an evasive response, something along the lines that each of us has to find our own path. I fully realized as I was saying this that I was just giving a pat answer. The student looked puzzled and walked away. But it got me thinking about what I could do *right now*.

I spent the past few weekends working and staying at a homeless shelter on Skid Row. I like to think that I've seen and done it all, but I wasn't prepared to digest the power of the stories I heard from the residents. To be honest, it scared the crap out of me, not because of any fear of personal safety but because I realized how easy it could be for any of us to end up in a similar predicament.

Sure, I provided some counseling assistance. I passed out food. I brought young people with me to talk to those living on the street and supply some meager support. But anything we did to be helpful seemed to pale in comparison to what I learned about myself and others. Given the kinds of tragic stories I hear in therapy sessions, or in lands far, far away, I think there is very little that could ever surprise or shock me. Yet sometimes it is my own arrogance or even good intentions that trip me up.

We had organized a food distribution in the streets that were lined with people sleeping or passed out on the sidewalk, smoking crack, conducting nefarious business transactions involving sex, drugs, or gang enforcement. I had led my group of volunteers into a park to distribute fruit and snacks, most of which were politely or angrily declined, which I found a bit perplexing. It was only later that I learned from a police officer who patrols the area that most of the people in that park are not homeless but rather represent a drug cartel, and that is where their dealers congregate to drop off their money. The experience just reminded me of how clueless I can be, even with the best of motives, how sometimes the help that we offer is more to appease a guilty conscience than it is to really make much of a difference.

It isn't necessary to travel very far in order for us to reach out to others who would never choose to visit us in our offices. The homeless, the chronically mentally ill, those within immigrant communities, those who live in isolated or rural areas, and those who live in poverty or neglect would often never consider therapy as an option for their troubles. It turns out that the people who truly need help the most would rarely ever choose to see us, which means that we have to go to *them*.

CHAPTER 15

BEING A WORK IN PROGRESS

We never, ever "arrive" at being a master therapist, that is, a model of perfection; rather, we spend our lives striving to get as close as we can to that ideal. As our journey comes to a close, we revisit once again the central theme of this conversation with you: the unique role and opportunity we have to live what we teach to others.

We have found it difficult to separate the different professional roles we occupy as therapists, teachers, supervisors, administrators, and authors, just as we haven't been able to do so between our personal and professional lives. We always thought it was the biggest gift of our field that we could use everything we learned in our jobs to make ourselves more personally effective. Likewise, we have been big fans of life experiences (especially travel to foreign lands) as a better teacher than anything found in books or formal workshops.

Even though we plead guilty to being more responsible than most for contributing to the glut of books on the market, we've learned a heck of a lot more from other sources. Our secret confession is that we find most counseling and therapy books to be boring, repetitive, and without soul. They may inform us but they don't *move* us; they don't touch our hearts. Of course, we can say this now, we suppose, because we spent the first decades of our careers reading as many books in the field as we could.

What we mean to say by all this is that we are interested in *everything*. Being therapists made us that way. Every client has a different story to tell, a different world for us to explore. And we keep learning so much during this process that the curiosity becomes insatiable.

A Voracious Curiosity

We think that master practitioners must show a certain amount of courage to face things that others would prefer to avoid. We've always been interested in the *experience* of being a therapist, what it means for our lives, and how and why we process the things we do. This has never been just a job to us, but a calling, one that requires devotion and commitment to learning in all domains of life.

It is the taboo and forbidden that fascinate us, the things that most people don't talk about. These are the secrets of the profession that were rarely discussed in school or among colleagues: How is it possible that therapy can be effective when we appear to operate in such different ways? How can we pretend to understand a phenomenon of how change occurs when the complexity and multidimensionality are so complex? How do we live with our fallibility and imperfections, even feeling like a fraud? How can we ask our clients to do things that we don't do in our own lives? How can we actually help people when we are hardly listening about half the time?

We don't think it's a matter that "regular" therapists are subject to all these traps and foibles whereas so-called "masters" have them all together. Rather, we think that what separates ordinary from extraordinary practitioners is that the latter are willing to demonstrate a high degree of honesty in their self-reflections, as well as their interactions with others. We've already talked about that at length.

It is also easy to slide into complacency, to tell the same old stories over and over, employ the most familiar and time-tested interventions, and operate on autopilot, hearing ourselves repeat the same admonishments, give the same advice, and follow the same paths that lead to salvation. It is easy to become a technician, especially if you practice a style that emphasizes technique over relational engagement.

We feel like such hypocrites sometimes when we tell our clients or our students that if they really want to achieve a certain excellence in their lives, they must take risks and do what is most difficult; they must get outside their comfort zones and take risks that challenge them. We hear these words come out of our mouths, watch clients nod in terrified agreement, and think to ourselves: What have *we* done lately?

It is questions like this that have led us to become addicts to change. We just can't sit there and listen to our clients report all these exciting things they are doing in their lives, watching them transform themselves while we sit back as passive observers. We feel envious. We feel left behind.

Every few years we've got to change something significant in the ways we work and live. We've been through almost every major school of therapy, not because we found any one of them inadequate (which they are) but because we were bored with the same old routines. We've walked away from comfortable jobs just because we didn't feel like we were learning much new. We have lived in a dozen places around the world to satisfy our hunger for new stimulation that comes with immersion in a different culture.

All this might sound fun and interesting, but it is truly exhausting. It is hard to abandon what is most familiar in order to experiment with new ways of being that might prove more useful— or at least interesting. That is why our clients are so resistant to change as well; on some level, it is terrifying to face the unknown.

Each of us is a work in progress. And one area where we often fall short is in our narrow focus and parochial views of how change takes place. Whereas nowadays therapy training programs emphasize particular and limited professional identities (e.g., "I'm a clinical social worker," "counseling psychologist," "family therapist," "mental health counselor," "forensic psychiatrist," "substance abuse worker") and theoretical identities, our earliest heroes studied widely in a wide variety of disciplines, reading philosophy, medicine, literature, and humanities, as well as the social sciences.

Bob Wubbolding, a major figure in reality therapy, believes that much of his expertise and sense of competence comes from his commitment to reading widely, way beyond the therapy literature. "For example, I am currently reading a book on 17th-century French politics and foreign policy. I believe that pursuing a broad interest creates more innovative and effective clinical work. The most influential author for me is Teilhard de Chardin, the French anthropologist and theologian. He believed, as I do, that the world is evolving toward a *pleroma* or fullness. Each human act contributes to this grand evolution and therefore does not cease to exist when it is completed."

Wubbolding finds that other interests have permitted him to associate with a variety of professionals for all kinds of backgrounds and cultures: "I worked in political campaigns for local and congressional candidates. I functioned as a Catholic priest after nine years in the seminary where I studied philosophy, theology, history, and other subjects. During that time I encountered people at their deepest level of need: their spiritual search."

Wubbolding has followed a similar trajectory of voracious curiosity about all kinds of subjects, even though he is so strongly identified with one therapeutic approach. Somewhat unique to those who hold a strong affiliation with a single theory, he sees it as an open system continuing to evolve rather than a closed doctrinaire. "Many years ago a theologian made a statement that has impacted my life on a daily basis: 'Never miss a chance to teach.' I believe I have attempted to implement this without an attitude of righteousness. Of course, implementing this injunction implies having something to teach." That's not as easy as it sounds if this means truly staying current on research and trends in the field, as well as evaluating their appropriateness.

Confronting Despair Versus Hope

If there is one thing that therapists must confront on a daily basis, it is the sense of hopelessness that clients bring to sessions. Whether depressed, anxious, lost, or frustrated, people come to us in the first place because they can't find a way out of their struggles. Furthermore, they don't honestly believe that anyone else can help them either. Therapy often represents a last desperate chance before all hope is surrendered.

It is a paradox that while despair springs from an absence of hope, it is also the consequence of reaching for expectations that are beyond one's grasp. The British novelist Graham Greene claimed that despair is the price we all pay for setting grandiose goals. It is, he writes, "the unforgivable sin," but one that could never be practiced by someone who is corrupt or evil; such individuals always embrace hope. "He never reaches the freezing point of knowing absolute failure. Only the man of good will carries always in his heart this capacity for damnation."

Hope and despair are a therapist's constant companions. The price we pay for our optimism, our hope for the future, and our belief in our own powers to help others is that we must also live with the limits, disappointment, and failures of our best efforts. We must maintain optimism even as we recognize the depths of our own sense of discouragement. Clients find this incredibly annoying at times, not to mention unrealistic. We are selling them hope when they want us to join them in their misery, or at least admit that they are entitled to it.

Therapists are virtually required to keep a smile on our faces. Everything we understand about the way therapy works is that if we can convince clients that what we have to offer them is useful, and we believe this, then they will more likely respond to our interventions. The placebo effect is all about capitalizing on these positive expectations.

Yet in the privacy of our own minds and hearts resides an assortment of doubts. Do we really make a difference in anyone's life? Do the effects really last? What sort of impact can we really have on people who are wracked with such intractable, chronic problems?

And what can we do for those who will never really recover from traumas, illness, or disorders from which they suffer?

One answer is that we believe our own myths and illusions that we present to others. We deny our own sense of despair, disown our failures, and pretend as if we have everything fully under control. We believe our lies when we tell clients that everything will be fine, that we have the answers, that we can cure their suffering or relieve their pain. Oh, we reassure our colleagues and supervisors that we understand our limits and acknowledge our failings. But deep down inside we really do want to save people; on a good day, we actually believe this is possible.

And what of our personal despair, that which emanates from our own disappointments and failures? Apart from anything depressing that our clients bring us, we each have our own demons. Some of us suffer from chronic depression, and all of us from the kind of existential angst that comes with being alive. Let's face it: As therapists, there is no place to hide.

Every day, we must square off against precisely those same issues that terrify us the most—the fears of mediocrity, of failure, loneliness, meaninglessness, losing control, being responsible. Countertransference doesn't begin to cover the territory: We must live now only with our despair but also shoulder the burdens of all those who come to us for help.

A client confesses she has no reason to live, and a part of you agrees with her. You wonder if she will ever experience anything resembling happiness or even numbness. Another client suffers from a chronic disease for which there is no cure; you are only applying psychological compresses to ease a bit of the pressure. Another has been so traumatized by a host of early experiences that you have serious doubts about whether you can put a dent in what is needed.

There are those who come for the most pedestrian of reasons: to lose a few pounds, quit smoking, find another job, make a life decision, recover from a lost love, or stop drinking so much. Sure, the success rate in our work seems pretty high, approaching 8 in 10 among those who seek our services. But during moments of our own despair, we wonder whether these changes really matter much to the person, much less to the rest of the world.

How can you *not* feel despair when looking at the poverty, the starving, the oppressed and abused, the indigent in the world? How can you ever feel satisfied with the small efforts we make when confronting how much there is to do? How can you avoid despair when spending your working days with people who are miserable, conflicted, fragmented, dissatisfied, depressed, despondent, addicted, suicidal, sometimes even actively hallucinating?

Yeah, yeah, we know: You've had enough of this already. You're ready to skip this section and move on to the next one. So are we. And yet . . . there's something powerful to be acknowledged, even honored, in despair. Clearly, despair has been a neglected, taboo subject in our field, but it is one that is surely confronted by the masters. Certainly, there is plenty written about depression, but almost nothing about the more amorphous, intangible, desolate, intractable despondency. There have been a few books on the subject related to the practice of therapy, but most of the major contributions have been written by the likes of Mark Twain, Albert Camus, Jean-Paul Sartre, and those with an existential bent.

Despair, writes another English novelist, George Eliot, is "the painful eagerness of unfed hope." There can be no despair without yearning, without thoughts for the future. This point is only too obvious when attending any conference or gathering of therapists. In any staff room or meeting, you hear tales of discouragement and disillusionment, of desperate searches for the latest therapeutic technique or magic cure.

Therapists complain that managed care has taken the pleasure out of their work, or at the very least, robbed them of choices. There is too much paperwork and too little control. More and more clients want instant cures, if not from our efforts, then medications or some supposed technological breakthrough. "They just don't want to take responsibility for their own change," one therapist complains. "We are working with a generation of whining narcissists."

An undercurrent of this dialogue is the ripple of therapists in despair. This discussion gives voice to the many forms of despair that therapists may experience. By mirroring the reality of what many therapists may feel, there can be a collective sigh of relief that we are not alone. Despair is part of what we do; it may even be an asset to our work when transformed to heighten our empathic powers.

Our aim is to end our journey together on the most realistic note possible, even if this last discussion has been a bit depressing. As we draw to a close, let's review some of the things we've learned about what has been most and least helpful to those who have achieved some degree of excellence in their therapeutic work.

What Has Been Most Helpful Along the Way

Based on our interviews with master therapists, as well as our own experiences and review of the literature on the subject, this is what we've found has been most likely to contribute to mastery in our profession. Some of these conclusions are congruent with research conducted during the past few decades while others represent our own observations.

Sitting in the Client's Chair

We became therapists because we had such amazing experiences as clients. We couldn't believe that people actually get paid to do this work. We also became teachers and authors for parallel but different reasons: because we were so dissatisfied with the options that had been presented to us and so yearned for something quite different.

We wanted to become the kind of therapists and teachers and writers who spoke directly to people's hearts and souls, not just to their minds. We didn't just want to talk to people; we wanted to help them create direct experiences. And most of what we know and understand and do as therapists, we learned from sitting in the other chair, appreciating what worked best and least. This was especially true when participating in therapy groups, where we could watch carefully the impact of each person's behavior—including our own—and get such honest feedback afterwards.

Sitting at the Feet of Our Mentors

Each of us has been systematic and strategic in identifying mentors who had what we wanted in terms of their skills, expertise, confidence, and personal mastery. We sought them out and followed them around, so to speak. We discovered early in our careers that almost anyone is accessible if you can initiate contact in a respectful way. And it takes considerable courage and persistence to go after what you want most.

Over the years, we have internalized the best of our teachers and supervisors, while discarding aspects of their style that either didn't fit or didn't seem appropriate. It was a seminal breakthrough when we realized that our mentors were hardly perfect and that is what allowed us to critically evaluate what worked best for us and what didn't have much value.

Finding Our Own Voice

A few of our early mentors were so charismatic, so influential, and powerful in our lives that we tried our best to be just like them. We embraced their values and learned their style. We imitated their behavior. We became a junior version of them and, in so doing, lost ourselves (at least for a while).

During our first decade of practice we could constantly hear the voices of our teachers and mentors echoing in our heads, scolding us, reassuring us, advising us about what to do and how to be. As grateful as we were for this wisdom and guidance, eventually we rediscovered our own voice as distinct and separate from others. We actually reentered therapy for this process, initially going through a rebellious phase rejecting the past before we could refashion a new version of ourselves as a professional who had their own unique beliefs and style. This ongoing evolution is so important to us that by the time we publish anything we write (including this!) we've moved on to something else that is just as interesting.

Listening to Our Clients—Carefully, Very Carefully

It isn't just impatience or boredom that led us to change so often what we are doing, and how we are doing it. Our clients have been our most informative teachers about what works best for them. This realization is only useful to the extent we are paying close attention to their reactions.

We have worked in so many settings, in so many countries and communities, with so many different populations, using such a variety of interventions and levels of engagement, that we have learned to empty ourselves as much as we can before entering a new domain. But what we do know that helps make us most effective is paying attention, such close attention, to our audience. We prepare compulsively, do our homework, anticipate scenarios, formulate goals and desired outcomes, and then usually realize that this was mostly to appease our own anxiety rather than because the actual plan is workable.

Becoming a Voracious Reader

As we mentioned before, whereas once upon a time we devoured books about therapy, we eventually moved far outside that realm.

Because our early author mentors like Sigmund Freud, William James, Victor Frankl, Alfred Adler, and Rollo May found so much value in philosophy, fiction, and the sciences, it inspired us to read widely in our studies. It is stories that have always inspired us, and that is why we make them such an essential part of what we do in our work—help people to tell their stories, share the stories we've heard, and dive deep into the meanings and lessons of these narratives.

One of the original attractions of this field that is so unlike other professions is that *everything* that we read, view, hear, sense, and experience helps us to become more worldly and wise, more knowledgeable about human experience in all its forms and manifestations. There is also some impressive research that reading fiction is far more influential and impactful because of the ways we are willing to suspend disbelief and criticism in order to immerse ourselves completely into the story. Such vicarious experiences provide us with opportunities to try on different roles and live in other worlds, all without the leaving the comfort of a chair.

Living What We Teach, Teaching What We Live

As we've said frequently as the major theme of this book, one of our greatest fears was being seen (or seeing ourselves) as hypocrites. This motivated us to constantly challenge ourselves to take new risks, experiment with new things, and move beyond complacency. We *hate* hearing ourselves talk about things that we haven't yet lived. We feel so uncomfortable telling people to do things that we don't do in our own lives. We love—and hate—the feeling after a session when we realize that we've just talked about some issue that we haven't yet resolved. We love the permission we feel, the *urgency*, to push ourselves beyond what is comfortable so that we can grow in ways that are similar to what we advocate for others.

Living and Working in Other Cultures

We have spent a lot of time working and living in cultures that have tested our most familiar and cherished assumptions. This has helped us to develop a level of flexibility, resilience, and curiosity that makes it easy for us to begin again—over and over. In many of the places we work we can't rely on verbal language to communicate and be understood; most of our work involves gestures, touch, and play. Jeffrey took a group of students to work in an orphanage in Ghana, an English-speaking African nation, only to discover upon arrival that their clients were profoundly disabled, most of whom couldn't speak. Their work involved holding the children, hugging them, singing to them, and loving them. It is the purest work he has ever done.

As we've mentioned, it isn't necessary to travel outside of our own region, or even local community, in order to experience a different culture. It is really about getting outside our own comfort zone, pushing ourselves to expand our worldview, broadening our horizons to include more varied facets of human interests, behavior, and values. Far more impactful than any workshop we could attend, any book we would read, or any supervision session, are the ways we are challenged by living, working, or traveling into novel environments that test our flexibility and entrenched assumptions.

Reinventing Ourselves—Over and Over Again

At least every decade, if not more often, we have made radical shifts in our job, professional identity, and career focus. This has provided a breadth of experience for us in a dozen different clinical and academic settings, as well as geographical and cultural contexts for our work. Jon began his career working in schools as a teacher and counselor, and then found himself teaching at the university, and then working in the community and became immersed in private practice.

He enjoyed running and the next thing he knew he was the coach of the university cross-country team and competing himself. He became interested in wellness, couples, families, teens, parenting, media, television, Eastern religion, writing, and all sorts of other things.

We have long admired those who stick with one mission, in one place, and enjoy the satisfaction that comes from sustained commitment to a cause—but that has not been our path. We are too concerned we'll miss something and so we want to see/live/experience as much as we can in a single lifetime.

Feeling Uncertain and Acknowledging Doubt

We're not being modest or playing games when we have said (and still insist) that most of the time we really don't know what we're doing (including right now). We really mean that (and feel it). It is this hesitance that protects us from becoming too attached to any idea and encourages us to keep experimenting with new ways to become more effective. We're not saying that we don't know things, and can do some things really well, it's just that we're often feeling uncertain about whether what we did was the best option at the time. We admit we spend *way* too much time reflecting on what we do, its impact and relative effectiveness. But we also think this is what makes us good at what we do: We work so damn hard at it. And we're willing to pay the price.

Really, Really, Really Wanting to Be Good at What We Do

Excellence is so important to us that motivation has never been a problem. That is one reason why much of what we do has never felt much like work but rather is so much fun. We know we are not alone in this attitude because so many other therapists we know feel so passionately about how privileged they are to be part of our special guild.

There is a lot at stake for us to achieve and maintain high standards of excellence. If we are honest, it isn't just about wanting to do the best job possible for our clients; it's also about bolstering our own self-esteem and sense of worth. We sometimes feel a degree of urgency to achieve greater excellence in our work, not as a choice but rather as an self-imposed imperative. We feel only as good as what we've done lately.

Many of the notable theorists and prominent practitioners we've interviewed over the years seem also to care a lot about their legacy. Like them, we hunger for acknowledgment and respect. There are thus often dual motives for the drive to be truly great—on the one hand to do the best job we can while serving others, and on the other hand to serve our own needs for recognition.

Remaining Fully Present

After more than a decade of studying mastery in therapy, Barry Duncan has been struck by the simplicity of one core factor. He is reminded of a story about two apprentice Zen monks who are comparing their respective masters while cleaning their temple. "The first novice proudly tells his companion about the many miracles that he has seen his famous master perform. 'I have watched,' the young novice says, 'as my master has turned an entire village to the Buddha, has made rain fall from the sky and has moved a mountain so that he could pass.'

"The other novice listens attentively, nods his head in acknowledgment, and then demonstrates his deeper understanding by responding, 'My master also does many miraculous things. When he is hungry, he eats. When he is thirsty, he drinks. When he is tired, he sleeps.'

"Like the first monk," Duncan concludes the parable, "many therapists have become too enamored with 'miracles' touted by the masters. Thousands of clients, and years of research about change, have taught me to discard the claims of the gurus and snake oil salesmen, and instead honor more simple but enduring acts: believing in clients, the power of partnership, and the ability to remain fully present. These simple but magical acts are the eating, drinking, and sleeping of effective therapy."

What Has Been Least Helpful Along the Way

If the things we just mentioned have been most instrumental in our continued growth, then we are also clear about what has gotten in our way and blocked creativity and deeper development as professionals. One of the worst "offenders" has been dense, turgid, incomprehensible books that claim to explain how therapy works. We won't mention names but our greatest inspiration to become authors came from our frustration with the works that we were forced to read. They just didn't describe our experience, and this led us to try to write as clearly and simply as we could, especially about what we felt was ignored or neglected.

We also had some models of terrible supervision. Jeffrey's first supervisor used to listen to his sessions with her ear to the wall and knock loudly when he said or did something she didn't like. Jeffrey would have to whisper conspiratorially to his clients to avoid her intrusions, which actually made for great relationships with his clients. Many of our other supervisory relationships were not safe enough for us to talk about what was really bothering us most. We had to be careful what we revealed, hide our feelings of ineptitude, and feed the supervisors what they most wanted to hear.

Staff meetings in places we have worked often take on a competitive tone in which colleagues are trying to undermine and humiliate one another. We have had the misfortune to work in places, both within academic and clinical settings, in which people were really mean to one another. We don't know why some people we've known in the field are hurtful to others they find threatening in some way, but we have always had a thin skin to tolerate that sort of behavior.

While we are on the subject of standard continuing education structures, we would be remiss if we didn't mention the status of many workshops we are required to attend to maintain licensure. It has become a game to find the easiest pathways to meet the mandated number of continuing education units, either through online programs or mind-numbing days spent trapped in conference rooms. Indeed, sometimes we do learn new and significant things to update our knowledge base, but so often the programs are boring and the presenters self-promoting. Maybe we're projecting here since we do more than our fair share of presentations but we just haven't gotten much enduring, useful stuff from formal programs. All too often, the presenters seem to be selling some idea, usually one we've heard before in other forms.

This brings up the subject of therapist narcissism—our own mostly, but also the self-inflated images that are common to others in our field. Many of us think we are so important. We are used to being in charge and fascinated by our own favorite ideas. We are critical of this trait in others because we're reluctant to admit it for ourselves. We pretend to be modest, but how can we not entertain fantasies of being special when clients sometimes treat us like godlings? The uncomfortable truth is that we sometimes do feel like we know more and understand more than most others, and this severely limits our openness to new learning.

Scott Browning, who has done a lot of research and clinical work with stepfamilies, has observed the ways that therapists get in their own way because of overconfidence: "Psychotherapy, because it is never an exact science, causes many people to feel continuously insecure. This insecurity, interestingly, may be masked as hubris. Someone may become more rigid and unwilling to adjust his or her clinical direction because of that drive to cling to what seems like the best, and possibly, only option. Or else the other common mistake is to frantically try to learn every new model with the assumption that the "real" answer is one continuing education workshop away. It is this lemming mentality that stops people from finally trusting themselves. If you are always searching, it is hard to refine what you are actually driven to do. The expert realizes that great therapy is a collaboration of multiple theories, a deep understanding of oneself, and a unshakable respect for the person seeking help."

It's About Relationships, Not Content

We suppose we could revisit almost every one of these points and talk about how each has helped or hindered us. Although we have not much enjoyed the *content* of programs, conference presentations, and workshops we've attended in recent years, we thrive on the informal interactions that take place during breaks, transitions, and other social encounters. We have always believed as workshop presenters that our main job is to do or say something stimulating, if not provocative, then put people in small groups and let them process and personalize the ideas. We can't learn much through passive learning—reading books like this, sitting in crowded, stuffy rooms, or listening to someone drone on and on for more than a half hour about almost anything, no matter how dynamic and interesting they might be.

So, whereas we don't learn as much as we could from many sessions at conferences or workshops, we learn a lot from conversations we have with old friends and new acquaintances while sitting in nooks and crannies or strolling through the hallways and streets. No surprise: It is all about relationships for us. Maybe this is true for you as well.

JC I was always more interested in all the kids in the school—what they were doing and their life stories—than the courses I took. I knew most of the kids at our large high school and still have contact with many of them although we live in different communities. I was also interested in the teachers and what their lives were like outside of the school. Maybe all of this was the beginning of my counseling apprenticeship.

I've always been one who wanted to speak up. I never could understand my friends who wondered how I could have said something. I was always wondering how they could just sit there and smile. I have challenged and confronted people my entire life. I've always been the one to tell the emperor that he didn't have any clothes on. In school I was always being shushed and told that I had to wait my turn to talk or raise my hand to talk or just plain couldn't talk—but I did it anyway. In high school my counselor was so ineffective that I started a petition to have him fired. Our school team name was the "Maroons," and I started a movement to remove the name because I had never seen a maroon. Have you? Our town and over a century of Maroon alumni were incensed.

I didn't like to write between the lines and had a hard time believing things that didn't seem right or make sense to me, especially when I would ask for clarification and frequently was told "because." I realized early in life how little many people knew and how often they were just faking it. I find many of the counseling and therapy conferences I attend to be really silly. People get up and talk about things that they really do not know much about (but wish that they did). They have slides and handouts and other interesting props to distract or entertain the participants from getting too close to realize that they really do not know much about their topic. Most of the experts practiced therapy for a very short time and, frankly, were not very good at what they did, so they chose to teach it. I know this because I was that way for a long time. I would obsess for weeks about my presentations and worried that someone would ask a question I couldn't answer and that my ignorance would be uncovered and my façade destroyed.

One day, one of the senior therapists in our counseling practice told me in a staff meeting that I didn't know what the hell I was doing after we did co-therapy together. He said I was a nice guy, had a lot of knowledge, and was a great teacher, but didn't know "shit" when it came to therapy. After my initial shock, and then defensiveness, I had to agree with him. I began to read more, went back to school, got back into intense supervision, and learned a lot that I didn't know. This guy has since died, but I was pleased to have had the chance to thank him for his honesty many years ago. Although it was not easy to hear his message, it sent me back to school. After the staff meeting when he blasted me, other colleagues discredited him and said he was a real jerk and that I shouldn't listen to him. However, I am glad that I did. Since then, I've wondered how many other people have been confronted in their careers and hated the messenger in order to avoid hearing the message?

Today, I usually attend only a few of the counseling and therapy conferences or the various professional association meetings. They are usually held at the huge convention centers where all the experts are lined up and other therapists and students are allowed to take our photos and to get our autographs. We are able to fantasize that we are pseudo rock stars. I am not sure why people want to deify famous therapists. I suppose this happens in all other fields whether it is mortuary scientists, fireworks purveyors, bass fishermen, or clowns for Jesus (yes, there really is such a group!). There seems to be something crazy about this, but we seem to be looking for someone to model, to look up to, or to lead us, someone outside of ourselves.

I have worked hard to become an expert on some things— whether it was distance running, coaching, couples therapy, or Buddhism—because I was curious and wanted to know all that I could about whatever my passion was at the moment. Like Jeffrey, I move from one area of interest to another with no larger purpose other than curiosity and the desire to make the world a better place. Okay, I also want to move myself into a better place as well.

Mastery Means Being Able to Accept Mystery

Although much of the therapist's role is devoted to meaning making and explaining things, sometimes what is required involves not so much making sense of situations but rather appreciating the eternal mystery of life. The master therapist is able to tolerate ambiguity and appreciate complexity; even more significantly, these attitudes can be taught to clients. This requires patience, presence, and confidence in the therapeutic process. Sometimes it means taking a position of not knowing everything.

JK One interesting outcome from this journey has been to examine the impact it has had on my own reflections and behavior about who I am and how I function as a person and a professional. I was recently reading a research study by Len Jennings and several colleagues on the ethical values of master therapists. Whereas there were the usual and expected outcomes that experts have higher order moral decision making, I was surprised and delighted to learn that one finding was that exceptional practitioners also have a much higher standard of respect and caring in *all* their relationships. They are more likely to demonstrate a sense of justice, compassion, and caring with anyone they encounter in their daily lives, applying the main theme of this book in that they really do practice what they preach.

At first, I felt affirmed by this result: I've been preaching this idea most of my life in almost everything I've taught and written. I've often felt alone advocating this idea that has often been ignored. I remember being influenced by the early moral development theorists like Lawrence Kohlberg, who talked about the highest level of functioning operates at a justice orientation in *every* aspect of life, not just when the meter is running. I've tried so hard to treat everyone I meet with respect and consideration and actually believe that I have mostly succeeded in this endeavor. But then I recall one line from Jennings's article in which the researchers mentioned that master therapists constantly reflect on the impact of their actions in all facets of life: They show respect and caring as much with a clerk or salesperson as they would with their clients (perhaps that is not exactly what was said but that's how I remember it).

Soon after I finished reading about the study, I went to the grocery store to pick up a few items. On the way, I couldn't help thinking about ways that I fall short in my interpersonal actions. I am impatient and usually in a hurry. Those close-door buttons on elevators that probably don't work were installed just for me, so I can proceed vertically just as urgently as I move through the rest of the world. I am critical of others who don't measure up to my standards. I can appear standoffish when I am actually quite shy. The list goes on and on. But the main point is that as much as I would like to think that I am nice and considerate to everyone I encounter, I know that is not the case. So as I stood in line to check out, I realized that I was actually in no hurry at all. I invited the man behind me to go ahead of me since he had fewer items. I made a point to smile and show him courtesy. I thanked the cashier and the guy who bagged my groceries more profusely than they probably felt was appropriate. But I resolved in that moment that I would work a lot harder at this every day.

Will I follow through on my commitment? *That* is the question. That's one thing I love (and hate) about our profession. We feel like such hypocrites when we don't follow through on what we say is important. Or I'll own it: *I* feel so dishonest when *I'm* not practicing what I preach to others.

This study of master therapists has been a gift to me at a latter stage in my own professional and personal development. I've been forced to reexamine what I really believe most passionately. Far more than that, I've challenged some of those beliefs that haven't necessarily been translated into constructive action. And more than ever before, I appreciate and honor the mystery in what we do.

Many of us have endured weekly case conferences at our clinics or other therapeutic setting. We are sitting at the long table, squeezed between the other therapists and interns, while we watch and listen attentively to the "chief" psychiatrists and psychologists debating furiously the "correct" diagnosis of each patient. The interns take turns presenting the results of their intake interviews, conducted over the course of 90 minutes, and then the senior staff take turns skewering their inadequate and incomplete data. Nevertheless, they seem to have little difficulty formulating hypotheses, clinical impressions, and treatment plans for the patients.

We are in awe. We have been living with ourselves our whole lives and we barely have a foggy idea about who we are and our life struggles. After taking the various diagnostic classes, we recognize parts of ourselves in at least a half-dozen different categories. Yet these experienced experts, most of whom speak in the language of sages, appear to have an informed, detailed, and confident vision of *exactly* what is happening with the patients and the best way to proceed with them. What's amazing to us is that they haven't even met these individuals, and yet they have such brilliant ideas about what their problems might be and what to do to help them.

There is a precision and certainty about the comments made by our supervisors that is so incongruent with our own experience— and with the realities that we witness before us. This only gets worse over time as we move from one mental health setting to another. Since we are in a perpetual state of bewilderment about our clients' "real" issues, and the best way to work with them, we constantly seek reassurance and feedback from colleagues.

We are convinced that one of the things that professional therapists need to be reminded of is the greater appreciation for the complexity of human experience. This means embracing ambiguity rather than needing to destroy it with simplistic theories; it means honoring that which we don't understand instead of seeking easy answers to phenomena in which we aren't even sure how to properly ask the questions. We need to continue to be honest with ourselves if we wish to grow as professionals and human beings. We can accept that mystery and complexity are a significant part of our journeys, facets of being a master therapist that are just as important as what we do know and understand. Certainly, confidence is a huge part of mastery in any domain or context, but so is humility. We find it more than a little intriguing that so many truly master therapists would never recognize themselves as such: They are just going about their days doing the absolute best they can to make the most difference in the time they have been granted.

EPILOGUE

JC Well, I'm still here. I haven't died yet. In fact, I feel better than I've felt in a very long time. And this book has helped significantly with my recovery, urging me to reflect on my life's work, my priorities, and my most important values. One result is that I've created a completely new lifestyle. I've learned to exercise with greater moderation, rest more, spend more time with friends, be attentive to my constant dog companions, and be more generous with my time as well as resources. I feel a deeper love and respect for my wife and family. It's not so much that I really changed the composition of my daily life; rather I reassigned the importance of each of the things that I do.

Recovery is not an end but a process. I worked hard at living with cancer and illness, and I have been able to avoid an illness identity even as I've had multiple setbacks and ongoing medical crises. I have watched too many clients overidentify with their disease to the point that they see themselves as a victim or survivor of cancer, multiple sclerosis, or some other intractable health problem.

I am honestly okay with dying, but as long as I am alive, I am more interested in living more fully. I do this to enrich my own life but also because it's important to practice what I preach for my clients, students, friends, and family. If one theme in this project has been hammered hard for me, it is how important it is to be a model of what I advocate for others. If I truly believe that it is crucial for my clients to be fearless and courageous risk takers and explorers, then I must demonstrate that in my own life. If I think it is important to show compassion, caring, respect, and love toward my clients, I have to constantly monitor the extent to which I am doing that with everyone else. Jeffrey and I work hard on this every day, push one another, inspire and support one another, and call out one another when we think we are wandering astray. We also fully recognize that we will never, ever satisfy ourselves in this regard: There is always more work to do.

I sometimes grieve over who I was before I got sick. I used to be much more physically vital and capable. I can't remember what it's like to live without pain. I rarely reached the limits of what I could handle or how hard I could push myself, the remnants of being a competitive athlete. Things I could previously do without a thought now require a lot of planning and assistance. As much as I hate to ask others for help, I notice how much they enjoy taking care of me. I am learning how to receive help with much greater appreciation, accepting gifts of love with my dignity intact. But I'm still also struggling with acceptance that I've become old and frail. People treat me like I'm invisible, or even worse, they keep asking me if I'm okay, if I need help, if I can do things on my own. However well intended such offers might be, they reinforce the idea that I'm less than capable than I've ever been before. That's hard to acknowledge.

Over the 3 years Jeffrey and I have been working on this project, I've become much more clearly aware of the ways a master therapist, like any exceptionally functioning person, creates action and movement by whatever means possible. Master therapists are, above all else, resilient, creative, willing to do whatever it takes to make a difference. More than ever before, I feel permission to stretch my limits, perhaps not physically, but in the domain of my internal functioning as a spiritual, loving human being.

Jeffrey and I thank you sincerely for joining us on this journey together, one that we hope has triggered for you some interesting, provocative questions. Perhaps you may also feel a greater commitment and dedication to practicing what you preach to others.

References

Adler, A. (1964). *Social interest: A challenge to mankind.* New York, NY: Putnam.

Alarcon, R. D., & Frank, J. B. (2012). *The psychotherapy of hope.* Baltimore, MD: Johns Hopkins University Press.

Alpert, J. (2012, April 21). In therapy forever? Enough already. *New York Times.*

Ariely, D. (2012). *The (honest) truth about dishonesty.* New York, NY: HarperCollins.

Baumeister, R. F. (1994). The crystallization of discontent in the process of major life change. In T. F. Heatherton & J. L. Weinberger (Eds.), *Can personality change?* Washington, DC: American Psychological Association.

Beer, E. G., & Young, D. M. (1998). *The silent language of psychotherapy: Social reinforcements of unconscious process* (3rd ed.). New York, NY: Aldine/Transaction.

Betan, E. J., & Binder, J. L. (2010). Clinical expertise in psychotherapy: How expert therapists use theory in generating case conceptualizations and interventions. *Journal of Contemporary Psychotherapy, 40,* 141–152.

Bien, T. (2006). *Mindful therapy: A guide for therapists and helping professionals.* Somerville, MA: Wisdom.

Binder, P., Holgersen, H., & Nielsen, G. H. (2009). Why did I change when I went to therapy? A qualitative analysis of former patients' conceptions of successful psychotherapy. *Counselling and Psychotherapy Research, 9*(4), 250–256.

Bjornsson, A. S. (2011). Beyond the psychological placebo: Specifying the nonspecific in psychotherapy. *Clinical Psychology: Science and Practice, 18*(2), 113–118.

Bohart, A., & Tallman, K. (1999). *How clients make therapy work: The process of active self-healing.* Washington, DC: American Psychological Association.

Burton, A., & Associates (Eds.). (1972). *Twelve therapists: How they live and actualize themselves.* San Francisco, CA: Jossey-Bass.

C'de Baca, J., & Wilbourne, P. (2004). Quantum change: Ten years later. *Journal of Clinical Psychology, 60*(5), 531–541.

Calhoun, L. G., & Tedeschi, R. G. (2013). *Posttraumatic growth in clinical practice.* New York, NY: Routledge.

Carlson, J. (2000) Individual psychology in the year 2000 and beyond: Astronaut or dinosaur? Headline or footnote? *Journal of Individual Psychology, 56*(1), 3–13.

Carlson, J., Watts, R. E., & Maniacci, M. (2006). *Adlerian therapy.* Washington, DC: American Psychological Association.

Castonguay, L. G., & Beutler, L. E. (Eds.). (2006). *Principles of therapeutic change that work.* New York, NY: Oxford University Press.

Castonguay, L. G., & Hill, C. E. (Eds.). (2012). *Transformation in psychotherapy: Corrective experiences across cognitive, behavioral, humanistic, and psychodynamic approaches.* Washington, DC: American Psychological Association.

Chi, M. T. H. (2006). Two approaches to the study of experts' characteristics. In K. A. Ericsson, N. Charness, P. J. Feltovich, & R. R. Hoffman (Eds.), *Cambridge handbook of expertise and expert performance* (pp. 21–30). New York, NY: Cambridge University Press.

Clarke, H., Rees, A., & Hardy, G. E. (2004). The big idea: Clients' perspectives of change processes in cognitive therapy. *Psychology and Psychotherapy: Theory, Research, and Practice, 77,* 67–89.

Colvin, G. (2010). *Talent is overrated: What really separates world-class performers from everybody else.* London, UK: Portfolio.

Cooper, G. (2009). Can therapists spot liars? *Psychotherapy Networker,* May/June, 14.

Corey, M. S., & Corey, G. (2010). *Becoming a helper* (6th ed.). Belmont, CA: Wadsworth.

Cormier, S., Nurius, P. S., & Osborn, C. J. (2009). *Interviewing and change for helpers: Fundamental skills and cognitive–behavioral intervention* (6th ed.). Belmont, CA: Brooks/Cole.

Cornell, A. W. (1996). *Power of focusing: A practical guide to emotional self-healing.* Oakland, CA: New Harbinger Books.

Coyle, D. (2009). *The talent code.* New York, NY: Random House.

Csikszentmihalyi, M. (1990). *Flow: The psychology of optimal experience.* New York, NY: Harper Collins.

Curtis, R. C., & Stricker, G. (Eds.). (1991). *How people change: Inside and outside therapy.* New York, NY: Springer.

Dalai Lama (2002). *Live in a better way: Reflections on truth, love, and happiness.* New York, NY: Penguin.

Dalai Lama & Hopkins, J. (2006). *How to expand love: Widening the circle of loving relationships.* New York, NY: Atria Books.

Darwin, C. (2010). *The descent of man, and selection in relation to sex.* New York: New York University Press.

Duncan, B. L. (2010). *On becoming a better therapist.* Washington, DC: American Psychological Association.

Duncan, B. L., Miller, S. D., & Sparks, J. (2004). *The heroic client: Principles of client-directed, outcome-informed therapy* (Rev. ed.). San Francisco, CA: Jossey-Bass.

Duncan, B. L., Miller, S. D., Wampold, B. E., & Hubble, M. A. (2010). *The heart and soul of change: Delivering what works in psychotherapy* (2nd ed). Washington, DC: American Psychological Association.

Ekman, P. (2009). *Telling lies: Clues to deceit in the marketplace, politics, and marriage* (3rd ed.). New York, NY: Norton.

Ekman, P. (2010). Darwin's compassionate view of human nature. *Journal of the American Medical Association, 303*(6), 557–558.

Ericsson, K. A., Charness, N., Feltovich, P. J., & Hoffman, R. R. (Eds.). (2006). *The Cambridge handbook of expertise and expert performance.* New York, NY: Cambridge University Press.

Frank, J., & Frank, J. B. (1991). *Persuasion and healing* (3rd ed.). Baltimore, MD: Johns Hopkins University Press.

Frankel, Z., & Levitt, H. M. (2009). Clients' experiences of disengaged moments in psychotherapy: A grounded theory analysis. *Journal of Contemporary Psychotherapy, 39,* 171–186.

Fromm, E. (1956). *The art of loving.* New York, NY: Harper & Row.

Gediman, H. K., & Lieberman, J. S. (1996). *The many faces of deceit: Omissions, lies, and disguise in psychotherapy.* Northvale, NJ: Jason Aronson.

Gendlin, E. (1982). *Focusing.* New York, NY: Bantam Books.

Germer, C. K., & Siegel, R. D. (2012). *Wisdom and compassion in psychotherapy.* New York, NY: Guilford Press.

Germer, C. K., Siegel, R. D., & Fulton, P. R. (2005). *Mindfulness and psychotherapy.* New York, NY: Guilford Press.

Gladwell, M. (2008). *The outliers: The story of success.* New York, NY: Little, Brown.

Goh, M. (2005). Cultural competence and master therapists: An inextricable relationship. *Journal of Mental Health Counseling, 27,* 71–81.

Goleman, D. (2003). *Destructive emotions: A scientific dialogue with the Dalai Lama.* New York, NY: Bantam Books.

Goleman, D. (2006). *Emotional intelligence.* New York, NY: Bantam Books.

Gottman, J. (2011). *The science of trust: Emotional attunement for couples.* New York, NY: Norton.

Greenberg, L., & Johnson, S. (1988). *Emotionally focused therapy for couples.* New York, NY: Guilford Press.

Greenberg, L. S., Rice, L. N., & Elliott, R. (1993). *Facilitating emotional change: The moment-by-moment process.* New York, NY: Guilford Press.

Greene, R. (2012). *Mastery.* New York, NY: Viking.

Guy, J. D. (1987). *The personal life of the psychotherapist.* New York, NY: Wiley.

Haley, J. (1984). *Ordeal therapy: Unusual ways to change behavior.* San Francisco, CA: Jossey-Bass.

Haley, J. (1993). *Uncommon therapy: The psychiatric techniques of Milton Erickson, MD.* New York, NY: Norton.

Hanna, F. J., & Ritchie, M. H. (1995). Seeking the active ingredients of psychotherapeutic change: Within and outside the context of therapy. *Professional Psychology, 26*(2), 176–183.

Hansen, J. T. (2007). Counseling without truth: Toward a neopragmatic foundation for counseling practice. *Journal of Counseling and Development, 85*, 423–430.

Hatfield, D., McCullough, L., Plucinski, A., & Krieger, K. (2010). Do we know when our clients get worse? An investigation of therapists' ability to detect negative client change. *Clinical Psychology and Psychotherapy, 17*, 25–32.

Helson, R., & Stewart, A. (1994). Personality change in adulthood. In T. F. Heatherton & J. L. Weinberger (Eds.), *Can personality change?* Washington, DC: American Psychological Association.

Higginson, S., & Mansell, W. (2008). What is the mechanism of psychological change? *Psychology and Psychotherapy: Theory, Research, and Practice, 81*, 309–328.

Hodgetts, A., & Wright, J. (2007). Researching clients' experiences: A review of qualitative studies. *Clinical Psychology and Psychotherapy, 14*, 157–163.

Hoorens, V. (1993). Self-enhancement and superiority biases in social comparison. *European Review of Social Psychology 4*(1), 113–139.

Hubble, M. A., Duncan, B. L., & Miller, S. D. (1999). *Heart and soul of change.* Washington, DC: American Psychological Association.

Hwang, P. O. (2000). *Other esteem: Meaningful life in a multicultural society.* New York, NY: Routledge.

Joseph, S. (2011). *What doesn't kill us: The new psychology of posttraumatic growth.* New York, NY: Basic Books.

Kabat-Zinn, J. (2012). *Mindfulness for beginners: Reclaiming the present moment—and your life.* Boulder, CO: Sounds True.

Kazdin, A. E. (2009). Understanding how and why psychotherapy leads to change. *Psychotherapy Research, 19*(4–5), 418–428.

Keeney, B. (2009). *The creative therapist: The art of awakening a session.* New York, NY: Routledge.

Keltner, D. (2009). *Born to be good.* New York, NY: Norton.

Kirby, S. (2003). Telling lies? An exploration of self-deception and bad faith. *European Journal of Psychotherapy, Counselling, and Health, 6,* 99–110.

Kohlberg, L. (1981). *The philosophy of moral development: Moral stages and the idea of justice.* New York, NY: Harper & Row.

Kornfield, J. (2012). *Bringing home the dharma: Awakening right where you are.* Boston, MA: Shambhala.

Kottler, J. A. (1991). *The compleat therapist.* San Francisco, CA: Jossey-Bass.

Kottler, J. A. (1992). *Compassionate therapy: Working with difficult clients.* San Francisco, CA: Jossey-Bass.

Kottler, J. A. (1997). *Travel that can change your life.* San Francisco, CA: Jossey-Bass.

Kottler, J. A. (2001). *Making changes last.* Philadelphia, PA: Brunner-Routledge.

Kottler, J. A. (2010). *The assassin and the therapist: An exploration of truth in psychotherapy and in life.* New York, NY: Routledge.

Kottler, J. A. (2010). *On being a therapist* (4th ed.). San Francisco, CA: Jossey-Bass.

Kottler, J. A., & Carlson, J. (2002). *Bad therapy: Master therapists share their worst failures.* New York, NY: Brunner-Routledge.

Kottler, J. A., & Carlson, J. (2003). *The mummy at the dining room table: Eminent therapists reveal their most unusual cases and what they teach us about human behavior.* San Francisco, CA: Jossey-Bass.

Kottler, J. A., & Carlson, J. (2006). *The client who changed me: Stories of therapist personal transformation.* New York, NY: Brunner-Routledge.

Kottler, J. A., & Carlson, J. (2007). *Moved by the spirit: Discovery and transformation in the lives of leaders.* Atascadero, CA: Impact.

Kottler, J. A., & Carlson, J. (2008). *Their finest hour: Master therapists share their greatest success stories* (2nd ed.). Bethel, CT: Crown.

Kottler, J. A., & Carlson, J. (2009). *Creative breakthroughs in therapy: Tales of transformation and astonishment.* Hoboken, NJ: Wiley.

Kottler, J. A., & Carlson, J. (2011). *Duped: Lies and deception in psychotherapy.* New York, NY: Routledge.

Kottler, J. A., Carlson, J., & Englar-Carlson, M. (Eds.). (2014). *Helping beyond the 50-minute hour: Therapists involved in real social action.* New York, NY: Routledge.

Kottler, J. A., Carlson, J., & Keeney, B. (2004). *American shaman: An odyssey of ancient healing traditions.* New York, NY: Brunner-Routledge.

Krumboltz, J. (2010). *Luck is no accident: Making the most of happenstance in your life and career.* Atascadero, CA: Impact.

Lambert, M. J., Harmon, C., Slade, K., Whipple, J. L., & Hawkins, E. J. (2005). Providing feedback to psychotherapists on their patients' progress: Clinical results and practice suggestions. *Journal of Clinical Psychology, 61,* 165–174.

Lambert, M. J., & Shimokawa, K. (2011). Collecting client feedback. *Psychotherapy, 48*(1), 72–79.

Lampropoulos, G. K., & Spengler, P. M. (2005). Helping and change without traditional therapy: Commonalities and opportunities. *Counselling Psychology Quarterly, 18*(1), 47–59.

Lemov, D., Woolway, E., & Yezzi, K. (2012). *Practice perfect: 42 rules for getting better at getting better.* San Francisco, CA: Jossey-Bass.

Maguire, J. (1998). *The power of personal storytelling: Spinning tales to connect with others.* New York, NY: Jeremy Tarcher.

Mahrer, A. (1985). *Psychotherapeutic change: An alternative approach to meaning and measurement.* New York, NY: Norton.

Manthei, R. J. (2005). What can clients tell us about seeking counselling and their experience of it? *International Journal for the Advancement of Counselling, 4,* 541–555.

Manthei, R. J. (2007). Clients talk about their experience of the process of counselling. *Counselling Psychology Quarterly, 20*(1), 1–26.

Martin, J. (1994). *The construction and understanding of psychotherapeutic change.* New York, NY: Teachers College Press.

McCormick, I. A., Walkey, F., & Green, D. E. (1986). Comparative perceptions of driver ability—A confirmation and expansion. *Accident Analysis & Prevention, 18*(3), 205–208.

Miller, S. D., Duncan, B. L., Brown, J., Sorrell, R., & Chalk, B. (2006). Using outcome to inform and improve outcomes. *Journal of Brief Therapy, 5,* 5–22.

Miller, S., & Hubble, M. (2011). The road to mastery. *Psychotherapy Networker,* March/April, 22–31.

Miller, S., Hubble, M., & Duncan, B. (2007, November/December). Supershrinks: What's the secret of their success? *Psychotherapy Networker,* 27–35.

Miller, W. R., & C'de Baca, J. (1994). Quantum change: Toward a psychology of transformation. In T. F. Heatherton & J. L. Weinberger (Eds.). *Can personality change?* Washington, DC: American Psychological Association.

Mozdzierz, G. J., Peluso, P. R., & Lisiecki, J. (2009). *Principles of counseling and psychotherapy: Learning the essential domains and nonlinear thinking of master practitioners.* New York, NY: Routledge.

Nepo, M. (2012). *Seven thousand ways to listen: Staying close to what is sacred.* New York, NY: Free Press.

Nhat Hahn, T. (1997). *True love.* Boston, MA: Shambhala.

Nhat Hahn, T. (1998). *Teachings on love.* Berkeley, CA: Parallax Press.

Nichols, M. (2009). *The lost art of listening: How learning to listen can improve relationships.* New York, NY: Guilford Press.

Norcross, J. C. (2011). *Psychotherapy relationships that work: Evidence-based responsiveness* (2nd ed.). New York, NY: Oxford University Press.

Norcross, J. C. (Ed.). (2011). *Psychotherapy relationships that work* (2nd ed.). New York, NY: Oxford University Press.

Norcross, J. C., Bike, D. H., & Evans, K. L. (2009). The therapist's therapist: A replication and extension 20 years later. *Psychotherapy: Theory, Research, Practice, Training, 46*(1), 32–41.

Norcross, J. C., Krebs, P. M., & Prochaska, J. O. (2011). Stages of change. *Journal of Clinical Psychology, 67*(2), 1–12.

Norcross, J. C., & Wampold, B. E. (2013). Compendium of treatment adaptations. *Psychotherapy in Australia, 19*(3), 34–37.

Orlinsky, D. E., & Rønnestad, M. H. (2005). (Eds.). *How psychotherapists develop: A study of therapeutic work and professional growth.* Washington, DC: American Psychological Association.

Pink, D. H. (2011). *Drive: The surprising truth about what motivates us.* New York, NY: Riverhead Books.

Pipher, M. (2005). *Letters to a young therapist.* New York, NY: Basic Books.

Pipher, M. (2010). *Seeking peace: Chronicles of the worst Buddhist in the world.* New York, NY: Riverhead.

Prochaska, J. O., Norcross, J. C., & DiClemente, C. C. (1994). *Changing for good.* New York, NY: Morrow.

Reese, R. J., Toland, M. D., Slone, N. C., & Norsworthy, L. A. (2010). Effect of client feedback on couple psychotherapy outcomes. *Psychotherapy Theory, Research, Practice, and Training, 47*(4), 616–630.

Reik, T. (1983). *Listening with the third ear.* New York, NY: Farrar, Straus & Giroux.

Richeort-Haley, M., & Carlson, J. (2010). *Jay Haley revisited*. New York, NY: Routledge.

Rifkin, J. (2009). *The empathic civilization: The race to global consciousness in a world of crisis*. New York, NY: Jeremy Tarcher.

Robb, C. (2006). *This changes everything: The relational revolution in psychotherapy*. New York, NY: Farrar, Straus & Giroux.

Rogers, C. (1961). *On becoming a person*. Boston, MA: Houghton Mifflin.

Rogers, C. R. (1980). *A way of being*. New York, NY: Houghton Mifflin.

Rønnestad, M. H., & Skovholt, T. M. (2013). *The developing practitioner: Growth and stagnation of therapists and counselors*. New York, NY: Taylor & Francis.

Roth, A., & Fonagy, P. (2004). *What works for whom? A critical review of psychotherapy research*. New York, NY: Guilford Press.

Sapyta, J., Reimer, M., & Bickman, L. (2005). Feedback to clinicians: Theory, research, and practice. *Journal of Clinical Psychology, 61*(2), 145–153.

Satir, V. (1998). *The new peoplemaking*. Palo Alto, CA: Science and Behavior Books.

Segal, D. (2010). *Mindsight: The new science of personal transformation*. New York, NY: Norton.

Segal, D. J. (2012). *Pocket guide to interpersonal neurobiology*. New York, NY: Norton.

Seligman, M. P. (2011) *Flourish: A visionary new understanding of happiness and well-being*. New York, NY: Free Press.

Shapton, L. (2012). *Swimming studies*. New York, NY: Blue Rider Press.

Siegel, R. (2013, March/April). Wisdom in psychotherapy: Can we afford it? *Psychotherapy Networker*, 18–25.

Siegel, R. D. (2010). *The mindfulness solution: Everyday practices for everyday problems*. New York, NY: Guilford Press.

Skinner, B. F. (1976). *About behaviorism*. New York, NY: *Vintage Books*.

Skovholt, T. M. (2012). *Becoming a therapist: On the path to mastery*. Hoboken, NJ: Wiley.

Soloman, A. (2012). *Far from the tree: Parents, children and the search for identity*. New York, NY: Scribner.

Stern, D. N. (2004). *The present moment: In psychotherapy and everyday life*. New York, NY: Norton.

Tallman, K., & Bohart, A. C. (1999). The client as a common factor: Clients as self-healers. In M. A. Hubble, B. L. Duncan, & S. D. Miller (Eds.), *The heart and soul of change*. Washington, DC: American Psychological Association.

Tan, C. M. (2012). *Search inside yourself: The unexpected path to achieving success, happiness, and world peace*. New York, NY: Harper One.

Tedeschi, R. G., Park, C. L., & Calhoun, L. G. (Eds.). (1998). *Posttraumatic growth: Positive changes in the aftermath of crisis*. Mahwah, NJ: Erlbaum.

Trivers, R. (2011). *The folly of fools: The logic of deceit and self-deception in human life*. New York, NY: Basic Books.

Wachtel, P. (2011). *Therapeutic communication: Knowing what to say when* (2nd ed.). New York, NY: Guilford Press.

Wallas, L. (1985). *Stories for the third ear: Using hypnotic fables in psychotherapy*. New York, NY: Norton.

Wallerstein, R. S. (1986). *Forty two lives in treatment*. New York, NY: Guilford Press.

Wampold, B. (2010). *The basics of psychotherapy: An introduction to theory and practice*. Washington, DC: American Psychological Association.

Wampold, B. E. (2001). *The great psychotherapy debate: Models, methods, and findings*. Mahwah, NJ: Erlbaum.

Watzlawick, P., Weakland, J., & Fisch, R. (1974). *Change: Principles of problem formation and problem resolution*. New York, NY: Norton.

Wegela, K. K. (2009). *The courage to be present: Buddhism, psychotherapy and the wakening of natural wisdom*. Boston, MA: Shambhala.

Whitaker, C. (1989). *Midnight musings of a family therapist*. New York, NY: Norton.

White, W. L. (2004). Transformational change: A historical review. *Journal of Clinical Psychology, 60*(5), 461–470.

Wilson, E. O. (1998). *Consilience: The unity of knowledge.* New York, NY: Knopf.

Yalom, I. (2009). *The gift of therapy: An open letter to a new generation of therapists and their patients.* New York, NY: HarperCollins.

Zuckerman, E. W., Jost, J. T. (2001). What makes you think you're so popular? Self-evaluation maintenance and the subjective side of the "friendship paradox." *Social Psychology Quarterly, 64*(3), 207–223.

Zupancic, A. (2007). Lying on the couch. In J. Mecke (Ed.), *Cultures of lying* (pp. 155–168). Madison, WI: Galda.

ABOUT THE AUTHORS

Jeffrey A. Kottler, PhD, is one of the most prolific authors in the fields of psychology and education, having written more than 80 books about a wide range of subjects during the past 35 years. He has authored more than a dozen texts for counselors and therapists that are used in universities around the world and dozens of books for practicing therapists and educators. Some of his previous titles include: *On Being a Therapist; The Compleat Therapist; Travel That Can Change Your Life; Creative Breakthroughs in Therapy: Tales of Transformation and Astonishment; The Therapist's Workbook: Self-Assessment, Self-Care, and Self-Improvement Exercises for Mental Health Professionals; Learning Group Leadership; The Assassin and the Therapist: An Exploration of Truth in Psychotherapy and in Life; Changing People's Lives While Transforming Your Own: Paths to Social Justice and Global Human Rights; Divine Madness: Ten Stories of Creative Struggle;* and *Change: What Leads to Personal Transformation.*

Jeffrey has worked as a teacher, counselor, and therapist in preschool, middle school, mental health center, crisis center, university, community college, and private practice settings. He has served as a Fulbright Scholar and senior lecturer in Peru (1980) and Iceland (2000), and has worked as a visiting professor in New Zealand, Australia, Hong Kong, Singapore, and Nepal. Jeffrey is professor of counseling at California State University, Fullerton, and founder of Empower Nepali Girls, an organization that provides educational scholarships for at-risk children in Nepal.

Jon Carlson, PsyD, EdD, is distinguished professor of psychology and counseling at Governors State University, University Park, Illinois, and a psychologist with the Wellness Clinic in Lake Geneva, Wisconsin. Jon is the author of 60 books in many areas, including psychotherapy, family therapy, marital enrichment, consultation, loneliness, and Adlerian psychology. Some of his best known works include: *How Master Therapists Work, Adlerian Therapy, Never Be Lonely Again, Creating Connection, Love Intimacy and the African American Couple, Inclusive Cultural Empathy,* and *Time for a Better Marriage.* Jon has also produced 300 video programs that feature the most prominent leaders in the field demonstrating their theories in actions. These videos are used to train the next generation of practitioners. He has received lifetime achievement awards from several professional associations, including the American Psychological Association and the American Counseling Association.

Together, Jeffrey and Jon have collaborated on several other books, including *Bad Therapy, The Mummy at the Dining Room Table, The Client Who Changed Me, American Shaman, Their Finest Hour, Moved by the Spirit, Creative Breakthroughs in Therapy, Duped: Lies and Deception in Psychotherapy, Helping Beyond the 50-Minute Hour: Therapists Involved in Meaningful Social Action,* as well as *The Master Therapist: Practicing What We Preach.*

INDEX